Environmental Overkill

Environmental Overkill

Whatever Happened to Common Sense?

Dixy Lee Ray

with Lou Guzzo

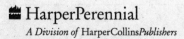 HarperPerennial

A Division of HarperCollins Publishers

First HarperPerennial edition published 1994.

Library of Congress Cataloging-in-Publication Data

Ray, Dixie Lee.
    Environmental overkill : whatever happened to common sense / Dixy Lee
Ray with Lou Guzzo. — 1st HarperPerennial ed.
        p.   cm.
    Originally published: Washington, D.C. : Regnery Gateway, c1994.
    Includes bibliographical references and index.
    ISBN 0-06-097598-9 (pbk.)
    1. Environmental responsibility. 2. Environmental policy. I. Guzzo,
Louis R., 1919–   . II. Title.
GE195.7.R39   1994
363.7—dc20   93-42982

94 95 96 97 98 RRD 10 9 8 7 6 5 4 3 2 1

Dedication

One of the most profound obligations of scientists is to provide factual information about basic science, technology, the environment, and human health in a manner that can be understood by policy makers and the public at large. We feel this obligation very deeply, as do many of our fellow scientists. But too few have the unique talent required for this very special kind of communication. Paramount among those who do are two great men—both physical scientists.

One is Dr. Petr Beckmann and the other is Dr. Edward Teller.

Although these two accomplished scientists have had strikingly different careers, each in his own specialty, they share many attributes. Both are foreign-born; they chose America. Like so many adopted citizens, they display an unabashed patriotism that reminds us native-borns that, whatever her faults, America is a unique and wonderful country, one that continues to be receptive to good science.

Through their research and writing, Dr. Beckmann and Dr. Teller have demonstrated their passionate devotion to truth in science and their unshakable belief in its remarkable power to improve the lot of human beings. Above all, they have used their considerable skills to make complex science understandable to the common man.

For all these reasons—and with profound gratitude—we dedicate this work to Petr Beckmann and Edward Teller.

—DLR and LRG

Contents

Preface

FIRST, a few words about what this book is not. It is not a scientific treatise. It is not a report of original work. It is not an encyclopedic treatment of all the environmental ills that plague the Earth. It is not an apology for modern civilization; nor does it seek to condemn human progress. It takes the position that good intentions are not enough in developing public policies; we need scientific facts.

We have chosen to give special attention to the uncertainties in science and to those policies that favor action above understanding. Unless they are based on a solid body of established facts, widely accepted perceptions may be faulty. We therefore emphasize many of the often-neglected consequences that result when actions are taken, even though evidence is missing or overlooked.

In taking this approach, we are aware that some may conclude that we are "anti-environment." That would be wrong. We acknowledge that there are problems of pollution and other environmental assaults, but we believe that they are amenable to solution when we use the knowledge that science can provide.

We believe that it is just as wrong to exaggerate the seriousness of environmental issues as it is to downplay the remarkable resilience and recovery powers of nature. We also believe that intrusive, punitive government controls are self-defeating. In sum, we believe in the basic goodness of our fellow humans; we believe that problems should be proved to be real before we lavish money on them. And we believe that it's important to demonstrate that a proposed solution is appropriate, practical, and affordable.

That's what this book is about; it is called common sense.

—DLR and LRG

PART ONE

The Air Above Us

CHAPTER 1

The Future According to Rio

UNCED Proposes to Save the Planet

In the first two weeks of June 1992, thousands of people converged on Rio de Janeiro, Brazil, to attend the United Nations Conference on Environment and Development (UNCED). Most of the 20,000 to 30,000 participants were there for the "Global Forum" part of the conference, which was billed as a "world's fair of environmentalism." This consisted of motley exhibits and short programs on every conceivable environmental and social program. It occupied a tent city that was erected in Rio's downtown Flamingo Park. Global Forum provided an opportunity for individual expression and for special interests to demonstrate environmental technologies, but was otherwise unrelated to the official conference agenda.

UNCED's serious work was done at the "Earth Summit" meetings. There the government representatives of 178 nations and the official delegates of hundreds of nongovernmental organizations (NGOs) met in separate sessions to consider a program of wide-ranging measures. The overall goal was to "Save the Planet." Save the planet from what? From human beings, of course!

The tone for these discussions was set by Maurice F. Strong, the UN's official spokesman and secretary general for the conference.

In his opening remarks on June 3, he referred repeatedly to serious deterioration in the natural world and to the pressing need for action. He spoke of "patterns of production and consumption in the industrialized world that are undermining Earth's life-support systems. . . . To continue along this pathway could lead to the end of our civilization. . . . This conference must establish the foundations for effecting the transition to sustainable development. This can only be done through fundamental changes in our economic life and in international economic relations, particularly as between industrialized and developing countries. . . . This planet may soon become uninhabitable for people."[1]

This theme—that nature has been irreparably damaged by industrialization and that the only remedy is to reduce progress and economic growth in the industrialized world—was one of the two underlying principles that guided UNCED. It was repeated over and over. The United States was generally singled out as the primary culprit. Curiously, the other guiding principle for UNCED was that the industrial nations, accused of causing all the problems, must now pay for them by transferring large sums of money and technical know-how to the Third World.[2] How this is to be accomplished by the industrialized nations while they simultaneously lower living standards and retrench economically was not explained or even discussed.

The year before, 1991, Strong had set the tone while the UN agenda was in preparation:

> In this transition to a more secure and sustainable future, the industrialized countries must take the lead. They have developed and benefited from the unsustainable patterns of production and consumption which have produced our present dilemma. And they primarily have the means and responsibility to change them. . . . It is clear that current lifestyles and consumption patterns of the affluent middle class—involving high meat intake, consumption of large amounts of frozen and convenience foods, use of fossil fuels, ownership of motor vehicles and small electrical appliances, home and workplace air-conditioning, and suburban housing—are not sustainable. A shift is necessary toward lifestyles less geared to environmental damaging consumption patterns.[3]

It appears that no proof is needed for these assertions and that simply saying so establishes their validity. Throughout the entire period of the conference, they were repeated like a mantra.

Planning for the Earth Summit began at the 1987 Stockholm conference that produced the report *Our Common Future*.[4] That meeting was chaired by Norway's Prime Minister Gro Harlem Bruntland, who was also the vice president of the International Socialist Party. *Our Common Future* is a green internationalist manifesto that brings the political philosophy of socialism into the environmental movement. The socialist approach to problems, along with the kind of remedies proposed, was evident in Mrs. Bruntland's remarks at Rio. She told the delegates to the Earth Summit that "We in the North consume too much."[5]

As reporter Ron Bailey of *Reason* magazine observed drily, "Fortunately, the activists at Earth Summit have a solution for this problem: Let the government divest you of your excess goods, such as your carbon dioxide-emitting automobile; your alienating, too-big house or apartment; and foods imported from outside your 'bioregion'. . . . The assertion by many Third World representatives that 'because you are rich, I am poor' was never doubted in the discussions. . . ."[6]

The Honorable Mrs. Bruntland, who served as vice chairman of UNCED in Rio, reinforced such attitudes in her opening remarks. She spoke of "the burden they [industrial nations] impose on the carrying capacity of the Earth's ecosystems by their unsustainable consumption and production patterns." In a stunning answer to a question from a Brazilian reporter following her prepared remarks, Prime Minister Bruntland freely acknowledged that the Earth Summit agenda was based upon the International Socialist Party's platform. This went largely unreported, although more than 7,000 journalists covered the conference.[7]

A few, however, dissented from the prevailing socialist propaganda. Again, Ron Bailey, contributing editor to *Reason* magazine, wrote:

Although I am generally not much of a nationalist, the patience of even the most laid-back, even-tempered American (excuse me, *North* American) wore thin under the unrelenting onslaught of virulent anti-Americanism at the Earth Summit. Even the ultraliberal Representative Gerry Sikorski, Minnesota Democrat, lashed out after a Zambian made a particularly vicious attack on the United States for not giving more money to the South. Sikorski told the Zambian that he would "feel a whole lot better about asking my consituents for money for the Third World if you would clean up your corrupt governments first."[8]

It would be interesting to know how Representative Sikorski's constituents feel about providing any of their tax money to Zambia. And, indeed, why should they?

In contrast to the predictions of impending ecological doom from Strong, Bruntland, and other UN leaders of the Earth Summit, more than 250 of the world's leading scientists, including 27 Nobel laureates, released a statement on June 1, 1992, called the Heidelberg Appeal.[9] It was directed to the heads of state that were attending the Rio Conference and appealed for the use of common sense and reliable science in making recommendations for action on environmental problems. As background, the scientists pointed out that it is neither reasonable nor prudent for major political decisions to be based on presumptions about issues in science, which, in the current state of knowledge, are still only hypotheses. They pointed out that in the more than two years of preparation for the Earth Summit, there was no significant involvement of scientists who specialize in the specific problem areas under consideration, nor were the competent scientists even informed. The Heidelberg statement, now signed and supported by hundreds of scientists worldwide, says, in part:

We are worried, at the dawn of the 21st Century, at the emergence of an irrational ideology which is opposed to scientific and industrial progress and impedes economic and social development. We contend that a Natural State sometimes idealized by movements with a tendency to look toward the past does not exist and has probably never existed since man's first appearance in the biosphere, insofar as humanity has always progressed by harnessing nature to its needs, and not the reverse. . . . The greatest evils which stalk our Earth are ignorance and oppression, and not Science, Technology, and Industry, whose instruments, when adequately managed, are indispensable tools of a future shaped by Humanity, by itself and for itself, overcoming major problems like overpopulation, starvation, and worldwide diseases.

Unfortunately, this appeal was neither acknowledged nor considered at the Earth Summit. All of the actions taken there were without the benefit of competent scientific input. By every measure the conference represented a signal victory for the foes of scientific progress, knowledge, and economic development.

What did happen? Two formal treaties were adopted. One, on global climate change, was signed by the United States; the other, on biodiversity, was not. It is worth noting here that when an international treaty is signed by the President and ratified by the Senate, it becomes the law of the land, overriding all domestic law. The Global Climate Change Treaty, though based on flimsy and repudiated science, was signed by President Bush and ratified by the U.S. Senate on October 15, 1992 during the final hours of the congressional session. We are stuck with it.

The administration congratulated itself on eliminating specifics of compliance that relate to how soon and at what cost the requirements of the climate treaty will be met—but it was a hollow victory. Simply signing the treaty implies acceptance of the theory that human production of carbon dioxide through burning fossil fuel causes catastrophic global warming. No solid evidence supports this position. But compliance with the treaty will be expected sooner or later, at enormous cost to U.S. taxpayers. Either we pay or we admit hypocrisy in accepting the treaty. Already William Reilly, administrator of the Environmental Protection Agency, has presented Congress with a compliance plan, complete with a plea for wholly unjustified and burdensome taxes on the production of carbon dioxide.[10] As reported in *The New York Times* June 14, 1992, Richard Benedick of the U.S. State Department and advisor to Maurice Strong admonished: "Don't worry about the blandness of the final treaty, because it has hidden teeth that will develop in the right circumstances." And Jessica Tuchman Matthews of the World Resources Institute, a major voice of alarm on global warming, said the treaty "has the potential of forcing governments to change domestic policies to a greater degree than any international agreement I can think of."[11]

The Biodiversity Treaty was rejected by the U.S.—for good reason. Quite aside from the question of whether many species of plants and animals really are being driven into extinction by human activities, its main requirement was for money to be provided by industrialized countries and controlled by Third World countries.[12]

According to Gareth Porter of the Environmental and Energy Study Institute, "the majority of the environmental groups believe that the Rio meeting was by and large a success. . . . Even if the agreements adopted by the Earth Summit fall short of what is needed, they do provide institutional mechanisms and benchmarks for holding governments accountable for progress in integrating environment and development and in forging more effective North-South cooperation. Moreover, the Earth Summit itself represents a fundamental transformation of world politics."[13]

Into this category of active internationalism fall the three agreements that were reached during the last days of the Rio conference: Protection of the World's Forests, the Rio Declaration, and Agenda 21. The forest agreement failed to achieve binding restrictions and international control because of objections from Third World countries that have extensive tropical forested areas. The agreement calls for international concern and programs to preserve forests, but it falls short of intruding on national sovereignty. To this international effort, President Bush pledged $150 million.

The Rio Declaration, consisting of 27 Principles, is expected to lead eventually to a more binding Earth Charter.[14] In its present form, it affirms the "integral and interdependent nature of the Earth, our home," and proclaims in Principle 1, "Human beings are at the center of concerns for sustainable development. They are entitled to a healthy and productive life in harmony with nature." It is hard to disagree with such sentiments.

Many of the principles follow in this spirit of altruism and deal with cooperation, fairness, and equality. But then they become more specific. Principle 6 calls for special priority for developing countries. Principle 7 declares the developed countries should acknowledge "the responsibility they bear in the international pursuit of sustainable development in view of the pressures their societies place on the global environment and of the technologies and financial resources they command." Principles 8 through 12 reinforce the requirement for transfer of money and technologies to the Third World.

Principle 13 justifies laws setting liability and compensation for "the victims of pollution and environmental damage . . . with international law to extend liability and compensation . . . to areas beyond their jurisdiction." Principle 15 states that "lack of scientific certainty shall not be used as a reason for postponing cost-effective measures to prevent environmental degradation." And so it goes, through principles on the rights of women (No. 20), youth (Nos. 22 and 23), against war (Nos. 24 and 25), and finally to Principle 27 with a call to all people and all states to "cooperate in the further development of international law in the field of sustainable development."

To further the objective of Principle 27, the formation of a Sustainable Development Commission within the United Nations was announced.[15] The Commission will function as a subsidiary of the existing Economic and Social Council and will be "empowered to have hearings, to have public proceedings, and receive evidence about the behavior and policies of countries around the world in order to assess whether and to what extent they are consistent with the agreements reached." Senator Al Gore, in a report to the U.S. Senate on June 16, 1992, expressed his enthusiastic approval of this extension of UN authority.[16]

The United States signed the Rio Declaration, which of course implies acceptance of all 27 Principles. And who will interpret the responsibilities and commitments that have been undertaken? And who will enforce the agreements? The UN bureaucracy. Murray Weidenbaum of Washington University's Center for the Study of American Business put it this way: "When the Earth Summit is all over, the UN agencies will have achieved a substantial accretion of power over economic activity and will start planning on the next round of such endeavors."[17]

More on this point later. We have still to consider Agenda 21. This is an 800-page agreement that lays out 115 specific programs to put into effect all the major issues discussed at Rio.[18] The Agenda is designed to facilitate (or force) the transition of the economies of all nations to "sustainable development."

Besides declaring that it is essential to eliminate poverty world-wide and to reduce human populations, Agenda 21 proposes ambitious and costly programs to set up a Global Environmental Facility to receive funds from industrialized countries *with no strings attached*. Its purpose is to "effect resource transfer." Agenda 21 would also force more efficient use of energy. Specifically it would "wean the developed countries off an overdependence on fossil fuels," "remove all trade barriers and subsidies," and bring about "large-scale reduction of current debt burdens" in the Third World.

The objective, clearly enunciated by the leaders of UNCED, is to bring about a change in the present system of independent nations. The future is to be world government, with central planning by the UN. Fear of environmental crises, whether real or not, is expected to lead to compliance. If force is needed, it will be provided by a UN green-helmeted police force, already authorized by the Security Council.

There's no mistaking the intentions plainly stated in the words of Michel Rocard, former prime minister of France and a leader at the Earth Summit: "Let's not deceive ourselves. It is necessary that the community of nations exert pressure, even using coercion, against countries that have installations that threaten the environment. International instruments must be transformed into instruments of coercion, of sanctions, of boycott, even—perhaps in 15 years' time—of outright confiscation of any dangerous installation. What we seek, to be frank, is the legitimacy of controlling the application of the international decisions."[19]

Rocard reinforced his belief that world government is the ultimate goal: "We need a real world authority, to which should be delegated the followup of the international decisions, like the treaties signed [at Rio]. . . . This authority must have the capacity to have its decisions obeyed. Therefore, we need means of control and sanctions. I well know the nervousness of some countries when they consider their sovereignty to be threatened. But we are not dealing with national problems. These problems are international.

Pollution knows no borders and the sea level cannot change in one place without changing in another.... Obviously, this supranational authority must be a world authority. It is precisely this international character that constitutes an advantage for the poorer countries, which will thus benefit from extra resources."

But if any doubts remain about the global intentions of the architects of the Montreal Protocol and the Earth Summit, those doubts are quickly dispelled by the chilling words of Maurice Strong, primary designer and Secretary General of the Rio conference. In answer to a magazine interviewer's question about his "unfulfilled ambition," he said he wanted to write a novel with an environmental plot, then explained:

> What if a small group of world leaders were to conclude that the principal risk to the Earth comes from the actions of the rich countries? And if the world is to survive, those rich countries would have to sign an agreement reducing their impact on the environment. Will they do it? The group's conclusion is "no." The rich countries won't do it. They won't change. So, in order to save the planet, the group decides: Isn't the *only* hope for the planet that the industrialized civilizations collapse? Isn't it our responsibility to bring that about? This group of world leaders form a secret society to bring about an economic collapse.[20]

And, in Mr. Strong's fantasy, the interviewer added, they succeed.

A confirmed internationalist, Matthews wrote, in the Spring 1989 issue of *Foreign Affairs* that there must be "new institutions and regulatory regimes to cope with the world's growing environmental independence" and that "our accepted definition of the limits of national sovereignty as coinciding with national borders is obsolete." The U.S. plan has already been communicated to the UN Secretariat, as reported in the Federal Register, Volume 57, No. 236, December 8, 1992.

Is this what Americans want? Are environmental issues so serious and imminently catastrophic as to require that we give up a significant part of our independence, our liberty? What is the scientific evidence that supports or refutes severe deterioration in nature? Must we destroy our nation in order to "save the planet"?

CHAPTER 2

Global Warming

Who Should We Believe?

THERE is no issue in environmental science that has so captured the public's imagination—and sparked so much fear—as the claim that the earth is warming up, with catastrophic consequences. Some scientists agree with the theory of "Global Warming" and some do not. Who should we believe?

There is almost universal agreement among atmospheric scientists that little, if any, of the observed warming [less than one-half degree Centigrade] of the past century can be attributed to the man-induced increases in greenhouse gases.[1]

> —HUGH W. ELLSAESSER, participating guest scientist,
> Lawrence Livermore Laboratory

Each year now the level of greenhouse gases in the atmosphere reaches a new high and the ozone layer grows thinner. These fundamental assaults on the atmosphere are caused almost entirely by rich nations that use most of the fossil fuels and ozone depleting chemicals. Yet long term costs will be borne by humanity as a whole. Ozone depletion may cause skin cancer among Andean peasants, who never used aerosol spray cans, while global warming could flood the homelands of Bangladeshis, who have never used electricity.[2]

> —LESTER BROWN, director of the Worldwatch
> Institute, *Saving the Planet*

*Current forecasts of the man-made greenhouse effect do not appear to
be sufficiently accurate to be used as a basis for sound national policy
decisions.*[3]

> —ROBERT JASTROW, WILLIAM NIERENBERG,
>   FREDERICK SEITZ, *Global Warming Update: Recent
>   Scientific Findings*

*Global warming is no longer a distant threat, but a shockingly present
reality.*[4]

> —JON ERICKSON, *Greenhouse Earth*

*Global warming is an outright invention. It is absolutely unproven,
and in my view it is a lie. A lie that will cost billions of dollars
annually. . . . There is no danger from the CFCs to the ozone layer, nor
is there any danger from CO_2, no greenhouse effect, nor any risk of
any kind of global warming. It is, to me, a pure falsehood.*[5]

> —HAROUN TAZIEFF, volcanologist, geologist, former
>   Secretary of State for Prevention of Natural and
>   Technological Disasters, French Government,
>   Champs Elysees, Paris, 1991

*The scientific basis for greenhouse warming includes some facts, lots
of uncertainty, and just plain ignorance—requiring more observation,
better theories, and more extensive calculations. . . . There is major
uncertainty and disagreement in the scientific community about
predicted changes as a result of further increases in greenhouse gases:
The models used to calculate future climate are not yet good enough.
As a consequence, we cannot be sure whether the next century will
bring a warming that is negligible or a warming that is significant.*[6]

> —S. FRED SINGER, atmospheric and environmental
>   scientist; director, the Science and Environmental
>   Policy Project, Washington, D.C.

And so it goes. For every assertion made by a reputable scientific
expert that the world is warming up, there is another one from an
equally qualified scientist who says that it is not. And many respected leaders in the field of atmospheric science take the position

that we simply do not understand climate phenomena well enough to take drastic actions. Who should we believe? Why is there so much disagreement? The answer is not easy, but there are two things to keep in mind.

First, whenever there is so clear a difference of opinion among experts, the conclusion must be: No one really knows. And when no one knows, it is best to withhold judgment and avoid precipitous action. The other thing to remember is that no scientific issue can be resolved by strongly held belief—however eminent the authority. Opinion polls are useless; *only evidence counts*. Facts, measured and described and independently verified, constitute the only basis for drawing conclusions in science.

Unfortunately, the debate about global warming has become highly politicized and used by the government as a basis for making policy decisions.[7] That means allocation of huge sums of public money, your money, to deal with a "problem" that may not exist.

But charges that human activities have altered the composition of the atmosphere, causing the earth to warm, with catastrophic results, have captured the imagination of the public and politicians.

Demands for government to "do something" to stop or to reduce the purported warming and its drastic consequences contributed to the organization of the "Earth Summit," the international conference held in Brazil in June 1992. This UN-sponsored meeting was more than two years in the planning and resulted in treaties that could cost the industrialized nations from 3 to 5 trillion dollars.

That's a lot of money to spend on global warming, especially since it was only 15 years ago that scientists were warning about global *cooling* and the return of an ice age. Lowell Ponte, author of the book, *The Cooling*, published in 1976, was one of many scientists who believed that the "Earth's climate has been cooling rapidly for the past three decades, and this has already caused drought and famine in major areas of the world. . . . At least a thousand people will have starved [in the near future] because of the impact climate instability already has had on food production."

Many studies predicted that a cooling trend had set in, as indeed it had, but the temperature drop was very small. From 1940 to the mid-1970s, average northern hemispheric temperatures dipped by a fraction of a degree Centigrade. This was seized upon by a number of scientists and journalists, who predicted dire consequences. Here are just a few:

The facts have emerged, in recent years and months, from research into past ice ages. They imply that the threat of a new ice age must now stand alongside nuclear war as a likely source of wholesale death and misery for mankind.

> —Nigel Calder, former editor of *New Scientist*, "In the Grip of a New Ice Age," *International Wildlife*, July 1975

There are ominous signs that the earth's weather patterns have begun to change dramatically and that these changes may portend a drastic decline in food production—with serious political implications for just about every nation on earth.

> —Peter Gwynne, *Newsweek*, April 28, 1975

According to the academy [National Academy of Sciences] report on climate, we may be approaching the end of a major interglacial cycle, with the approach of a full-blown 100,000-year ice age a real possibility ... with ice packs building up relatively quickly from local snowfall that ceases to melt from winter to winter.

> —*Science*, March 1, 1975

The continued rapid cooling of the earth since World War II is also in accord with the increased global air pollution associated with industrialization, mechanization, urbanization, and an exploding population, added to a renewal of volcanic activity....

> —Reid Bryson, "Environmental Roulette," *Global Ecology: Readings Toward a Rational Strategy for Man*, John P. Holdren and Paul R. Ehrlich, editors, 1971

The sensitivity of climate was pointed up independently by a Soviet and an American scientist, who concluded that a permanent drop of

only 1.6 to 2 percent in (solar) energy reaching the earth "would lead
to an unstable condition in which continental snow cover would
advance to the Equator . . . [and] the oceans would eventually freeze,"
according to a recent U.S. scientific advisory report.

>—SAMUEL W. MATTHEWS, "What's Happening to
>Our Climate?" *National Geographic*, November
>1976[8]

Now more than 15 years have passed. The very small cooling in the 1970s has been replaced in the 1980s by an equally minute warming—and once again calamity and catastrophe are forecast.

Human society has always had its Cassandras and Jeremiahs who predict the end of the world. How similar those ice age warnings sound to what is being said today about global warming. Are our memories so short? And are all these claims about climate changes, whether cooling or warming, as serious and as frightening as the activists in these areas would have us believe? I think not. From another viewpoint, can human beings really influence the *overall climate*—or "stabilize" it, or cause or prevent significant warming or cooling? I do not believe that we can or that we have done this. After all, there are one million tons of air per capita for every person on earth. All the claims about climate change are based on computer projections. But to reach an informed conclusion, we must look at the facts.

It appears that nearly everyone now believes that the Earth is heating up or soon will. But what is the evidence? It comes down to three simple but basic issues:

1. Either the earth is getting warmer or it is not. If there is a persistent temperature change, then it is either within natural variability or it is not. What do the facts tell us?

2. If the earth should warm, either that is caused by increased carbon dioxide in the atmosphere or it is not. What does the record tell us?

3. Either the acknowledged increase in atmospheric concentration of carbon dioxide is caused by industrial activity or by natural phenomena, or by both. What is the evidence?

Before considering these three fundamental issues, we need to remember that our Earth, together with its enveloping atmosphere, does indeed constitute a "Greenhouse." The atmosphere is a porous blanket. Heat, light, and other radiation from the sun—and remember it *all* starts with the sun—reach the upper atmosphere. Roughly 30 percent of the incoming solar radiation is reflected back into space; 20 percent is absorbed in the atmosphere, and 50 percent penetrates to the surface to cause warming. A fraction of the heat that reaches Earth returns to the atmosphere as infrared radiation, which contributes to further warming by being absorbed by certain constituents of air called "greenhouse gases." These gases are, mainly, carbon dioxide, methane, hydrocarbons, aerosols, and, above all, water. Indeed, although carbon dioxide is getting all the attention in greenhouse discussions, it is really water—the water vapor of the atmosphere, and droplets in the clouds—that is the *main* greenhouse gas. Water is responsible for 98 percent of all greenhouse warming. The other gases, including carbon dioxide, do function to absorb infrared and thus contribute to warming, but their effect is minor compared to water's.

The combined effect of solar radiation and the "greenhouse effect" is to moderate surface temperatures to an overall rough average of 60 degrees Fahrenheit, making the Earth very amenable to life. If Earth lacked an atmosphere, its temperatures would resemble those of the moon, which reaches a scorching 211 degrees Fahrenheit during the lunar day and drops to an uncomfortable −270 degrees Fahrenheit during the lunar night.

The Greenhouse theory holds than an increase in the concentration of any of the greenhouse gases will lead to increased warming. No one disputes this, but the question is how much will it warm and are there naturally occurring corrective phenomena? Nature is always unexpectedly complex, and we all too frequently underestimate its powers. Given the increases in carbon dioxide since the beginning of the Industrial Age, temperatures, according to the Greenhouse theory, should have gone up from 2 degrees to 4 degrees Centigrade over the past 100 years. They have not. The measurable overall increase is a trivial 0.5 degrees Centigrade or less.[9]

Actual temperature records, taken on land mainly in North America and Western Europe, show no consistent, significant upward trend. There are indeed ups and downs. A slight warming occurred between 1910 and 1938. The year 1938 was, until the present, the warmest year on record. During the post-World War II industrial boom, and over the period when carbon dioxide was continually increasing, there was a slight drop in temperature from 1940 until the 1980s, when it started up again. Now the warmest years on record are 1988–91. Conversely, the summer of 1992 is the third coldest on record in the American Midwest and East Coast. The overall result is that the *measured* net change in temperatures recorded on land over the past 100 years is an increase of no more than one half of one degree Centigrade, with most of that increase being accounted for by warmer nighttime temperatures. This is certainly not indicative of the catastrophic heating that has been predicted by some scientists and environmental activists.[10]

This lack of significant warming is corroborated by 135 years' worth of analysis at M.I.T. of sea surface temperatures (1850–1987).[11] Finally, perhaps the most accurate and most comprehensive recorded temperatures come from space-based instruments orbiting the Earth since 1978.[12]

Tiros II, a temperature-measuring satellite, has orbited from pole to pole, over oceans and land, making continuous temperature records 24 hours a day. These voluminous data show no significant temperature trend, either up or down. The actual increase, again in nighttime temperatures measured from space, is no more than 0.065 degrees Centigrade, and that is no more than a natural variation. Another interesting fact emerges from these data: The slight nighttime warming trend was restricted to the winter months.

This is hardly the environmental disaster that the global warming theory predicts. Moreover, even if further warming should occur over the next 100 years, the total is not predicted to exceed the temperatures that prevailed during the period 900 to 1100 A.D., a time known as the "Medieval Optimum." Both human society and plants and animals survived that climate very well.

Indeed, climate does not stay the same for long; change is nature's rule. During the early Middle Ages, the weather was so mild that wine grapes grew in England. The terraces built there by the Romans can still be detected. And the ups and downs of temperature in Europe can be deduced from the French records of wine grape harvests.

Official temperature records in Europe began in 1781, with the widespread measurements initiated by the Meteorological Society of the Palatinate. Their data showed mild oscillations in temperatures, with a decade or two of cooling, always followed by a decade or two of warming. Their net result was that between 1800 to 1880 there was a slight cooling, roughly 0.5 to 1.0 degrees Centigrade. Obviously, these fluctuations cannot be blamed on human industrial activities. Again, it's interesting to note that these 19th century temperature data showed that when warming occurred, it took place in all seasons except the summer.

Although instrument-measured temperature variations do not exist before 1780, there are other records from which relative changes may be inferred. These include the ice extent of various Swiss lakes, the harvest dates of several important food or fodder crops, the behavior of glaciers, and, on the other side of the world, the dates of the blossoming of cherry trees in Japan, where records go back at least 1,700 years.

All available evidence shows that climate varies naturally.[13]

Coming back to the well-known medieval warming, it was during this time that Vikings sailed across on an iceberg-free North Atlantic Ocean. They discovered, colonized, and named "Greenland." It was indeed green at that time, not covered with glacial ice, as it is today.

After a few hundred years of Middle Ages warming, the Earth then turned cold and entered the "Little Ice Age" (1450–1850). Temperatures in England were so low during some of those winters that trees in the forests of Somerset in Southern England froze solid and sometimes exploded from the buildup of internal ice. The Thames River also froze solid all the way up to London. The last time that happened was 1814. The dreadful winter suffered by General Washington's troops in 1777–78 at Valley Forge is another example of the severe cold that was often experienced during this time. By about 1850, a gradual warming trend set in, continuing to the present. But there are, as always, ups and downs. The years 1881 and 1882 are some of the coldest on record.

As another example of ever-shifting temperatures, we should

heed the words of Dr. Marc Cathay, director of the National Arboretum, who said in 1989: "The trees and the plants have been telling us, unambiguously, that the U.S. climate has [recently] been *cooling* in some areas, *not warming.*"[14]

He cites the fact that it used to be possible to grow citrus fruit in the American Southeast all the way up to the Carolinas. Nowadays commercial orange groves aren't sustainable north of Orlando, Florida. And in Florida itself, there have been 24 "Arctic outbreaks" in the past 30 years. (An "Arctic outbreak" is a period of severe killing frost.) There had been only six such episodes in the previous 50 years. In the Midwest, Mark Twain wrote of the delicious oranges that grew in the Mississippi Valley as far north as Natchez. Today there are none even in the Southern Mississippi River delta.

In 1990, the U.S. Department of Agriculture put out its first revised hardiness report for commercial crops since 1965. Taking temperature data from 14,500 different measuring stations, the new map shows that the area in which crops can be grown without certain danger of a killing frost has moved southward 100 miles in the past 50 years.

Such data should come as no surprise. The entire history of Earth is one of climatic change. A few hundred years ago in America's arid Southwest a flourishing culture of native Americans lived on the mesas, supported by verdant agriculture. And, taking a longer view, there have been 17 ice ages over the past 10 million years. Each lasted a few hundred thousand years and was followed by an abrupt warming that brought glacial retreat and a period of moderate climate lasting about 10,000 to 12,000 years. It has been about 11,000 years since the end of the last ice age, so that from a purely statistical basis and assuming that the natural cycles of temperature change continue, we may be in for some cooling in the next few hundred years or so. The Earth, over its entire history, has been covered with ice (in the Northern Hemisphere) 80 percent of the time.

Long-term natural oscillations in temperature seem to occur at about 2,500-year intervals.[15] From cave paintings in the Sahara Desert, dated about 6,000 years ago (a period that meteorologists refer to as the "Climate Optimum"), we know the climate must have been different. The paintings show elephants, giraffes, hippopotamuses, and crocodiles. Other warm periods occurred about 3,500 years ago and 1,000 years ago. The significance of these episodes is that, even though no one knows what caused them, any more than anyone knows what caused the ice ages, we can be certain of one thing: They were not due to human activities, industrialization, or the burning of fossil fuels. Nor could humans have prevented those weather and climate changes that are part of the planet's history. Climate changes occur naturally.[16] They take place so slowly over decades or centuries that they are hardly noticed, and most people believe that whatever weather prevails over their lifetime is "normal."

Examination of temperature records, whether current or in the distant past, reveals a history of continual temperature oscillations. The facts do not support a claim of significant global warming. The less than one-half degree of temperature rise, which is all that the global warming enthusiasts can find, is probably part of the slow recovery from the Little Ice Age of 1450–1850.

Still, the belief that the Earth will undergo dramatic warming persists, even in the absence of supporting temperature data. Some scientists have concluded that mankind, through industrialization that pumps out carbon dioxide, has acquired the ability to alter the composition of the atmosphere. This, they say, will sooner or later force temperatures to rise.

There is still much that is unknown about the role of carbon dioxide, but it's an unlikely candidate for causing any significant worldwide temperature changes.[17] Why?

First, because it is a minor Greenhouse gas; as we mentioned earlier, its effect is far less than that of water.

Second, industrialization and the burning of fossil fuels also add sulfur dioxide and other compounds to the atmosphere. Recent research reveals that sulfur oxides are probably incorporated into clouds, thus increasing their reflectivity and causing some cooling.[18]

Third, both historic and prehistoric levels of carbon dioxide have shifted and changed—in the absence of human intervention.

Fourth, whereas the historic increases in carbon dioxide have occurred at about the same time as temperature increases, careful scrutiny of the historical record and the most recent data shows that the rise in temperature precedes the increase in carbon dioxide, not the reverse.[19] We know that from 1880 temperatures rose to their high point in 1940. But between 1940 and 1980, when CO_2 buildup was rapid, temperatures dropped slightly.

Fifth, in the distant past, there were times when the carbon dioxide content of the air was more than ten times what it is today. That was the time of the emergence and evolution of most land plant species.

Sixth, increasing the amount of atmospheric carbon dioxide contributes to greater and healthier plant growth and helps plants resist drought and disease. Controlled atmosphere experiments show that a doubling of the carbon dioxide concentration results in a better than 30 percent increase in crop and seed production.

Seventh, when scientists try to draw up a carbon balance, calculating all sources of production and absorption, they have been unable to account for about 50 percent of the carbon dioxide known to be produced annually. More recent research reveals that both land plants and ocean water may sequester far more carbon dioxide than previously believed. But, so far, the available measurements do not support this conclusion. The puzzle remains: What happens to the missing CO_2?[20] One of the intriguing possibilities has been proposed by Sherwood Idso[21] and by Bert Drake,[22] who independently have proved through plant growth experiments with controlled atmospheres, that in many species, growth is stimulated by elevated CO_2 concentrations. If this phenomenon proves to hold for plants worldwide, it could account for a very large amount of the carbon dioxide.

From all of this we can conclude that our knowledge of the role of carbon dioxide in weather and climate is far from complete. Certainly, there is insufficient understanding to justify costly programs for carbon dioxide control.

On the other hand, there is a phenomenon that we know has a direct and significant effect on weather. That is El Niño, a sudden warming of the waters of the eastern tropical Pacific Ocean. El Niño occurs irregularly, at intervals of about seven to eleven years, and each episode tends to differ in the magnitude of warming. When it is larger, it correlates with drastic or unusual weather changes mainly throughout the Northern Hemisphere, including Alaska and even as far away as Africa and India. In some years, a similar phenomenon, La Niña, occurs, but it involves cooling, not warming, of the surface ocean waters.[23] Why are we not pursuing a study of the cause and effects of El Niño and La Niña at least as vigorously as we are looking at carbon dioxide, whose claimed effect on climate is based wholly on theory and computer simulation and is not substantiated by direct study of nature and by measurements?

Some recent research suggests a possible connection between the appearance of stratospheric aerosols derived from volcanic eruptions that occur in the low latitudes and cooler temperatures on the earth's surface. The effect appears to be regional, rather than global, and may explain the cool, wet summer in parts of North America and Europe following the eruption of Mount Pinatubo. Handler and Andsager of the University of Illinois suggest that the increased aerosol in the stratosphere blocks some of the incoming solar radiation and that this, in turn, stimulates the onset of El Niño.[24]

Finally, we must consider the question: Where does the increased concentration of carbon dioxide come from? Is it from fossil fuels burned by humans? Or is it from natural sources? Or both?

First, the human contribution. It comes mainly from the direct burning of fossil fuels, coal, petroleum, and natural gas. The activities that use fossil fuel are vast, numerous, and important. They range from the liquid fuels for transportation, coal for generating electricity, many manufacturing processes, and space heating. Carbon dioxide is also produced from burning wood and charcoal and from decaying vegetation as a result of land clearing.

Calculations show that man is responsible for adding about 7 billion tons of carbon dioxide annually to the atmosphere. This may seem like an enormous amount until we consider the contribution from nature, which may be as much as 200 billion tons annually.[25] Nature's contribution comes from the respiration of countless organisms, from hot springs, fumaroles, rifts, and geysers that abound around the world, and from volcanic eruptions. And the amount of carbon dioxide locked up in limestone exceeds that of the atmosphere by many thousandfold. The earth exudes carbon dioxide. Many will remember the tragic episode at Lake Nyos in Africa a few years ago, when carbon dioxide accumulated in the deep lake waters that were fed by "soda springs." Unexpectedly during the night, the lake "burped," suffocating with carbon dioxide all the humans and higher animals in the surrounding valley. Similar incidents have been reported many times from the open oceans; the carbon dioxide released from the ocean bottom has been shown to be responsible for extensive fish kills.

Eruptive volcanoes also add carbon dioxide to the atmosphere. During the major eruption of Mount St. Helens on May 18, 1980, no one could get close enough to measure the gases emitted. In the remainder of 1980, however, the mountain released 910,000 metric tons of carbon dioxide, as determined by direct measurement.[26] These results were possible to obtain because Mount St. Helens is relatively accessible. That's not the case for most volcanoes in the Pacific "rim of fire."

Prodigious amounts of gases are emitted whenever volcanoes erupt. When the eruption is an explosive one, the gases and ash may be injected directly into the high troposphere or even into the stratosphere. We are now living in a period of vastly increased volcanism, the greatest in the past 500 years.

Certainly far more carbon dioxide is produced by natural phenomena than by any human activity. And, until we can account for the cause of high atmospheric carbon dioxide levels in the historical and geological past, why should we assume that today's increase is due solely to human causes?

Indeed, some scientists, like Roger Revelle and Robert White, have stated that our understanding of the role of carbon dioxide in possible "global warming" is woefully inadequate.

Revelle, who initiated the program of carbon dioxide monitoring in 1958, said in a 1991 article in *Cosmos*: "The scientific base for greenhouse warming is too uncertain to justify drastic action at this time. There is little risk in delaying policy responses."[27]

White, former head of the U.S. National Weather Service and the National Oceanic and Atmospheric Administration and present president of the National Academy of Engineering, joined 55 of the most respected atmospheric scientists in America in an extraordinary statement of scientific principle before the beginning of the United Nations Conference on Environment and Development in Rio in June 1992:

> As independent scientists researching atmospheric and climate problems, we are concerned by the agenda for UNCED (the United Nations Conference on Environment and Development) being developed by environmental activist groups and certain political leaders. This so-called Earth Summit is scheduled to convene in Brazil in June 1992, and aims to impose a system of global environmental regulations, including onerous taxes on energy fuels, on the population of the United States and on other industrialized nations.
>
> Such policy initiatives derive from highly uncertain scientific theories. They are based on the unsupported assumption that catastrophic global warming follows from the burning of fossil fuels and requires immediate action. We do not agree.
>
> A survey of U.S. atmospheric scientists, conducted in the summer of 1991, confirms that there is no consensus about the cause of the slight warming observed during the past century. A recently published research paper even suggests that sun-spot variability, rather than a rise in greenhouse gases, is responsible for the global temperature increases and decreases recorded since about 1880.
>
> Furthermore, the majority of scientific participants in the survey agreed that the theoretical climate models used to predict a future warming cannot be relied upon and are not validated by the existing climate record. Yet all predictions are based on such theoretical models.
>
> Finally, agriculturalists generally agree that any increase in carbon dioxide levels from fossil fuel burning has beneficial effects on most crops and on world food supply.
>
> We are disturbed that activists, anxious to stop energy and economic growth, are pushing ahead with drastic policies without taking notice of recent changes in the underlying science. We fear that the rush to impose global regulations will have catastrophic impacts on the world economy, on jobs, standards of living, and health care, with the most severe consequences falling upon developing countries and the poor.

Turning again to the role of the sun, recent research reveals a strong correlation between temperature changes on the surface of the earth and variations in magnetic activity on the surface of the sun. Enormous magnetic storms (sun spots) appear on the sun at fairly regular intervals of approximately 11 years. The investigations by Friis, Christensen, and K. Lassen[28] of the Danish Meteorological Institute, published in *Science*, November 1, 1991, reveal that whereas the number and intensity of sun spots vary with each cycle, so also does the cycle length. It is the variation in the length of the solar cycle that correlates closely with long-term temperature variations on earth. The Danish scientists make a good case that solar activity directly influences global climate. Their analysis covers a period of 130 years and focuses on Northern Hemisphere air temperatures. Clearly, much more research over several sun spot cycles is necessary to evaluate this interesting correlation properly, but it makes good sense.

Finally, two quotations—one old and one new—from two scientists deserve emphasis in closing this discussion of the global warming controversy.

One is the assertion of Dr. Stephen Schneider, who is today one of the most ardent supporters of the theory of global warming by elevated levels of carbon dioxide. Here is what he wrote more than two decades ago, in 1971, when his position, in a paper written with Dr. N. Rasool, was that CO_2 and the greenhouse effect were overrated:

"Temperatures do not increase in proportion to an atmospheric increase in CO_2. . . . Even an eight-fold increase over present levels might warm earth's surface less than 2 degrees Centigrade, and this is highly unlikely in the next several thousand years."[29] Dr. Schneider also predicted a 25-foot rise in the sea level from melting polar ice caps. Ice sheets in Greenland and Antarctica are actually growing.

The second statement is from Dr. Robert E. Stevenson, secretary general of the International Association for Physical Sciences in the Ocean, who reported at an April 1992, conference on "Climate Volcanism and Global Change" in Hilo, Hawaii:

Mean sea level has not changed in the past century (which puts the lie to the ecologists' argument that global warming is melting the polar ice caps); atmosphere temperatures, though having up-and-down cycles, have not established a trend in either direction; ozone holes are natural reactions to ultraviolet-light variation and volcanic matter in the stratosphere; and the gases in the stratosphere caused by humans' activities are insignificant.

Should we worry about global warming? Best that we clear away some of the real uncertainties before we devote significant resources to a phenomenon that may exist only in computer simulations.

CHAPTER 3

Stratospheric Ozone and the "Hole"

Now You See It; Now You Don't

"The world now knows that danger is shining through the sky. The evidence is overwhelming that the earth's stratospheric ozone layer— our shield against the sun's hazardous ultraviolet rays—is being eaten away by man-made chemicals far faster than any scientist had predicted. No longer is the threat just to our future; the threat is here and now...."

NONSENSE, but so began *Time* magazine's cover story, "The Ozone Vanishes," in the February 17, 1992, edition.[1] Typical of the sort of "scientific" information available to the public, this article is so full of emotional hype, exaggeration, half-truths, and unsupported dogma that it is more propaganda than reporting. The only evidence that is referenced comes from the press releases of the National Aeronautics and Space Administration. And NASA, despite all our sentimentality about it, is hardly a reliable source. Like any other government agency, it is interested primarily only in those facts that justify more research and more federal dollars. The only scientists quoted in the *Time* magazine story are those who support the ozone-depletion-by-chlorofluorocarbons (CFCs) theory. No dissenting opinions, although there are plenty of them among reputable scientists, are mentioned.

By contrast, another cover story, "The Ozone Scare," appearing in the April 6, 1992, issue of *Insight* magazine, quotes many scientists who dispute the fashionable theory of ozone depletion.[2] Even more dissenting scientists were featured in a June 1992 article, "The Hole Story—The Science Behind the Scare," published in *Reason*.[3]

But it's typical of so much science reporting today that every issue is presented as one side of a great debate—a fundamental misreading of the nature of science. Lawyers might sway juries with rhetorical genius, ministers might inspire their flocks, and political talk shows might be enlivened by the cut and thrust of debate. But science is about the sober weighing of evidence. To the scientific mind, argument seems to have replaced reason in our public discourse—as if important questions of science or technology could be resolved by which scientific celebrities have the most charisma and media appeal. But science isn't a popularity poll, and sincere and impassioned rhetoric won't change reality. Only evidence counts. Eventually, the facts, clearly established and independently verified, will prevail. But until that time, the public is not well served by the airing of conflicting and untested scientific theories—especially when the theories amount to scaremongering, a vocation that can be quite profitable for those who manipulate it.

No wonder thoughtful people ask: "Who should we believe?" My only advice is this: Look for evidence, not for arguments; discount any unsupported assertions, even if they come from an eminent authority, and then make up your own mind based on what facts you can assemble and on your own common sense.

Now, in an effort to follow my own advice, let's look at ozone.

The issue of stratospheric ozone depletion comes down to just two basic, very simple questions: (1) Is ozone really disappearing from the stratosphere? (2) If it is, is the ozone loss caused by CFCs?[4] These questions are important, especially since freon-12, probably the most widely used CFC, is used extensively in refrigerators and air-conditioners.

Many atmospheric scientists uphold a theory that the answer is "yes" to both questions, and their theory has been widely reported as *fact* in the media. But according to a significant body of scientific opinion that is based on evidence and measurements, the answer is "no." Who is right? And does it matter?

To answer the second question first, it does indeed matter. It matters a great deal, because our entire food transportation and marketing system depends upon refrigeration, which, in turn, depends upon CFCs. The integrity of many medicines, vaccines, inoculations, and the entire supply of blood for surgery and transfusions also depends upon refrigeration.

It matters, too, because of the importance of air-conditioning in most modern buildings—a convenience that makes healthful living possible in the hotter parts of our country. These two industries, refrigeration and air-conditioning, will be affected drastically by political decisions regarding the use of CFCs and related substances. But so will other industries. Halon, a related substance, is, for instance, an agent used by firefighters across the country. If decisions about CFCs and halons are not based on good, solid scientific evidence, the result will be a tragic mistake that could cost the jobs and endanger the lives of countless Americans.

But the lives of many people could also be affected if CFCs are drilling a hole in the ozone layer and flooding the Earth with ultraviolet radiation, which we know can cause skin cancer.

So let's start at the beginning. Is ozone disappearing or isn't it?[5] Why the difference of opinion among scientists? The easy answer is that everyone is partly right, because ozone is being formed and destroyed all the time; the important question is whether there is a long-term trend that could ultimately lead to serious loss. Much of the answer to that question depends upon exactly when, where, and by what means ozone is measured.

Increasingly in modern research, scientists tend to divide themselves into two groups, each with a different way of analyzing natural phenomena. On the one hand, there are the theorists. They develop intellectual models of how nature is believed to work and then, using very highly sophisticated (and expensive) supercomputers, they make computer simulations from which conclusions and predictions are derived. On the other hand, there are the realists; these are the data-collecting and data-measuring people. They believe that natural phenomena can best be understood by gathering evidence from nature itself. They believe in studying what actually happens in the natural world.

There is no unanimity, no universal agreement about which is the better way to explain natural phenomena.[6] My obvious bias is toward direct evidence and measurement. So let's see what data are available, and then compare them with the conclusions drawn from computer models.

What do we know for sure about stratospheric ozone?*

First, we know that ozone is formed from oxygen. The oxygen molecule is very stable; it consists of two atoms of oxygen and hence is always referred to as O_2. Ozone, on the other hand, is not stable. It consists of three oxygen atoms, O_3, any one of which can easily react with either another ozone molecule to form three oxygen molecules or with other substances to form an oxygen molecule and some other oxygenated molecule.[7]

Now for some simple, common sense chemistry. It is the presence of oxygen in the high atmosphere and in the stratosphere that really protects us from ultraviolet radiation. In a very simplified manner, it works this way: Incoming ultraviolet radiation strikes and divides an oxygen molecule (O_2). The two separate oxygen atoms are very reactive and quickly combine with other oxygen molecules to form ozone (O_3). Ultraviolet energy is thereby absorbed by oxygen and prevented from penetrating to the Earth's surface. As long as there is sufficient oxygen in the stratosphere and as long as the sun puts out ultraviolet radiation at the right wavelength, ozone will be produced. Several tons of ozone are produced every second, mainly in that part of the stratosphere that is 10 to 40 kilometers above the earth's surface.

That's the basic reaction, but the reality is somewhat more complex. As already noted, ozone molecules are very unstable and reactive. Once formed, they can react with other substances commonly present in the stratosphere like chlorine monoxide, which is formed by oxygen atoms from ozone combining with the chloride ion.

---

* Note that here we are concerned with ozone *in the stratosphere*. Ozone that forms at ground level is a different problem and will be considered separately, as a factor in urban air pollution.

Technically, that makes chlorine monoxide an "ozone destroyer." There is always a certain amount of chlorine present in the stratosphere, but it is believed by some atmospheric scientists that the stratospheric chloride that starts this process comes from chlorofluorocarbons. That's why some scientists support a ban on CFCs (more about this important topic later).

The important thing to remember is that ozone is constantly being formed and constantly being broken down. The *amount* that is present at any one time is the result of these reactions, and they can be influenced by many factors.

For example, the amount of ultraviolet radiation reaching the stratosphere—and affecting ozone production—depends upon the season, latitude, and solar cycle.[8]

Given the many chemical and photochemical reactions constantly taking place in the stratosphere, the expression, "ozone layer," is misleading. Ozone does not stratify into a discrete band. It is simply more abundant in the 10 to 40 kilometer area of the stratosphere than in the atmosphere below, because that is where the ultraviolet radiation at a wavelength of 240 nanometers is intercepted. Nevertheless, since the phrase, "ozone layer," is so commonly used, we will continue the practice.

It should also be noted that the amount of ozone can change rapidly. The amount present on any particular day may differ dramatically from the next. These changes in ozone concentration occur naturally and can vary by as much as 50 percent, depending on the weather. In the northern latitudes, ozone concentrations differ as much as 40 percent, even within a few days, while in equatorial regions, there is almost no annual variation in the amount of ozone.[9]

By convention, a decrease in the amount of ozone of 50 percent or more is called a "hole," even though there is no ozone "gap." The regular, annual ozone "hole" that appears over Antarctica was first measured and described in 1956–57, long before CFCs were in common use.[10] The "hole" appears at the end of the dark, cold Antarctic winter, lasts about three to five weeks, and then disappears. There is no overall or permanent depletion of ozone. Among other likely causes, the appearance of the Antarctic ozone hole requires intense cold (−80 degrees Centigrade) and is closely correlated with the onset of the annual Polar Vortex, a severe, late winter cyclonic storm. A similar but less severe storm occurs over the North Pole, with accompanying, though much smaller, temporary reduction in the amount of ozone.

Conclusions about long-term trends in the amount of stratospheric ozone cannot be based on single-day or short-term measurements. Even so, that is exactly what the U.S. Congress did.

A recent announcement by NASA, the U.S. space agency, that an aircraft-borne instrument had detected a high reading of chlorine stampeded the U.S. Senate into passing an amendment, 96 to 0, calling for an accelerated phaseout of the manufacture of chlorofluorocarbons. A week later, the White House ordered a phaseout of CFCs by 1995, five years ahead of schedule.

All this was accomplished by two NASA press releases and a lot of attention from the news media. It is discouraging to see public policy driven by press releases, rather than proved science.

What really happened? As best as one can tell—absent any published information that can be checked by independent scientists—a chlorine detector instrument, flying on a NASA research aircraft in the northern stratosphere, encountered high concentrations of an active form of chlorine, *capable* of attacking ozone.

But, of course, it required careful reading of the artfully worded document to discover that nothing at all was happening to ozone.

The NASA announcement was based on a peak chlorine reading, which occurred on January 20. "Peak" implies, however, that readings were lower—perhaps much lower—both before and after that date. The document was silent on this important point. Nor did it reveal that similar measurements in 1989, the date of the last such experiment, also encountered high chlorine values. Although widely anticipated and discussed at the time, there was no Arctic ozone "hole" in 1989, nor in any other year. Nor did one occur in 1992.[12] Research conducted, not by NASA but by Scandinavian scientists, tells an important story: No Arctic or high northern ozone "hole."[13]

The NASA press release may have told the truth, but it didn't tell the whole truth. It did not reveal that chlorine atoms cycle back and forth between an active and inactive form, depending on the presence of stratospheric ice particles, which, in turn, depend on whatever happens to be the temperature.

In spite of the facts concerning constant fluctuations in the amount of stratospheric ozone, Congress and the White House have accepted the ozone depletion theory that ozone is disappearing over time. This has not been established.

It is known that in addition to ultraviolet radiation and chloride, intense cold, ice particles, nitrogen compounds, and other factors might be involved in the oxygen-ozone interactions. Although the presence of chloride appears to be directly involved in ozone breakdown, the origin of that chloride is open to question. The assumption that it comes from CFCs is based upon hypothesis only. No breakdown products of freon have been identified in the stratosphere.

Chloride is one of nature's most abundant ions. Sea water evaporation provides the atmosphere with 600 million tons of chloride per year. Volcanic eruptions emit millions of tons of chloride. And at least another million tons of chloride are produced naturally every year. Now let's put this in perspective. World production of CFCs at its peak reached 1.1 million tons per year. At this rate there would be roughly 750,000 tons of chloride available from CFCs annually.

When Mount Tambora in Indonesia erupted in 1813, it ejected 211 million tons of chloride. At the highest rate of worldwide CFC production, it would have taken about 282 years to produce as much chloride-yielding CFCs as this one eruption.

Although measurements of chloride are not available for many modern volcanic eruptions, we know that Mount Erebus in Antarctica has been producing 1,000 tons of chloride daily since 1972.[14] Mount Erebus is located 10 kilometers upwind of McMurdo Sound, where ozone measurements are made. The volcano pumps out 50 times more chlorine annually than an entire year's production of CFCs. And, interestingly enough, the amount of chloride calculated to be in the stratosphere at any one time is 50 to 60 times higher than the chloride that comes from CFCs every year.[15]

If chloride is in fact necessary to the stratospheric breakdown of ozone, whose chloride is it? Man's or nature's?

Some scientists believe that ozone-destroying chloride must come from freon and related substances because CFCs rise through the atmosphere until they encounter stratospheric ultraviolet radiation at 20 to 40 kilometers. There they release their chlorides. Most natural chloride, on the other hand, is in the air and dissolves easily in water droplets and is rained out. But if this theory is true and if freon breaks down and releases its chlorine in the stratosphere, what happens to the rest of the molecule?[16] At least 192 chemical reactions and another 48 photochemical reactions have been identified in the stratosphere, but none involves CFCs.

Several questions are obvious: How does CFC rise when its molecules are four to eight times heavier than air? All experience with freon and related CFCs shows that they are non-volatile and so heavy that you can pour CFCs from a container and if some of them spill, they will collect at the lowest point on the ground, where soil bacteria will decompose them. Of course, some molecules will be caught in upward air eddies or otherwise carried upwards, but this is a very small fraction of the total.

We do not know how these heavier-than-air molecules cross the equatorial counter currents to accumulate at the South Pole and do the most ozone destruction there. And until the transport mechanism for CFC molecules is explained and until the full spectrum of CFC breakdown products is identified and measured *in the stratosphere*, the case for CFC destruction of ozone has not been made.

Again, what about the chloride coming from volcanoes? Chloride is hard to measure in the atmosphere and even harder in the eruptive plumes from volcanoes. Even so, David A. Johnston (who died at Mount St. Helens), in a posthumously published paper (*Science*, July, 1980), brought many previous estimates up to date and refined the measuring techniques for chloride in volcanic emissions.[17] He pointed out that a single eruption of Mount Augustine in Alaska in 1976 put more chlorine into the stratosphere than was contained in the worldwide production of CFCs for the entire year 1975.

Johnston also claimed that chlorine in many volcanic emissions is 20 to 40 times more concentrated than formerly believed. "Volcanic contribution of chlorine to the stratosphere [is] more significant to ozone than previously estimated," he wrote. "Clearly volcanic sources of stratospheric chlorine may be significant in comparison with anthropogenic sources."

Also, recent work has added emphasis to the important role of the sun in altering the ozone layer.[18] Solar flares play a major role, as do planetary waves, and even a major storm crossing the United States on the jet stream can result in a large, temporary ozone reduction.

The occurrence or absence of the El Niño warm current in the Eastern tropical Pacific Ocean is also related to the amount of ozone; any or all of these natural phenomena may reinforce or cancel each other out.

We also know that ozone was at a lower level in 1962 than it is today. An analysis of recent satellite data shows the overall amount of ozone in the stratosphere hit a high in 1969–70 and then dropped. It has been increasing steadily at 0.28 percent annually since 1986. It becomes more and more clear that to discern any real trend beyond normal fluctuations requires measurements that continue over a period of at least 20 to 30 years.[19]

In contrast to the press release publicity from NASA, the Norwegian scientists, Larsen and Henrickson in a January 1990 paper, published in *Nature*, discuss the ozone variations in the Arctic and point out that their work in the North Polar region going back to 1935 reveals "that anthropogenic gases, such as CFCs, have, up to the summer of 1989, had a negligible influence on the Arctic ozone layer. The general balance between formation and destruction of ozone has not changed, at least not to an extent that is apparent in the long-term observations."[20]

We conclude that measurement data do not support the theory that stratospheric ozone is being depleted by human-produced freons or any other CFCs. The theoretical computer models, however, tell a different story.

After ten years of computer predictions about depletion of ozone, it's time to look back and see how accurate these warnings have been.

If models—computer simulations—have any practical usefulness, it would be in their ability to predict phenomena or trends before they are revealed by measurements. In this they have failed dismally. For example, they failed to predict the Antarctic ozone "hole" that appeared in 1985—even though the phenomenon had been discovered and described on several occasions by a number of atmospheric scientists going back to 1956. When it was finally recognized, "new" chemistry had to be invented to explain the phenomenon so that it would fit the CFC theory.[21]

Moreover, in 1980, the National Academy of Sciences conducted a study based on the model developed by Rowland-Molina, the originators of the CFC-caused ozone destruction theory. This model predicted an 18 percent ozone decrease. By 1984, this prediction dropped to 7 percent and shortly thereafter to 2 percent. Recently, the best models now claim that ozone will decline by 5 percent over the next 100 years. After measurements in January 1990, the predicted ozone loss was announced by NASA and the Environmental Protection Agency as proceeding "faster than expected." Note that all of these dire predictions fall well within normal annual variations of 20 to 40 percent.[22]

Maybe it's time to remember that unexpected thinning of ozone in the Antarctic was first described not in 1985 but in 1956 by Gordon Dobson of Oxford University during the International Geophysical Year. CFCs had been developed but were not in widespread use. Not only was Dobson the first scientist to measure and describe the late winter formation of the Antarctic ozone "hole" and its sharp recovery with the onset of spring, but he also devised the instruments and system for measuring and quantifying the ozone amounts (Dobson units). He is recognized as the founder of research on ozone in the stratosphere. At first, he considered the Antarctic phenomenon to be an anomaly, but when it was repeated in 1957, Dobson concluded that it was a natural phenomenon.[23] Moreover, in 1958, the French scientists, P. Rigaud and B. Leroy, described the "hole" and concluded, "the thinning [is] related to the Polar Vortex ... and the recovery is sharp and complete."[24]

Since the ozone depletion enthusiasts claim that the Antarctic "hole" dates only from 1985, these French scientists reviewed their earlier work, verified the results, and published it again in 1990. They also related the ozone "depletion" to increased solar activity.

Although for many practical applications the radiance from the sun is considered to be "constant," there are detectable variations. It is important to measure both long- and short-term variations in the total solar irradiance, as well as changes in solar output at specific wavelengths, particularly in the ultraviolet and X-ray components. Long-term variations in total irradiance and in high-energy output take place over the years-long solar cycle, while short-term variations occur on a days-long time frame. Both these cycles and types of variations can have important effects on the temperature and chemical composition of the upper atmosphere and the stratosphere.

Although total solar irradiance is thought to be relatively constant over time, recent measurements have determined that it can vary by nearly 0.1 percent during an 11-year solar cycle, the period during which the occurrence of solar flares, sun spots, and other magnetic activity on the sun changes from one extreme to the other and back.

We are now living in a period of greater solar flares and larger sun spots than at any time since measurements began. In addition to Dobson and Rigaud and Leroy, several Japanese scientists have described and discussed the annual Antarctic ozone "hole" as a natural phenomenon.[25] None of these investigations is cited by the ozone depletion theorists, nor are these earlier workers given credit for their discoveries. Yet their research puts the whole "CFC-caused-ozone-depletion" theory into question.

But as far as the news media are concerned, what makes a better story: "Man-Made Chemicals Punch Deadly Hole in the Sky" or "Sun Spots Lead to Natural Fluctuation of the Ozone in the Stratosphere"? It all began with Chicken Little.

CHAPTER 4

The Ozone and Ultraviolet Rays

Why the Fuss?

IF we are losing stratospheric ozone and being bombarded with ultraviolet radiation, the fear is that we'll endure higher rates of skin cancer.

The problem with this theory is that ultraviolet radiation levels at the earth's surface are going down, not up.[1]

According to scientists from the National Oceanic and Atmospheric Administration (NOAA), the University of Colorado, and the National Center for Atmospheric Research, the amount of ultraviolet radiation reaching the earth has, in some urban areas, decreased by 5 to 18 percent. How has this happened? Probably because of industrial sulfur dioxides, which, the scientists believe, might scatter the incoming ultraviolet radiation.[2]

Measuring instruments set up across the U.S. in 1974 by the National Cancer Institute show that over two test periods—1974–79 and 1980–85—the amount of ultraviolet "B" (UVB) reaching the earth actually decreased by an average of 0.7 percent per year since 1974. In an article in *Science* (1988), the institute also reports that data from Mauna Loa, Hawaii show no increase in UVB radiation from 1974 to 1985. Similar results were obtained by Penkett in East Anglia, England, and Bavaria, Germany. Measurements taken between 1968 and 1982 show UV decreases of from 0.5 to 0.9 percent. During this period, the ozone layer should have thinned 1.5 percent, causing a 3.0 percent increase in ultraviolet radiation—if the ozone depletion theory were correct.

To explain the significance of these results, we need to consider some more detail about UV radiation. Nothing in nature is simple. This certainly applies to ultraviolet radiation.[3] In the heat, light, and other radiation that flow outward from the sun, UV radiation comprises about 5 percent of the total energy radiated and is itself a spectrum of wavelengths. This spectrum is separated arbitrarily into three groups, A, B, and C. UVA is the longest, with wavelengths from 400 to 320 nm, UVB from 320 to 286 nm, and UVC, the shortest and most energetic, with wavelengths from 286 to 40 nm.

As already described, it is mainly UVC at wavelength 242 nm that splits oxygen molecules (O_2) into two oxygen atoms that immediately combine with other oxygen molecules to form ozone (O_3). There is also a similar interaction of oxygen with UVB at 293 nm. This reaction results in the production of billions of tons of ozone every second. The ozone molecules they create then become the "shield" that blocks nearly all of the remaining UVC and much of the UVB radiation. UVA, by contrast, is not absorbed by either oxygen or ozone, and it passes through the stratosphere virtually unaffected, nearly all of it reaching the Earth's surface. Since it is UVB that is believed to cause sunburn and, presumably, also the most common kinds of skin cancer, most attention has been focused on it. Available evidence does not, however, link UVB directly to malignant melanoma, and there is a growing suspicion that UVA may be implicated in this most serious type of skin cancer. As noted below, there are other possible causes of malignant melanoma, casting doubt on whether the amount of ozone in the stratosphere influences the incidence of this disease.

Even so, William Reilly, administrator of the Environmental Protection Agency, claimed on April 4, 1991, that ozone depletion of 4 to 5 percent would permit increased UV radiation to reach the earth so that "over the next 50 years about 12 million Americans will develop skin cancer and 200,000 of them will die." Such scare statements by a high government official are utterly irresponsible.[4]

Of course, overexposure to ultraviolet radiation can cause skin cancer; this is well established. But that's not the whole story. Two basic types of skin cancer are apparently related to too much ultraviolet exposure, presumably UVB. People who sunbathe or who frequent tanning salons increase their risk of acquiring these cancers. The most common skin cancer is *basal cell carcinoma*. It affects about 400,000 light-skinned individuals a year. The tumors are small, fleshy bumps or nodules that do not spread quickly. They generally occur on the face, neck, trunk, or hands, and, with treatment, basal cell carcinoma is curable in 99 percent of the cases. Then there is *squamous cell carcinoma*. It affects about 100,000 light-skinned people annually. Typically, this type of skin cancer occurs on the ear rim, face, nose, or lips. It can spread and often forms large masses of cells. These common skin cancers may be unsightly, irritating, and annoying, but they are curable.

A third, rarer form of skin cancer is malignant melanoma. Despite considerable investigation, this type of skin cancer has not been correlated with exposure to UVB. It has also been increasing. It is usually fatal and may be, to some extent, genetically determined. There is clear evidence that cases of malignant melanoma occur more frequently among people living close to the Equator.[5]

Melanoma is increasing at about 5 percent per year, and, curiously, its incidence is much greater in the higher social classes. This suggests that a person's lifestyle might have a significant influence on susceptibility to the disease. Studies in Australia, for example, show that melanoma is considerably more common in indoor workers than in outdoor workers.

Malignant melanoma starts with a black mole or a lesion that usually appears on the trunk, buttocks, or other parts of the body that are not often exposed to sunlight. To imply that ozone loss (even if it has occurred) would lead to an increase in malignant melanoma is obviously false.

The extent of ozone loss that EPA Director Reilly called "grim" would result in a 4 to 5 percent increase in exposure to ultraviolet radiation. This is, in fact, far less than normal, annual variations in ultraviolet radiation, and far less than the increased dosage one would absorb if one made a simple move to a lower latitude.

For every six miles that one goes closer to the Equator, one's ultraviolet exposure increases by 1 percent. Humans accommodate very well to these changes. And if one moves from either the North or South Polar region to the Equator, ultraviolet penetration and consequent exposure increases 5,000 percent.[6]

Who would refuse a vacation in Hawaii, or Florida, or to the South Seas, or along the French Riviera because of such increases in the ultraviolet exposure? Yet these trips mean exposures many times in excess of the amounts that the EPA and NASA are using to frighten Americans. When people from Scandinavia go to Spain's Costa del Sol or the English and Scottish move to Australia, they subject their lightly pigmented skins to amounts of UV radiation to which they are not adapted by nature. The intensity of UV radiation in northern Australia is 300 percent greater than in England.

It is not surprising, given the sunbathing fad of the past few decades, that there is an increase in common skin cancer among white people. The same phenomenon has not appeared among brown or darkly pigmented peoples or among those who are native to more tropical climates.

UV radiation can be very damaging to unpigmented cells; this is the basis for the long-known sterilizing properties of direct sunlight—it kills bacteria. And UV radiation has many positive effects. Exposure to UV rays from sunlight is absolutely essential for young children in order to develop a normal, strong skeleton. Absence of sufficient ultraviolet exposure results in a dreadful childhood disease, rickets. It is UV radiation acting to catalyze a chemical reaction in the skin that leads to the formation of Vitamin D, which is required for the growth of strong bones. Provision of synthetic Vitamin D can help to overcome lack of UV exposure, but some UV exposure remains important.

While rickets is the expression of severe lack of Vitamin D, less extreme reactions may include the onset of adult osteomalacia (also known as osteoporosis or "brittle bones"), particularly prevalent in women.*

It is worth noting that although the EPA speaks pompously and probably erroneously of 400,000 to 800,000 new cases of common

---

* Question: Could this be related to the "little girls don't romp half-naked in the sunshine as much as little boys do" phenomenon?

skin cancer in the U.S., there are 1,200,000 bone fractures annually among the elderly—many of them are hip or legbone breaks—and 20,000,000 Americans are afflicted with osteomalacia. It's likely *more* exposure to UV would have helped. Recent research has revealed a strong possibility that both colon cancer and breast cancer are inversely related to exposure to sunlight.[7]

Further, those who would protect us from UV rays by banning the production and use of CFCs on the basis of computer simulations and undocumented theory overlook the reasons CFCs were developed and put into use in the first place. CFCs are non-volatile and non-toxic and present no direct hazards to living organisms. Until CFCs were developed, many people died from the toxic fumes of ammonia, methyl chloride, and sulfur dioxide, which were often used as refrigerants.

In 1929, more than 100 people died in a Cleveland hospital from a leak in the refrigeration system. The dangers of home refrigerants stimulated the search for a safe substitute. It was a division of General Motors—Frigidaire—whose scientists, led by the chemist, Thomas Midgley, succeeded. The CFC now called "freon" was introduced in 1930.[8]

Not only are CFCs safe, but all of the proposed substitutes have turned out to be very expensive, and some are toxic, flammable, and corrosive. All are inefficient compared to freon. Use of any of them or a return to cumbersome, ineffective refrigerants like ammonia or sulfur dioxide would require a thorough redesign of home, commercial, and industrial equipment.

In the U.S. alone, there are thousands of companies that use CFCs. They produce billions of dollars' worth of goods every year. There are millions of individual and commercial refrigerators, air-conditioning units, refrigerated transport trucks, rail cars, and ships.

Replacing *just* the refrigerated transport for food moving to market would cost more than $150 *billion*. Some estimate the cost of banning CFCs for refrigeration at $800 per person per year.[9]

Melvyn Shapiro, an atmospheric scientist at the National Oceanic and Atmospheric Administration, has said that President Bush's decision to speed up the phaseout of CFCs by five years (1995, instead of 2000) was "A terrible thing. . . . The President reduced the time scale for the elimination of CFCs based on the politics of the day. . . . The costs to the country for the termination of CFCs are going to be phenomenal. Globally, it will cost hundreds of billions of dollars."

"What you have to understand," Shapiro added, "is that this is about money. If there were no dollars attached to this game, you'd see it played in a very different way. It would be played on intellect and integrity. When you say that the ozone threat is a scam, you're not only attacking people's scientific integrity, you're going after their pocketbook, as well. It's money, purely money."[10]

The manufacturers of CFC have glibly assured everyone that substitutes for freons and halons can and will be found, because they hope to make a killing on new, more expensive products. One possible replacement for freon, being touted by DuPont, is Suva (CFC 134a). But it has a few problems. It is inefficient, compared to freon. It cannot be used in existing equipment. Tools that have been used in units containing freon cannot be used with Suva. It is toxic and hazardous to handle. It reacts with the desiccant used to keep water out of air-conditioning units; no solution to this problem has been found. It is corrosive and attacks lubricants, leading to early failure of compressors; it requires a specially fabricated lubricant. And its use will be temporary, because Suva is a hydro-chlorofluorocarbon and will come under the hydro-chlorofluorocarbon ban by the year 2000. And, of course, it will cost a lot more than freon; it is about ten times more expensive. Is it worth it?

Suva will require the complete redesign and re-engineering of all existing refrigeration and air-conditioning equipment. Given the flimsy and dubious scientific basis for banning CFCs, it doesn't make good sense to throw away all our present refrigeration and air-conditioning equipment just to accommodate environmental bureaucrats. If leaking freon *is* a problem, it would be simpler and wiser merely to improve the sealing of refrigerators and air-conditioning units. But simple solutions and common sense aren't the point. News media play and big dollars are, even if human lives are endangered in the process.

The effects on human health should also be considered. Loss of food through spoilage will increase if the use of refrigeration is reduced, and at the same time cases of food poisoning will also increase. U.S. health statistics show a dramatic decline in stomach cancer deaths when refrigeration was introduced. Robert Watson, head of the Ozone Trends Panel (a strong supporter of banning CFCs), has admitted that "probably more people would die from food poisoning as a consequence of inadequate refrigeration than would die from depleting ozone."[11]

There is also an international health consequence. International refrigeration experts estimate that should the world's "cold chain" for food transportation collapse because of the ban on CFCs, hundreds of millions of people could die. Preventing Third World countries from building modern refrigeration systems is one of the stated purposes of the population-control environmentalists.

EPA chief William Reilly said in 1989: "The prospect of seeing countries move forward with major development plans involving, as we heard in China, a proposal for 300 million new refrigerators possibly based on CFCs, makes [it] very clear that we must engage them in the process [to ban CFCs]."[12]

Remember that CFCs also play a role in firefighting. These CFCs are called halons and are nonflammable. Their molecules are so heavy, they can be incorporated into foams that instantly smother fires. Countless lives have been saved by using halons to put out fires in aircraft, in ships and submarines, and in many industrial facilities. What will replace halon? The Montreal-London Treaty requires that production of Halons 1211, 1301, and 2402 be frozen at the 1986 level by 1992, reduced 50 percent by 1995, and phased out completely in the year 2000. It might have been helpful if the treaty also banned fires, or at least came up with a replacement for halon.[13]

Even though CFCs have been impugned only because of theories, computer models, simulations, and forecasts of disaster that are not substantiated by either the evidence or the measurements gathered in nature over the past 35 years, CFCs have already been effectively banned. Their production is being phased out by 1995, the price of freon has already gone up by 40 percent, and further increases are coming. The costs are enormous. The question is, again, is all this justified? Is the evidence of an irreversible loss of stratospheric ozone so overwhelming and the likelihood of worldwide damage so great that billions of taxpayer dollars must be spent? All the evidence points the other way.

Yet 59 nations signed an international treaty usually referred to as the "Montreal Protocol on Substances that Deplete the Ozone Layer." It was adopted in 1987 and revised, to cover more substances and make the restrictions and penalties more severe, in 1990.

Richard Benedick, deputy assistant secretary of state for environment—an unelected population-control bureaucrat—was the chief negotiator for America in forging the ozone treaty. In his account of the events leading to the treaty, recorded in his book, *Ozone Diplomacy*, Benedick writes with astonishing candor of how the treaty was agreed to even though a scientific basis for it had not been established.[14]

Ozone Diplomacy reveals how science can be, and has been, politicized; it is a clear example of how a little dubious science and zealously held theory can overwhelm available evidence.

"Perhaps," Benedick wrote, "the most extraordinary aspect of the treaty was its imposition of short-term economic costs to protect human health and the environment against *unproved future dangers* ... dangers that *rested on scientific theories, rather than on firm data*. At the time of the negotiations and signing, *no measurable evidence of damage existed*."*

No such evidence exists today.

"By their action," Benedick added, "the signatory countries sounded the death knell for an important part of the international chemical industry, with implications for billions of dollars in investment and hundreds of thousands of jobs in related sectors. The protocol did not simply prescribe limits on these chemicals based on 'best available technology'.... Rather, the negotiators established target dates for replacing products that had become synonymous with modern standards of living, *even though the requisite technologies did not yet exist*."†[15]

Not only does the protocol require replacement substances; the negotiators also established procedures for enforcement, including

---

* Emphasis added.

† Emphasis added.

severe penalties and fines for noncompliance. Who gave the negotiators the authority to establish police power?

Yet the treaty is in effect; it has the force of law. In the last analysis, it is based on two unproved assumptions: (1) that CFCs destroy ozone, which is not replaced, and (2) that CFCs are so resistant to change that nothing except ultraviolet radiation in the stratosphere breaks down the molecule. Neither of these assumptions has been corroborated. Many people believe them only because "everyone says so."

We have seen that the evidence for CFCs destroying ozone is flimsy and scant, and now it has been discovered that soil bacteria destroy CFCs very effectively.[16] This fact has not been taken into account in calculating the persistence of CFCs, whose *estimated* lifetimes range from 20 years to 1,000 years. For freons, the estimates are 75 to 120 years, or an average of 100 years, which is the figure most often quoted. These estimates are all based on the assumption that nothing disintegrates the CFC molecules. Enter the microbes. As already pointed out, CFC molecules are (depending on which CFC is considered) four to eight times heavier than air molecules; most CFC that escapes into the atmosphere falls to the earth. There, soil bacteria decompose CFCs within a few days or weeks. The history of this discovery is interesting.

In 1986, while measuring the production of carbon dioxide and methane in termite colonies in Australia, scientists Khalil and Rasmussen ran into an unexpected problem. Believing, as everyone did, that CFCs were indestructible outside the stratosphere, they were using this material to calibrate their instruments. To their surprise, they found that the calibration kept changing and concluded that something in the soil was destroying the CFC. Study of the soil microbes established that there was rapid breakdown of freon and many other man-made chlorofluorocarbons, including methylchloroform and carbon tetrachloride (both targeted for banning by the Montreal Protocol). Khalil and Rasmussen reported on the microbial removal of CFCs in 1989; their research has been substantiated by field work in China's rice fields and by considerable laboratory experimentation. These results have been largely ignored in the ozone controversy.

Further evidence that CFCs sink to the earth and are sequestered in soil or on plant materials comes from the results of testing the smoke from forest fires. Dean Hegg, et al, from the University of Washington report large amounts of CFCs in wood smoke—an amount equal to as much as 50 percent of all freon likely to have been released to the atmosphere.[17]

When all the research on CFCs is taken into account, the idea that all these molecules end up in the stratosphere and destroy ozone has less and less to recommend it. Yet millions of dollars have been spent to examine the minuscule amounts of CFC that do reach the ozone and very little has been spent to look at the real environmental sink—the ground and the oceans.

It is from the marine environment that information on the *natural* production of CFCs may be obtained. Indeed, nature does produce CFCs, as well as the bacteria that destroy them. What are we to make of the macroalgae and the invertebrates that produce and use halogenated organic compounds in the sea?[18]

The current fuss about ozone "depletion" is not the first. It is only the most recent, and judging by the degree of clamor and emotionalism engendered, the most successful. Some senior citizens may remember the public outcry during the 1950s about testing nuclear warheads (atom bombs, as they were then called) in the high atmosphere. Besides fallout of radioactive isotopes, the nuclear explosions were claimed to disrupt the stratosphere and destroy the ozone. They didn't.

Then in the 1960s came plans for a commercial supersonic transport plane. This development was vigorously opposed by environmentalists, who charged—among other supposed effects—that the exhaust gases would destroy the stratospheric ozone. The United States SST program was terminated, giving the activist environmentalists one of their early victories. France and Great Britain went ahead with their own program, the Concorde. Today there are hundreds of supersonic military aircraft flying. Their exhaust has not been shown to affect the ozone or the stratosphere.

Then in the 1970s came the Space Shuttle. Here, too, the ozone depletion enthusiasts attacked.

But NASA's political clout was sufficient to squelch them and, of course, the shuttle program has not depleted ozone or perturbed the stratosphere. And then, also in the 1970s, along came Sherwood

Rowland and his postdoctoral student Molina with their theory that man-made chemicals—CFCs—somehow found their way into the stratosphere and destroyed ozone.

This time the charge was widely reported in the popular press and soon received broad public support. Even such claims as increased UV radiation due to the Antarctic "ozone hole" causing cataracts and blindness in sheep and rabbits in New Zealand and South Chile received uncritical acceptance. Veterinarians have examined the afflicted animals and report that the eye problems are caused by an epidemic of the highly contagious bacterial infection commonly known as "pink eye."[19]

Meanwhile, we're stuck with the Montreal Protocol that bans human production and use of CFCs. If one adds up all the estimated costs from the different affected industries, it may be as high as $5 trillion worldwide by the year 2005. Because of the severe effect on transportation and storage of food due to the loss or greatly increased cost of refrigeration, estimates indicate that between 20 to 40 million people will die yearly from hunger, starvation, and food-borne diseases.

Why have so many nations signed the protocol? One reason could be Article 4, which imposes a total trade ban on any nation that does not abide by the protocol conditions. This amounts to very effective "persuasion." Also, all the countries that sign the treaty are prohibited from exporting or importing CFCs, and the penalties, in addition to the trade sanctions, are severe. "Illegal" use of freon carries a $25,000 per day fine, and five years in prison can be imposed on anyone who transports a refilled cylinder.[20] To counter the loss of refrigeration technology, many developing countries are, of course, demanding payment from the industrialized nations, mainly the USA, and free access to all manner of other development technology. Maneka Gandhi, India's environmental minister, delegate to the Montreal conference, and the daughter-in-law of former Prime Minister Indira Gandhi, has said, "The whole 21st Century's survival will be based . . . on knowledge . . . . Either you sell us the technology [at an acceptable price] or you change your laws or you change your patent rights. . . . Start working on it."[21]

Responding to this sentiment, expressed by many developing

countries, the protocol proclaims, "Industrialized countries affirmed their commitment to 'take every practicable step' ... to ensure that the best available, environmentally safe substitutes and related technologies are expeditiously transferred ... under fair and most favorable conditions."

Who pays? Especially since DuPont and others will patent their substances and processes? And, as Robert Watson said, commenting on the prospects of DuPont making so much money from substitutes, "Of course, they are going to make enormous profits."[22]

Since there was never an informed public discussion of the obligations undertaken by the U.S. under this treaty, it seems fair to ask the question: Precisely what is meant by the statements quoted above? Does this "protocol" override normal commercial practices in international trade? What about patent law? Benedick writes:

> The parties and non-parties to the Montreal Protocol had accomplished far more than significantly strengthening controls over ozone depleting substances: they had created the first financial mechanism dedicated to protection of the global environment, and, for the first time, the governments of industrialized nations had accepted a responsibility to help developing countries with modern technology.[23]

The president of the London conference, United Kingdom environmental secretary Patten, concluded that the Montreal Protocol "would become 'the model for ... future environmental diplomacy.'"

What will happen to this treaty should it turn out, as appears likely, that "ozone depletion" is nothing but an aberration of the research techniques? That perturbations occur in the ozone layer is well established. Some have been correlated with solar activity, and with stratospheric weather patterns, intense cold, and the presence of chloride and/or nitrogen. Of all these, stratospheric weather may be the most important.

Further long-term studies, especially those relying on satellite-based instrumentation, may reveal cyclic patterns and may help to determine what is cause and what is effect among the many phenomena that have been described. Maybe—just maybe—none of the earth-based data are reliable.

This startling statement is based on a 1992 research report by two Belgian meteorologists, D. DeMuer and H. DeBacker (published in the *Journal of Geophysical Research*), who contend that all ground-based measures of stratospheric ozone concentration are influenced by changing amounts of sulfur dioxide (SO_2) in the atmosphere. They conclude that the presence of SO_2—from volcanoes and from industry—produces a "fictitious" ozone depletion and point out that when the data for the past 30 years are corrected for SO_2 interference, all evidence of ozone depletion disappears.[24]

Should this surprising result be confirmed by other independent investigators, it would do away with all the worry over ozone depletion. It would also be an object lesson in the hazards of acting precipitously, before sufficient data are gathered and understood.

So where does that leave us on the question of ozone depletion? The facts do not support the notion that ozone in the stratosphere is being irrevocably destroyed. Nor do they support the supposed dire consequences that would result if the ozone doomsayers should be right.

We also know that the idea that CFCs destroy ozone is long on theory but short on facts. Yet, CFCs, specifically freon (CFC-12), are essential for the proper functioning of today's refrigeration and air-conditioning equipment, and halons are critical for fire suppression. Nevertheless, we're still faced with an early, forced phaseout, accompanied by enormous price increases of this important product. What to do?

Should we succumb to the plans of the duPont Company to introduce Suva (CFC 134a) at great cost to the consumer and great profit to duPont? By no means.

So far, the unsurpassable ingenuity of the human mind has not been taken into account. Faced with the CFC challenge, the proprietor of an automotive air-conditioner repair shop in Florida, Bob Holzknecht, has come up with a replacement for freon that is both inexpensive and effective. Experimenting in his own personally supported research laboratory, Holzknecht has found that a mixture of four parts propane and three parts N-butane is every bit as effective in air-conditioners as freon. The same should be true for refrigeration units.

The beauty of the propane-N-butane combo is that both components are readily available—and they cannot be patented. While it is well known that both of these gases are flammable, that can be controlled by proper sealing. After all, natural gas (which is both flammable and explosive) is safely used in many household appliances and gasoline likewise is safely controlled for use in automobiles. No chemical company, no matter how large, can monopolize this product and hence make enormous profits.

Holzknecht's results are supported by independent work in the former Soviet Union.[25] A report broadcast on the Moscow Home Service said, in part: "In accordance with the International Convention signed two years ago, the Soviet Union is taking steps to cut production of freon, which has a damaging effect on the ozone layer. This year, a large number of aerosols will be manufactured without freon, to be replaced by a mixture of propane and butane. In a year's time, five more Soviet factories will stop using freon in refrigerators."

Information on whether Russia and other countries that were formerly part of the U.S.S.R. will adapt propane-N-butane as a freon substitute is not currently available.

The case for or against freon and other CFCs, substitute refrigerants, and destruction of stratospheric ozone has not been made, and, until it is, we should be suspicious of those with an interest in reaping the profits of doom.

CHAPTER 5

Urban Air Pollution and Smog

Exaggerations and Overkill

AIR pollution in populated areas has two facets. One is smog, in which ozone is implicated. The other is a more general decline in air quality, doubtless determined by large numbers of people and all their activities crowded into relatively small areas. In addition, when cities are built, the original vegetation is replaced by buildings and paved streets, with the result that the heat balance is altered. Incoming sunlight is absorbed and reflected differently from asphalt and building materials than from green leafy surfaces, and so cities are always warmer than the neighboring areas. Cities, therefore, constitute "heat islands," and this, in turn, alters patterns of air circulation and the dispersion of pollutants.

City air has higher concentrations of sulfur and nitrogen oxides, various hydrocarbons and other organic compounds, particulates such as soot and dust, and carbon monoxide than does the surrounding countryside. It is these five components, plus lead, that were targeted in the 1970 Clean Air Act as the prime constituents of air pollution. To control them, strict ambient air quality standards were established, and deadlines were set for meeting them. How well have they worked?[1, 2]

There has been considerable progress. And for that we can be thankful, because the air we breathe is pretty important to all of us. Naturally, we want it to be clean, free from hazardous substances, and we like it to smell good or not to smell at all. Actions taken during the past two decades have succeeded in removing the heavy load of industrial pollutants that used to flow unchecked from the smokestacks of factories. Particulates, other than those that are extremely minute (10 microns or less) or come from volcanoes, wind, or sand storms, forest fires, and other natural events, have been brought under control. The sulfur oxides have been significantly reduced, but less progress has been achieved in the effort to cut back on levels of hydrocarbons, nitrogen oxides, carbon monoxide, and the formation of ground-level ozone. These are the remaining substances of interest.

Automobiles and buses—the internal combustion and diesel engines—are major contributors to these pesky pollutants. Nevertheless, there has been improvement here, too. Today's cars produce 96 percent less hydrocarbon and carbon monoxide, and 76 percent less nitrogen oxide than those built 20 years ago.[3] The removal of lead from gasoline has resulted in an 80 percent reduction. All this is a real achievement—but the air quality standards set by the EPA have not been met. The deadlines have been extended several times, and still many communities are declared to be "non-attainment" areas. How come?

After a 20-year effort and the expenditure of $30 billion, surely it is time for a critical review of the clean air programs. We need to ask, for instance: Is there a good justification, a solid base of scientific facts for the presumed relation between air pollutants and human health? Are the programs to reduce pollutants realistic and cost-effective? What benefits have been achieved?[4]

But instead of analyzing what we've learned and determining whether continuation of programs already under way is justified, government regulation has merely bred more regulation. The 1990 Clean Air Act amendments, for example, mandate spending an additional $12 billion per year. For what benefit?

In a recent review of the municipal ozone-smog problem submitted early in 1992, the National Academy of Sciences reported that "billions of dollars invested at refineries and gasoline stations and in the hardware of cars to reduce organic emissions ... have been misdirected because efforts to reduce nitrogen oxides have been neglected.... Smog is so poorly understood that much of the nation's effort to control it may [also] be misdirected."[5]

This startling comment from America's most prestigious science organization compels attention, since there has been intensive research on air pollution, smog formation, and human health for more than two decades. What has been learned?

With respect to human health, toxic levels of air pollution have historically been claimed to be the cause of more than the expected number of deaths in the famous air pollution episodes in the Meuse Valley of Belgium in 1930; Donora, Pennsylvania, in 1948, and London, England, in 1952.[6] Several other independent studies have failed to identify any single pollutant or combination of pollutants that could have caused the fatalities.

A more likely explanation for the deaths has been offered by Dr. Hugh Ellsaesser:

In each case there was an initial drop in temperature associated with the onset of autumn. The previous winter in each case had been unusually mild. The unusually mild winter allowed many people who were susceptible to respiratory illness to survive an additional year. When the first cold snap of autumn occurred, these were the people primarily affected. The deaths were concentrated in those under 1, over 45, and those suffering with pre-existing respiratory conditions. In all likelihood, the *air pollution was associated with, rather than the cause of,* the deaths from respiratory failure.*[7]

Nevertheless, the belief that air pollution, as defined for purposes of regulation and control, has an adverse effect on public health is well established in the public mind. Yet many careful studies, dating back to the 1960s, do not find such a relationship. In an analysis and critical review of the possible association between general urban air pollution and lung cancer, a member of the California Air Resources Board, John R. Goldsmith, reported in 1968:

* Emphasis added.

If such a relationship exists, a number of consequences should follow which have not been observed:

1. The urban factor should be largest in those countries where there is the heaviest urban pollution. It is not.
2. Assuming that the larger the city, the greater the population exposure will be to air pollution, then the urban factor should increase regularly with city population. It does not, at least in the United States.
3. If exposure to urban pollution causes an augmentation in lung cancer, then the rates should be higher in lifetime urban residents than in migrants to urban areas. They are not.
4. Correlations of lung cancer rates with measured pollution should be found by studies in the United Kingdom, where both lung cancer rates are high and pollution is great. A positive correlation is found with population density, but not with pollution.
5. If the urban factor were community air pollution, it should affect women at least as much as men. It does not.*

There may be other explanations of the urban factor (greater smoking, occupational exposure, population density, infections), but the evidence presently available that it is air pollution *does not confirm the suspicion of causality* which previously existed.†[8]

Despite evidence to the contrary, the "suspicion of causality" still exists—and it is still without proof. But what about carbon monoxide and ozone; aren't these two constituents of air pollution known to be toxic?

The answer for carbon monoxide (CO), of course, is "yes"—but at concentrations far beyond the levels set by the EPA's air quality standards, which require ambient air to have no more than nine parts per million of CO. But that doesn't tell the whole story about the EPA's standards. If only one CO monitor shows more than that amount for eight hours on any one day, then the EPA regulators consider that whole city to be a "non-attainment" area for the entire year.

---

* The more recent increase in lung cancer among women is related to cigarette smoking, not air pollution.
† Emphasis added.

Consider the situation that occurred recently in New York City, as reported by *The Wall Street Journal*, March 31, 1992.[9] Out of ten CO test sites near Columbus Center, where a construction project was proposed, one site was determined to have 12.9 parts per million (ppm) if the project were *not* built. If it were, the ppm would rise to 13.3. Following regular EPA procedures, these two results were averaged and rounded to 13 ppm CO, or 4 ppm above the EPA standard. A suit was brought and Judge Shirley Wohl Kram rendered summary judgment that the city must come into CO regulatory compliance by November 15, 1992, or deny *all* permits for *all* new construction throughout the city. Does the punishment fit the crime?

The physiological effects of breathing carbon monoxide are well known; they can be fatal, if enough CO is inhaled. Carbon monoxide combines irreversibly with the hemoglobin of red blood cells and thus effectively blocks the oxygen-carrying capacity of blood, which, of course, is essential for life. Fortunately, the human blood stream contains a large number of red cells, and it takes quite a bit of CO to saturate them. At 20 percent carboxy hemoglobin—which is equivalent to saturation at about 120 ppm CO—some impairment of activity occurs, but little performance degradation is observable at 10 percent saturation, equivalent to CO at 60 ppm. At 8 percent saturation—equivalent to 48 ppm CO— there is no convincing evidence of adverse effects. The permissible standard of 9 ppm CO can, therefore, be considered very conservative. This level is based on a 1967 study by Beard and Wertheim which claimed impairment of time-interval discrimination after human subjects were exposed for 90 minutes to 50 ppm of CO.[10] Their results have not been accepted, and even the authors recognized the shortcomings of their research. They have been unable to verify or repeat their results. Nevertheless, the EPA's air quality standards and non-attainment rules are based on this flawed study. It costs cities many millions of dollars.

Now, what about ground level ozone? It has long been claimed that breathing air with detectable levels of ozone is hazardous to our health. Ralph Nader's Public Interest Research Group has warned, "Lung damage from ozone-polluted air is a risk faced by roughly three out of five Americans."[11] How great a risk from how much ozone is not made clear by Mr. Nader, but, doubtless, many people believe that some harm is involved. What is the evidence?

In an interesting piece of historical research by three scientists from Michigan State University, Dale E. Linvill, W. J. Hooker, and Brian Olson found that ground-level measurements of ozone taken between 1871 and 1903 show that the patterns and levels of ozone in the lower atmosphere were the same then—before cars and widespread industrialization—as they are today. The records came from a statewide network of 20 recording stations throughout Michigan.[12]

Linvill, et al, say: "Day-to-day ozone levels exhibited patterns very similar to those patterns seen in today's data. Ozone concentration was lowest during the coldest part of the year and highest during warm months. . . . A strong argument can be advanced for plant-soil emissions as the major contributor of photochemical ozone precursors."

Since the actual ozone levels were the same in the 1870s as in the 1970s, there is every reason to believe that the major cause of ozone formation is not industrial or automotive emissions—then or now.[13]

What are the precursors of ozone? Or, to put it simply, where does smog-related ground-level ozone come from? It has long been known that ozone forms under the influence of high temperatures, 90 degrees Fahrenheit or above, bright sunshine, the presence of hydrocarbons, and low wind speed or temperature inversion. True enough, but, as usual, the conventional wisdom is an oversimplification. *Both* hydrocarbons and nitrogen oxides are required, but it is the ratio between these two chemicals that is crucial. This ratio cannot be controlled by law, no matter how stringent the regulations are, because nature intervenes.

In some places like Atlanta, Georgia; Baton Rouge, Lousiana; Tampa-St. Petersburg, Florida, and the entire Los Angeles basin, the natural production of hydrocarbons from trees and other vegetation far exceeds what we humans can be held responsible for.[14] Nitrogen oxides also come from both natural and human sources. William L. Chameides, an atmospheric chemist at Georgia Tech, found that regulatory controls succeeded in reducing man-caused hydrocarbons in Atlanta by 37 percent between 1979 and 1985, but since more than two-thirds of the ozone precursors consisted of natural emissions from plants, the ozone level in the city actually rose.

In other investigations, Phil Abelson[15] found that living plants emit from two to four times as much hydrocarbon as man produces. Moreover, vegetation releases its organic emissions preferentially on hot summer days that are favorable for ozone formation. Of course, if the naturally occurring hydrocarbons were produced by human activity, they would be classified as "air pollutants." Since they form in nature, they are ignored. In the rarefied atmosphere of bureaucracy, where computer models and simulations take the place of human brains, natural phenomena apparently don't count.

No matter, the possible health effects of elevated levels of ozone have been studied intensively for more than 20 years without finding problems beyond some temporary respiratory and eye irritation. Only among persons with pre-existing breathing problems—asthma, for example—does ozone appear to be harmful since it will trigger an attack. Even this can be avoided by refraining from vigorous exercise or other heavy physical activity during a smog episode. The EPA's own five-volume ozone review, published in 1986, concludes that no long- or short-term impacts on human health have been discovered or demonstrated.[16]

The National Ambient Air Quality Standard, required by the 1970 Clean Air Act, sets the limit for ozone concentration at 0.120 ppm. Ozone monitoring devices are maintained at several hundred locations around the country. If even one monitor registers ozone concentration over 0.124 ppm for one hour or more, that whole region is declared to exceed the standard for that day. Four such instances in any three-year period results in that region being declared an ozone non-attainment region.

Throughout the nation, 85 percent of all ozone exposures above 0.120 ppm are in California, and 82 percent occur in the Los Angeles Basin.

If elevated ozone causes health problems, we would expect to find the evidence in Los Angeles. The residents of that city have been exposed to air that has exceeded the EPA standards for ozone from between 100 to 200 days a year for at least 40 years. Where are the respiratory invalids? Where are the smog victims' bodies?[17]

Despite intensive research, health statistics for Los Angeles fail to show any distinction between the health of the residents of Los Angeles and any other American city.

If every human being, all automobiles, and all industry were to be removed from the Los Angeles Basin, it would still fail to meet EPA ozone standards on most days, due entirely to natural conditions and weather.[18]

Throughout the nation, human-influenced ozone levels have dropped by 74 percent since 1985. Today California is the only state with an important ozone regulatory problem. But especially since most of California's ozone is produced by nature, why should taxpayers throughout the U.S. continue to pay $10 to $15 billion per year for fractional further reductions that have dubious benefit?

The EPA's already strict rules about "non-attainment" have been made even more draconian by the 1990 Clean Air Act requirements. In a careful analysis of ozone and urban smog, K. H. Jones sums up the situation as follows:

The EPA's new regulatory program, particularly the nitrogen oxide control provisions, will not only bleed precious money from the economy; it will exacerbate ozone air pollution in America [by altering the O_3-NO_2 ratio] and slow progress in improving urban ozone air quality, as well.

Those effects have two causes. First, the ozone non-attainment regulations stipulated in the 1990 amendments to the Clean Air Act attack minor hydrocarbon sources that may contribute to urban ozone. . . . If imposed on all industrial sources of hydrocarbons or nitrogen oxide emitting 25 tons per year (which could shut many small businesses down), [the new mandates] would reduce stationary source emissions by only a few percentage points.

Similarly, rigid inspection and maintenance programs for automobiles are a total waste of time and money. Only 3 percent of all 1981–89 vehicles in Seattle failed the test. Review of other such data suggests that the same is true of other state programs, as well. Non-California-certified cars already emit about half of the legal standard of 0.41 grams per mile (gpm); hence, the new 0.25-gpm standard is meaningless. The federal clean fuels program will address sources that generate only 4 percent of total hydrocarbon emissions in the average city.

Stage II vapor recovery nozzles on gasoline pumps will reduce emissions by only about 2 percent. Because 70 to 80 percent of emissions in the commute cycle occur in driveways during initial ignition, controlling vehicle miles traveled is also of dubious value, since any transportation control measure that involves starting a car (e.g., park and ride) leaves most transportation emissions unaffected.

All of the above strategies taken together—even if they proved to be 100 percent effective—would result in less than a 0.01-ppm reduction in ozone concentration at the air quality monitor.

The EPA's regulations are counterproductive because auto fleet turnover is the only proven means of significantly reducing ozone pollution. Ten percent of America's cars are responsible for 50 percent of all emissions, and most of those cars are pre-1981 vehicles without catalytic converters and other emissions control devices. Regulations that increase the costs of new cars will simply delay the turnover of the auto fleet and unnecessarily postpone further improvements in air quality.

[The EPA's] rhetoric aside, America has made great strides in smog abatement over the past decade. Temperature-adjusted data indicate that ozone pollution outside California has been reduced by 74 percent since 1985.

Today only three urban areas outside California have serious or severe ozone non-attainment problems. Another 25 areas, which suffer only marginal to moderate smog problems, show every sign of achieving attainment within two to five years without the additional onerous regulatory controls spelled out in the 1990 amendments to the Clean Air Act.

Any major ozone-smog problem in America is confined to the state of California, particularly the Los Angeles Basin. It is ridiculous to treat all of America as if it faced the problems California does and to impose on the entire nation massive economic costs that are ultimately unnecessary and counter-productive.

In pursuit of greater budgets, increased regulatory authority, and the political benefits of front-page coverage, the EPA has perpetrated a fraud on the American people. The agency's refusal to acknowledge that the 1988 data on ozone were an aberration and its failure to publicize preliminary 1991 data in a timely manner could cost the economy $26 billion a year.

The result can only be continued economic stagnation, higher unemployment, and reduced international competitiveness. Three-quarters of the cost of the EPA's ozone non-attainment program is a total waste of money. Even under optimistic assumptions, the costs of the program outweigh any possible benefits by a factor of from 9 to 48.[19]

But nobody likes dirty air, even if illness can't be attributed to it. Isn't there some additional way of improving urban air quality without all the new, expensive regulations? Indeed there is—by using the same phenomenon that nature does: photosynthesis.

By planting lots of green growing plants downtown, we could bring to cities a breath of fresh air.[20]

There is precedence for such use of green plants. Best known is the band of Vienna Woods, surrounding Vienna, Austria. Established by Kaiser Franz Josef, they encircle much of the city proper. What is not so well known is that the "woods" were planned as an air freshener. Also during post-World War II reconstruction in the city of Karlsruhe, Germany, extensive planting was included for the purpose of combating air pollution. The city of Stuttgart also had such a program.

Suppose that in addition to city parks and parkways, tree-lined streets, and the occasional tubs with flowers (all at ground level), we were to make use of every building as a planting site. Roof gardens should abound. Most building roofs are sufficiently strong to support plantings, especially around the periphery, and water is generally available to serve air-conditioning systems. With plantings suspended from parapets and cornices, we could greatly augment the ground level plantings and make our buildings look better, too—bringing back memories of the hanging gardens of Babylon.

By judicious selection of species that use carbon monoxide, as well as carbon dioxide, such as Alder and English ivy, in addition to hardy species of leafy plants that consume quantities of carbon dioxide, the composition of urban air could be beneficially affected. Plants also absorb other air pollutants, including sulfur, nitrogen, and organic compounds and particulates. Since city temperatures are several degrees warmer than outlying areas, temperature moderation becomes another worthy goal achievable with green plants. And, finally, plantings on such a large scale would render the cities far more pleasant to the eye, ear, and nose of residents and tourists alike.

Another important advantage—a political one—should be mentioned. Such a plan would not only bring the positive results mentioned; it would prove to everyone that we can better reach the goal sought through natural means and voluntary cooperation than we have done thus far with punitive legislation, which hasn't done the job and whose enforcement grows continually more expensive.

PART TWO

About Food, People, Animals

CHAPTER 6

Of Food and Population

More Than Enough to Feed All

SOMETIME in the future, when the accomplishments of the 20th century are recorded for posterity, it may finally be acknowledged that our greatest achievement by far has been the introduction of high-tech, high-yield agriculture. Measured in terms of benefit to human society, an adequate diet of nutritious, abundant, and affordable food eclipses all other developments of this most remarkable century. Neither computer technology nor transistors, robotics, advances in communication and transportation, life-saving antibiotics and modern medicine, nuclear energy, synthetics, plastics, and the entire petro-chemical industry rank as high in importance as the advances in food production. And all these other wonderful breakthroughs probably could not have happened *without* a well-fed population.

No less an authority than Napoleon acknowledged the primacy of food when he observed that "an army marches on its stomach."

For the first time in history we can take for granted that food will be available whenever we wish to buy it. For the first time in the more than 6,000 years of recorded human progress, food self-sufficiency in the developed world has been achieved, and it happened on our watch! Modern society—that is, the Western industrialized world—is now able to feed itself and still have surpluses left over to help nourish much of the rest of the world.

Who points with pride to the fact that agricultural scientists and farmers have scored a monumental victory over the ancient scourge of hunger and malnutrition? Ironically, modern agriculture is, instead, under attack, and its most important tools and techniques are being questioned at a time we should be loudly singing its praises.

Dr. Norman Borlaug, a Nobel prize recipient who is considered one of the fathers of the "Green Revolution" because of his involvement in the early genetic development of the newer, shorter stiff-stalked wheat and rice varieties, has said, "I am concerned that the growing anti-science and anti-technology bias in affluent countries will adversely affect the prospects for agricultural development. . . . In effect, the 'haves' are telling the 'have-nots' that they should stay with current simple lifestyles since great material well-being isn't what it is made out to be. How many people in the First World would be willing to cut their life spans by one half, see up to half of their children die before reaching the age of ten, often as a result of minor and easily curable illness, live in illiteracy with substandard shelter, clothing and sanitation, and face bleak prospects of no improvement in economic well-being for themselves or their children? Unwittingly, this is the continuing fate that the affluent anti-technology groups are wishing for the Third World's people."[1]

Since 1960, the use of agricultural technology has doubled food output, tripled corn yields, and added 25 percent to per capita food supplies in poor countries. To be more specific, in the United States, corn crop yields have increased fourfold, wheat is up nearly 250 percent, soybeans have doubled, cotton has nearly tripled, and peanuts are up more than 450 percent—all in just 30 to 50 years.[2]

If we should try to produce today's crops without the tools of high-yield agriculture, it would be necessary to farm nearly three times as much land as is actually in present use. Without high-yield agriculture, we would already have had to plow up another ten million square miles—an area equal to the entire land mass of North America. But, by using our ever-expanding knowledge of food plants, by supplying their nutritional requirements, and by protecting them from pests and disease, modern farming takes a total of only about six million square miles.[3]

Even more astonishing is the fact that increases in agricultural output have been accompanied by significant decreases in the number of agricultural workers. Again, using the U.S. as an example, in 1800 farming required about 73.6 percent of the labor force; by 1980 it had dropped to 2.7 percent. This trend toward a smaller number of farmers producing much more food on much less land and feeding larger populations than at any time in the past continues in all the industrialized countries of Europe and North America, as well as in Japan.[4]

We should note that these figures may be somewhat misleading, because they refer only to those persons actually engaged directly in farming. What has actually happened is that, along with the abundant food crops that are grown in the specific geographical regions where they fare best, a whole new food-handling industry has sprung up. This involves transporting the harvest, warehousing it, packaging it, distributing it, and merchandising it nationwide and for export. The entire enterprise probably involves as many as one in five American workers.

Two key factors help to explain the remarkable productivity of modern agriculture. First, we have improved varieties of many food plants. Second we have vastly expanded our knowledge of their growing requirements. Soil science, and the informed, controlled use of fertilizers and pesticides targeted for specific applications have had a tremendous positive effect.

There is, of course, a long history of improving crops. Farmers have always selected the best plants to provide seeds for the next year's crops, and naturally occurring hybrids have long been recognized and valued. But it was the conscious breeding of desirable strains, despite the laborious and painstaking work involved, that led to the introduction early in the 20th century of many kinds of improved crops, including potatoes, fruits, and eventually the revolutionary hybrid corn. Then came the growing understanding of plant genetics, which opened the door to the possibility of designing and tailoring plants to have the characteristics desired by grower and consumer. It was probably the introduction of the genetically engineered strain of wheat with strong, short stems and built-in disease resistance that ushered in the "Green Revolution." Developed by Nobel laureate Norman Borlaug, the new wheat was

adapted to thrive in Third World countries with spectacular results.[5]

Expansion of the Green Revolution techniques—that is, high-
yield agriculture—to many different food plants has effectively
ended the era of chronic hunger and famine in most of the world.
Traditionally, up to 50 percent of the world's population has faced
the possibility of severe hunger; that number now has been reduced
to no more than five percent. Famine still occurs but only in those
countries that experience both drought and war. Providing enough
food for starving people is not a matter of production, because the
supply is sufficient; it is a political problem of bad government, bad
economic policies, inadequate transportation systems, and, all too
often, civil war.[6]

High-yield agriculture has already produced many successes like
the short-stemmed wheat, and many more innovations are ready
for wide-scale adoption. Among these are a new system of high-
yielding wet-rice farming that could utilize, for the first time, about
500 million acres of wetland in central Africa. With this development, Africa could become self-sufficient in rice production and be
able to release the low-yield upland areas, where rice is now
grown. This upland area, in turn, could then be used for the
cultivation of trees, to which it is far better suited.[7] Among other
success stories are these:

- In China, a new hybrid rice has been developed which has the
  potential to increase yields 25 percent for virtually all the
  world's rice plantings. Currently, it has to be hand-pollinated,
  but if a technique for male sterilization is found, this hybrid
  could become very important.
- Yields of field corn for livestock feed can be tripled with
  hybrids and agronomic varieties that are now on the shelf. One
  of these, a variety of high protein corn, has 90 percent of the
  food value of non-fat dry milk. It is ready for release.
- New shorter-season crop varieties have already pushed the
  world's corn belt 500 miles farther north; this benefits Canada, Russia, and China.
- India is adopting a new hybrid sunflower seed that has already
  tripled production and promises to double it again in 1993.

- Kenya's new high-tech coffee tree resists both coffee-berry disease and leaf rust; growers can, therefore, cut pesticide sprays by one-third.
- New pest-resistant varieties of the cassava plant yield from three to five times as much food as the wild types in Africa, Latin America, and Southeast Asia.
- Alfalfa and soybeans are benefiting from new, more vigorous high-tech strains of the nitrogen-fixing bacteria, Rhizobium, that can be induced to grow on the legume's roots and increase crop yields five to ten percent by making the necessary nitrogen readily available.
- Cloning and tissue culture are high-tech procedures that have been applied to some species of trees, shortening their breeding cycles from decades to months. This is especially important for tropical species, where the technique has also been used to quadruple yields of palm oil, cocoa, rubber, and wood.
- By exploiting gene modification techniques, acid tolerance has been bred into corn, rice, and forage crops that can then be planted successfully on much of the world's 400 million hectares of acid savannah land that is now considered worthless even for wildlife.[8]

In some instances, new ways of utilizing existing species have also made important contributions to agriculture. For example, the ubiquitous salt-tolerant weed, Salicornia, is found in temperate regions throughout the world and grows in both sandy and muddy salt marshes. It has long been thought to be useless. Recently it was discovered that its copious seeds yield an abundance of high quality vegetable oil, and the body of the plant, when chopped, provides fodder that is as nutritious as alfalfa. Among its most appealing characteristics is its ability to grow luxuriantly on desert sand when irrigated with sea water! Experimental crops are now being raised in the Middle East and other semi-arid regions.[9]

Developments in animal husbandry are also impressive; at least two of them are worthy of mention. The first is bovine somatotropin (BST), also known as bovine growth hormone (BGH). This substance is produced naturally in the body of cattle and functions to control milk production. Harmless bacteria have been genetically altered to produce the hormone so that it can supplement the amount found in the cow's body. Since it is identical with that originally present, the administration of increased amounts stimulates the volume of milk produced and increases the yield by as much as 25 percent on the same amount of feed. As early as 1985, the Food and Drug Administration, after extensive testing, determined that BST is safe both for cows and for people. With hogs, pork somatotropin can be bacterially produced, and use of this wholly safe, natural substance leads to pigs that, when slaughtered, have one-third less fat and 15 percent more lean meat. They also grow well on one-quarter less feed grain. But these important advances in the production of nutritious, healthful meat and milk are opposed by some farmers who fear the competition. And by some who have fallen victim to the fear-mongering of anti-technology folk who oppose all the techniques of high-yield agriculture. They forget, apparently, that before 1950 the average American dairy cow produced about 5,314 pounds of milk a year, while that same "average cow" today produces 14,300 pounds—the result of scientific farming. The use of BST simply continues this great tradition of continuous improvement.[10]

Like technological advances in many fields, high-yield agriculture is under severe attack from anti-science factions. Modern farming methods, we are told, are destroying topsoil and ground water. This charge is wrong on both counts.[11] Erosion of topsoil has been cut back at least 50 percent by conservation tillage and no-till techniques in North America and in western Europe. This has become possible through use of herbicides for weed control. Old-timers will remember the terrible soil erosion in the "dust bowl" of America's Midwest during the years of heat and drought of the mid-1930s. Similar climatic conditions occurred in the late 1980s and there were months of heat and drought again, but no "dust bowl." Modern tillage techniques saved the soil.

Anti-technology critics often cite the supposed loss of arable soil in the Amazon Basin, which they attribute to deforestation and "slash and burn" farming. It is now known that planting the legume vine called kudzu in the Amazonian rain forest adds organic material to the soil and increases soil fertility by 90 percent, providing as much nutrition as 14 years of bush fallow.[12] And kudzu is a weed largely out of control in much of the southeastern United States. Conclusion: For most problems there is a solution.

Salinization of soils, which is also blamed by critics on high-yield agriculture, is known to be caused by two factors, waterlogging the land and over-use or improper application of fertilizers. New irrigation techniques are replacing the old-style general flooding. Sprinkler, drip, and trailing tube irrigation systems double the efficiency of water use. Adoption of these newer procedures may sometimes seem slow, but they are happening—and modern high-yield agriculture is as involved in environmental conservation procedures as it is in increasing yields.[13]

As far as fertilizer is concerned, it is true that high-yield strains require additional nutrient, especially nitrogen. It would be difficult to find any procedure that has come under more persistent, ill-informed attack than the use of fertilizers and pesticides in today's agricultural practices.

Some opponents would have us return to the use of animal manures and crop rotation,[14] apparently disregarding the fact that such procedures were standard farming practices throughout history and that they were able to provide sufficient food for only small populations. The technique of growing food crops without using chemically formulated fertilizers and pesticides is variously called "sustainable" (at what level?) "alternative" (to what?), "low-input," or "organic"—as if there were any such thing as "inorganic" food! Many efforts at "organic farming" have proved to be effective only on small plots and for short periods of time. Not well known is the fact that China tried organic farming on a large scale during the regime of Mao Tse-Tung. It was a disaster, and China wound up with 200 million underfed people. Now China is among the nations that are most aggressively using high-yield agricultural techniques.[15]

Still, with respect to fertilizer, plant nutrients—and especially nitrogen—are not uniformly available in all cropland. What nature does not supply, man must provide. Improved varieties of food plants grow faster, become larger, and produce more harvest than the wild types from which they were developed. That means more nutrients move from the soil into the plant, and the seeds and fruits are more nutritious. Naturally, then, more replacement by fertilizer is required. Intelligent management of how much to add and the timing of applications are essential to a successful crop.[16]

Those who object to the modern formulations of pesticides that target specific pests choose to ignore the fact that, previously, food crops were either obliterated by insects, bacteria, fungi, or other problems (no food is better?), or were protected by compounds of arsenic, lead, mercury, or other heavy metals that retain their toxicity forever.[17]

The history of how Bordeaux mixture (copper sulfate and lime) came to be used as a fungicide is interesting enough to merit retelling. Angered by the public plucking grapes from vineyards that were too close to main thoroughfares, the farmers sprayed the grapes within reach with the copper sulfate-lime slurry to make them unpalatable.

When the fungus known as downy mildew (phytophthora infestans) was introduced inadvertently into the vintage wine areas of France, it destroyed the grape vines—all of them except for those near the roads. The Bordeaux mixture turned out to be an excellent fungicide and is still often used to control fungus disease.

Those who object to the proper use of modern pesticides never reveal what they believe the alternatives should be. They also overlook the fact that pesticide residues on food are well below the levels set as safe by the FDA and are effectively negligible. No fatalities, no serious illness, and no cancer has resulted from the approved uses of pesticides. Dr. Robert Scheuplein, the respected food-safety microbiologist with the FDA, concluded that the effective cancer risk from pesticide residues in food is 0.0000076.[18] That means that less than five hundredths of one percent of all cancers *might* be caused by pesticide residues. A comment from Dr. C. Everett Koop, former Surgeon General of the United States, is especially appropriate in this regard:

Consumer advocates, however well intentioned, continue to tell us that dangerous, cancer-causing pesticides are present in our food and that we and our children are at extreme risk. This is simply not true. There is no food safety crisis. While some pesticides are known to have caused tumors in laboratory animals when exposure occurs in concentrated doses, the residues which may be present on some foods occur at such minute levels that they present no risk of harm to human health. . . . Indeed, U.S. food supplies contain less than one-quarter of one percent of the allowable intake of pesticides.[19]

According to a report published in 1990 by Warren Brookes, eliminating pesticides would cost the average household $228 a year, while including chemical fertilizers in a ban would raise food costs $428 a year.[20] This would be in addition to the drop in crop yields. Yet the scare tactics against pesticides persist.[21]

The opponents of pesticides and many food faddists also ignore the existence of natural pesticides; yet these chemical compounds, produced by most food plants, do exist.[22] In fact, as pointed out by Dr. Bruce Ames, University of California biochemist, "We are ingesting in our diet at least 10,000 times more, by weight, of natural pesticides than of man-made pesticide residues. . . . Nonetheless, there has been relatively little interest in the toxicology or carcinogenicity of these naturally occurring compounds until recently, although they are by far the main source of 'toxic chemicals' ingested by humans."[23]

Remember that a simple cup of coffee contains at least a thousand known chemicals, of which only 22 have been subjected to animal carcinogenicity tests—and, of these, 17 turned out to be positive. Should we stop drinking coffee? Or insist that every cup be labeled with the message, "Contains at least 17 known carcinogens"? A little common sense is in order.[24]

Consider the unique case of celery.[25] The crisp, delicious flavor of this widely used salad vegetable contributes importantly to the taste of soups and stews and countless prepared dishes, as well as being a popular food item on its own. But celery has a problem. It is able to produce certain organic chemical compounds, called psoralens, to defend itself. This happens whenever the celery plant is attacked by specific disease-causing fungi or other plant-invading organisms. Now, fungi spores are everywhere in the natural environment, and unless celery is protected from them, it will inevitably become infected. That stimulates the celery to produce its protective chemicals, which, in turn, can cause a severe skin reaction in humans. This unfortunate sequence of events is prevented by spraying the celery crop with the proper fungicide.

Studies show that chronic exposure to celery which is not treated by fungicides increases the risk of skin cancer.

Celery is not the only food plant that becomes hazardous unless protected by agri-chemicals; it is simply the best documented. Many vegetables, herbs, and fruits also produce psoralens. In fact, whenever food starts to decay (usually caused by invasion of fungi or bacteria), any of several unpleasant chemical compounds may be formed. These contribute to the estimated 6.5 to 24 million cases of food-borne illnesses that occur each year in the U.S. The number of deaths that result exceeds 9,000 annually.[26] Should the Environmental Protection Agency be successful in its recently announced plan to ban the use of methyl bromide—now required to sterilize contaminated soils and to protect cereal grains in storage—the loss of much stored food and the increase in food-borne illnesses and deaths will be significant. There is no available substitute for methyl bromide, which is harmless in the quantities used.[27]

Given the extraordinary success of high-yield agriculture, why are there so many attacks upon it? Would the opponents and critics prefer that less food be grown? I believe the answer to that question is "yes." And the reason can be summed up in a single word— *overpopulation*.

As we have seen, high-yield agriculture can not only provide sufficient food for today's world population, it can supply enough for billions more. The idea of saving lives and providing for population growth upsets a lot of people. During the discussions that took place in the early 1970s about the banning of DDT, one of the cogent arguments put forward to retain and control the use of this remarkable insecticide was the number of human lives that had been saved. During the less than 30 years of its use (1944–72), DDT prevented more human death and disease than any other man-made chemical in all of recorded history.[28] Without any adverse effects on human health, then or since, DDT prevented thousands of Allied soldiers from contracting typhus (borne by body lice) during World War II and millions of people in the Third World were protected from mosquito-borne malaria in the decades of the 1950s and 1960s.

If we are to believe the statements of some people, including several well-known biologists, that was just the problem with DDT. It saved human lives. For example, in response to a reporter's question about banning DDT, Dr. Charles Wurster, who was then chief scientist for the Environmental Defense Fund, stated that in his opinion there are too many people, and "this is as good a way to get rid of them as any." Another statement of Dr. Wurster's was brought out in congressional testimony before the House Committee on Agriculture, 92nd Congress, first session, 1971: "It doesn't really make a lot of difference because the organophosphate (pesticide) acts locally and only kills farm workers, and most of them are Mexicans and Negroes." There is no record of any media or public reaction to this shocking statement.[29]

Dr. LaMont Cole, a respected environmentalist at Yale University, asserted that "To feed a starving child is to exacerbate the world overpopulation problem." And Dr. Van den Bosch of the University of California chided others about their concern for "all those little brown people in poor countries."[30]

Malthusian predictions about overpopulation and starvation have been made since the beginning of the 19th century. America's most ardent Malthusian is Paul Ehrlich of Stanford University, who, with his wife, proposes the following program to prevent or ameliorate the population explosion:

1. We must institute the Chinese Communist system of compulsory abortion and various forms of infanticide so that each couple will have only one child. We must hope that our government doesn't wait until it, too, decides that coercive measures can solve America's population problem. . . . The price of personal freedom in making childbearing decisions may be the destruction of the world.

2. As Barry Commoner recommended, we must go back to the spinning wheel, returning to a beatific state of endless drudge labor, six days a week, and exhaustion on Sunday. Most of the labor-saving devices and the appliances of everyday life consume fossil-fuel energy, which, of course, poisons the environment.

3. Air travel by businessmen must cease, with the world's executives linked instead by closed-circuit TV.

4. All this nonsense of getting into the family car and driving off on vacation must cease, too.

5. The "rich and the intelligent" must not propagate. They are "dangerous because they promote overproduction [and have] the heaviest impact on the planet." The rich are the cause of most of the world's ills. Poverty is beautiful.

6. The couple of the future must be good parents by having 1.5 children.

In a commentary on this Ehrlich program, Ralph De Toledano of *National Review* noted that they did not explain how violations of the China-like compulsory abortion rules would be punished.[31] Also, regarding the proposed crackdown on air travel by businessmen, De Toledano observed that the Ehrlichs seem to be unaware that the closed-circuit TV they propose "uses electric power, which must be generated and thus only worsens global warming."

In an overview of the Ehrlichs' program, De Toledano concluded: "And this about sums up the whole 'environmentalist' drive. These types do not want two blades of grass to grow where one did before. They are not interested in feeding the starving or clothing the cold. They don't care whether there will eventually be only one child in the playground where three once romped. They want a society in which the elite have organic strawberries and cream, and the rest of the people thank them each day for saving the tsetse fly and the precious mosquito."

The conviction that there are too many people, and that overpopulation causes a catastrophic loss of natural resources and severe environmental deterioration is inherent in the joint statement by the head of the U.S. National Academy of Sciences and the Royal Society of London, and was indeed a major driving force for the actions taken at the Earth Summit in Brazil in June 1992.[32] Reducing the size of human populations is one of the proposals in Agenda 21, agreed to by the participating nations. Of course, details of just how many humans will be eliminated, by what means the reduction would take place, and just who would be affected and who would not were not among the items discussed. Nor was the interesting question of who would make the life-or-death decisions.

But before we allow global bureaucrats to engage in this sort of tyranny over our private lives, we ought to examine their assumptions. The facts, including the record of actual food produced, show unequivocally that through using science and technology and taking advantage of the information and understanding inherent in modern agriculture, today's total world population can be fed adequately. This runs counter to the Malthusian theory that people will always out-produce their food supply. No matter how often Paul Ehrlich, the population guru of Stanford University, predicts widespread famine, he is wrong. He was wrong in 1968, when he said "The battle to feed all humanity is over. In the 1970s, the world will undergo famines—hundreds of millions of people will starve to death." He was wrong when he predicted the same worldwide famines by 1985. He continues to be wrong, and the popular press continues to treat him with great deference as an expert! Dr. Ehrlich is either ignorant of the facts about the successes of high-yield agriculture or he chooses to overlook them. Nor does he acknowledge that predicted population growth has not exploded, as he had predicted.[33]

In East Asia, for example, births per woman declined from 6.1 in the 1960–65 period to 2.7 from 1985–90. In Latin America, there were 5.9 births per woman in 1960–65 and by 1985–90 that figure dropped to 3.6. For all the developing countries, births per woman dropped from 6.1 in the 1960–65 time frame to 3.9 in 1985–90. According to United Nations figures, the total fertility rate has gone 59 percent of the way toward a level of no-growth in the developed world, and 62 percent of the way toward that level in the Third World—in just one generation.

Of course, world population is greater now than it has ever been. That is due in part to better nutrition that allows people to live longer and healthier lives. From a life expectancy of about 40–45 years at the beginning of the 20th century to about 76–78 years now, many more people survive to old age. This has made a significant contribution to total population size. And of course, that size is bound to increase somewhat in the near future. But to project, as so many do, that humans will continue to increase at the same rate indefinitely into the future has no basis in fact. Earlier in this century, the U.S. birth rate was so low as to fall behind replacement levels; then came the baby boom. The 1957 fertility rate was 3.76, which no one had predicted, followed by the 1976 fertility rate of only 1.72. This also was unpredicted. The entire history of human population increase shows periods of rapid growth followed by slowing to an almost plateau-like stability. Such a spurt followed the invention of tools, the introduction of agriculture, and the industrial revolution. But, what really drives the ups and downs of the fertility rate is not known. There is simply no reason to believe that the numbers of people will go up and up.[35]

As recently as 1991, the Public Broadcasting System program, "Race to Save the Planet," said flatly that world food production is falling behind population growth. That simply isn't so. The U.S. Agency for International Development's demographic survey published in 1991 shows birth rates slowing more rapidly than anyone had predicted. Third World food production continues to rise twice as fast as its population. The reality of the world's food and environmental gains are confirmed by all major published data series, including the UN's Food and Agriculture Organization and the U.S. Department of Agriculture. Every reputable study of the world's "carrying capacity" has concluded that the world can feed its expected population growth.

But the doomsayers are not placated. Recently, Ted Turner, owner of the CNN network, said in an interview with *Audubon* magazine, "Right now, there are just way too many people on the planet." His plan is to cut back from the current 5 billion human beings to no more than "250 million to 350 million people."[36] Will he and Jane Fonda lead the way?

In the same interview, Turner also revealed his opinion of his fellow Americans when he said, "When you look at us, we are a bunch of pigs ... and losers." Speak for yourself, Ted. How does he think we should live? According to Turner, with spears, loin cloths, and human sacrifices. "The indigenous people were the ones who were right!" he said. "I mean they had their own religion, their ethics, their own technology. We just went down the wrong road."[37] Surely no one listens to and accepts this drivel!

No one, that is, except the leaders and spokesmen for the environmentalist movement.

CHAPTER 7

Endangered Species

Are We Running Out of Plants and Animals?

Extinctions of plant and animal species will increase dramatically.
Hundreds of thousands of species—perhaps as many as 20 percent of
all species on earth—will be irretrievably lost as their habitats vanish,
especially in tropical forests.
Efforts to meet basic human needs and rising expectations are likely to
lead to the extinction of between one-fifth and one-seventh of all
species over the next two decades.

—Global 2000[1]

Without firing a shot, we may kill one-fifth of all species of life on this
planet.

—RUSSELL TRAIN, World Wildlife Fund[2]

Of the 3 to 10 million species now present on the earth, at least
500,000 to 600,000 will be extinguished during the next two decades.
At least 90 percent of all species that have existed have disappeared ...
the extinction rate has certainly soared, though details mostly remain
undocumented. *In 1974, a gathering of scientists concerned with the*
problem hazarded a guess *that the overall extinction rate among all*
species, whether known to science or not, could now have reached 100
*species a year.**

—THOMAS LOVEJOY, World Wildlife Fund[3]

* Emphasis added.

THIS last extraordinary statement, made without any supporting evidence, comes from the book *The Sinking Ark*. It is also the source cited as evidence by the authors of the previous quotations, which may account for the similarity in their predictions. But what's also similar about them is that they are hypotheses based on guesswork, unwarranted assumptions, and an apparent desire to excite public interest. They are not based on fact.[4]

Flimsy and uncertain though the predictions of large scale species demise may be, it is because so many people *believe* that so many plants and animals are in imminent danger of being exterminated that the Endangered Species Act was passed in December 1973. Adopted with the utmost good will, the act claims "to provide a means whereby the eco-systems upon which endangered species and threatened species depend may be conserved, to provide a program for the conservation of such endangered species and threatened species, and to take such steps as may be appropriate to achieve the purposes. . . ."[5]

Senator Mark Hatfield, one of the authors of the act, was quoted in the June 12, 1992, edition of *The Washington Post* as saying: "I have supported—and I continue to support—the Endangered Species Act. I helped write it. I offered the 1972 version of the act that eventually became law in 1973. I want it to survive."

But Senator Hatfield also admits that there are serious problems in the way the law is interpreted and administered. He points out: "But unlike many of my colleagues from urban areas, I also have to deal with the human side of this act, and thus have special reason to know that it has come to be an environmental law that *favors preservation over conservation*. There is no question that the act is being applied in a manner far beyond what any of us envisioned when we wrote it 20 years ago. . . . But today the act is being applied across entire states and regions, with the result that it now affects millions upon millions of acres of publicly and privately owned land, and many thousands of human beings. . . . The fact is that *Congress always considered the human element as central to the success of the ESA*. . . . The situation has gotten out of control."[*][6]

---

* Emphasis added.

One of the problems with the Act is its broadly inclusive definition of what is a species.

Consider the law: Under Section 3: *Definitions*:

- Paragraph (16) states: "The term 'species' includes any subspecies of fish or wildlife or plants, and any distinct population segment of any species of vertebrate fish or wildlife which interbreeds when mature."
- Paragraph (14) states: "The term 'plant' means any member of the plant kingdom, including seeds, roots, and other parts thereof."
- Paragraph (8) states: "The term 'fish or wildlife' means any member of the animal kingdom, including without limitation any mammal, fish, bird (including any migratory, non-migratory, or endangered bird for which protection is also afforded by treaty or other international agreement), amphibian, reptile, mollusk, crustacean, arthropod, or other invertebrate and includes any part, product, egg, or offspring thereof, or the dead body or parts thereof."[7]

These legal definitions may seem clear enough, but in the real world of biology, nature permits many variations and exceptions. As long as one deals only with the higher animals, it might seem that we are on firm ground, that species are well defined and distinctive. After all, anyone can tell the difference between an elephant and a tiger, between a horse and a cow. But consider the last two, horses and cattle. Within each of these clearly recognizable species, there is a range of physical characteristics—size, color of coat, body contour, and so on—that distinguish many types. If we're talking about horses, which type do we mean—Clydesdale, Thoroughbred, Arabian, Palomino, Quarter Horse, Shetland, Percheron, Appaloosa, or one of many others? And if we're talking about cows or cattle, is it a Holstein, Aberdeen Angus, Shorthorn, Galloway, Hereford, Guernsey, Brahman, Welsh, Highland, Jersey, or one of many others that we have in mind? But these are not different species or subspecies; because they are domesticated, they are called breeds.

Then there is the case of the horse-donkey cross. These two

clearly defined species are able to interbreed, but the hybrid offspring—the mule—is infertile. Is the mule a species? Or a sub-species? Or what? For the most part, taxonomists (biologists who specialize in the identification of species) ignore these complications because they are not found in nature. But that is by no means the end of the troubles.

With expert study, many more subtle differences among similar individuals can be distinguished than are seen with casual observation. Taxonomy is a sort of art—and what constitutes art? Some wag has said, "Art is what an artist says is Art!" It's also true that a species is what a taxonomist says is a species. And all taxonomists do not agree; the degree of subjectivity is great.

Since the study of systematics (another name for taxonomy) began, there have been lively debates—to be sure, mostly of academic interest only—over what really constitutes a species. In a general sense, taxonomists fall into one of two categories—splitters and lumpers. For example, some specialists in mammalian taxonomy (the lumpers) believe that all grizzly bears belong to the same species; others (splitters) claim to distinguish as many as 74 different species of grizzly bear.[8] Who is right? The controlled breeding of grizzlies, which might answer this question, would take a degree of courage and heroism that most of us do not possess. A similar situation obtains with many higher animals—birds, fish, reptiles; the confusion is common, and, until now, has had no practical consequences.

And then there are the recorded cases in which different species of insects were described and named—only to discover later that they were male and female of the same species. The two sexes among insects are often distinctly different in appearance. And among invertebrates, using reproductive behavior as a way to determine species poses special problems. There are many cases of hermaphroditism (male and female organs in the same body). Sometimes the anatomical bisexuality is simultaneous, as in most mollusks, and sometimes the young animal is male, and as the life cycle continues, it becomes female, as in shrimp.

Obviously the identification and describing of species is not straightforward or easy and *no one* knows how many species of animals there are or ever have been. The same can be said for much of the plant kingdom, especially the simpler forms.

Indeed, when one faces the problems of speciation among the so-called lower forms of life, including many worms, fungi, and single-celled organisms, the process becomes almost wholly subjective. Challenges to taxonomic descriptions that have been made of various invertebrates are not likely because the overwhelming number of insects, spiders, worms, and other "lower" animals are not generally popular critters, and because there are fewer experts able to question these categories than there are in the case of a duck or a trout or a bear.

All of this would be merely academic were it not for Congress' action in setting into law a definition of what is, in science and in nature, not definable. It is therefore possible for government agencies and their employees to identify any creature as a species—or subspecies—or geographical population—or whatever best suits their purposes for listing it as "endangered" or "threatened." And this action can have, and has had, devastating consequences.

There does indeed appear to be an increasing emphasis on listing subspecies and geographical populations, even though these categories are based on a high degree of subjectivity. In 1990 there were 14 mammal species and 36 mammal subspecies or populations listed as endangered or threatened. By 1991 the number of species had increased to 36, but the subspecies and population listings had grown to 199. The subspecies Santa Cruz Fox was one of these latter, as were five other "subspecies," one each for the five other islands found near Santa Barbara, California. Yet some experts consider that all these constitute a single species of gray fox whose range is from the East to the West Coast and into Mexico—a species that is abundant, not facing extinction.[9]

Probably no "endangered species" has achieved so much notoriety as has the Northern Spotted Owl, nor has any listing been so hypocritical and unjustified.[10] The Northern Spotted Owl is being used, quite cynically, as an excuse to stop logging in old growth forests, not to save the owl from extinction. Randall O'Toole of Portland, Oregon, who describes himself as an "eco-activist," is quoted in the September 30, 1991, issue of *Newsweek* as saying, "Cumulatively, the environmental movement is interested in shutting down the timber industry." Period.

Andy Stahl, resource analyst for the Sierra Club and Legal Defense Fund, represented the position of the Greens' contingent of anti-logging activists when he stated: "The Northern Spotted Owl is the wildlife species of choice to act as a surrogate for old growth [forest] protection, and I've often thought that thank goodness the Spotted Owl evolved in the Northwest or we would have had to genetically engineer it."[11]

Stahl erred in referring to the Northern Spotted Owl as a species. It is not. At best, it is claimed to be a subspecies of the much larger group of spotted or barred owls (*Strix occidentalis*). Even this is doubtful, since blood tests fail to show any genetic difference between the two presumed subspecies, Northern and Californian. The range of spotted owls is extensive, reaching from British Columbia to southern California and on into Mexico as far as Mexico City and eastward to the tip of Texas. In Washington, the Spotted Owl is also found in significant numbers east of the Cascade Mountains. The greatest concentration of nesting pairs of Northern Spotted Owls yet recorded inhabits not an old growth forest, but a privately owned tree farm in eastern Washington, where the oldest trees are 40 years old.[12]

Supposedly, the southern boundary of the "Northern species" Spotted Owl range is the Pitt River in California and a section of Highway 299, which borders the river. The owls, in fact, live on both sides of the highway, probably fly across it and most certainly interbreed.

Since the Spotted Owl's rise in media celebrity, significant new data have been obtained on the owl's abundance and distribution, its feeding, nesting, and mating habits, and its survival records in different types of forests.

These new investigations established that the Northern Spotted Owl is far more widely distributed than originally supposed. Lowell Diller, a geologist, has found some of the highest concentrations of owls on 400,000 acres of land owned by the Simpson Timber Company. Barely 2 percent of that land is old growth forest. His findings have been checked and accepted by the American Ornithological Union and, perhaps surprisingly, by a committee of government agency representatives. Steve Self, a wildlife biologist working to the east of the Redwood zone in California, reports "we have not found any areas where we do *not* have owls."[13]

The biological needs of Spotted Owls are few. They need a place to nest and lay eggs, and enough trees to provide cover, but open enough so they can fly after and capture suitable prey. For food, the owl prefers rodents; wood rats and brush rabbits are favorites. Spotted Owls—Northern or Californian or Mexican—can survive wherever these conditions exist; the age of the forest is of no consequence.

Many intensive surveys have also revealed that in the northern forests and woodlands, the Spotted Owl is far more abundant than originally believed. A recent count in Washington and Oregon revealed 2,170 nesting pairs and hundreds of single birds. In California, surveys conducted during 1990 showed 1,868 owls on public lands and 900 on private property. Both presumed "subspecies" were present.

Is the Northern Spotted Owl—or any spotted owl—truly endangered? All the evidence indicates that it is not. But by 1990, $9.7 million had already been spent by federal agencies, mainly the Forest Service, on the Northern Spotted Owl alone.[14] After having been listed for two years, no designated habitat has been drawn and no recovery plan prepared for the Spotted Owl. Seven different proposals have been made, but none has been adopted. In the meantime, timber harvest on federal lands has come to a standstill and uncertainty clouds the timber industry's future on other public land and in private forests.[15] In 1990 and 1991, the federal government spent $22.5 million on this one "species."

All the proposals to protect the Spotted Owl would end timber cutting in certain designated areas. These proposals would cost 23,000 to 103,000 jobs, depending upon the plan adopted. One year after the owl listing, 75 mills closed because they no longer had a stable wood supply. Forty thousand jobs were lost. And the number of closed mills and job losses in the timber industry continues to rise year after year. Timber sales have plummeted and prices have jumped—making the price of housing much more expensive for all Americans. Over the past two years, the rising cost of timber has added about $5,000 to the building costs of a three-bedroom home.

No one in the Fish and Wildlife Service seems to have considered the human cost of the agency's proposal to set aside 11.6 million acres of old growth forest to "save" the Spotted Owl. The land it has designated includes the municipal airport, three mobile home parks near the town of Forks, Washington, an accounting office, a logging supply store, and the Forks Timber Museum.[16]

The land already locked up by the federal government has meant $96 million in lost timber revenues per pair of owls. State taxes, known as "stumpage" fees in Washington State and totaling $27 million in 1991, had been going to counties for school support. Now those fees are lost, creating a funding crisis in the public schools. Since federal lands are tax-exempt, as compensation, 25 percent of timber sales have historically reverted to counties for schools and roads. That amounted to $46.7 million in 1989 and $36.8 million in 1990 for school funding and road construction and repair. Now it is going, going, gone?

Unemployment in timber communities is at an all-time high in the once timber-proud state of Washington. The figures sound as though they come from the Great Depression—34.9 percent unemployment in Skamania County, 12.7 percent in Pacific County, and 13.3 percent in Grays Harbor County.

Nationally, the well-organized preservationists do not relent. In 1990, there were 1,154 appeals filed against 585 proposed timber sales throughout the country. This resulted in a loss of federal taxes totaling nearly $200 million. One might be forgiven for wondering whether lawyers and radical environmentalists simply want to destroy the American economy.[17]

The Northern Spotted Owl is by no means the only example of protectionism gone wild; it is simply the best documented case. Here are a couple of other weird examples:

Up until a few years ago, the Fish and Wildlife Service (FWS) was using poison to get rid of four trash fish in Colorado—the squawfish, two types of chub, and a sucker. They are now listed, by the very same FWS, as endangered! And their recovery is estimated to cost $60 million. The extended economic impacts are expected to exceed $650 million.

But because the squawfish are attacking young trout and salmon in the state of Washington, the FWS actually pays fishermen $3 for every squawfish they catch that measures more than 11 inches!*[18]

In another story, an elderly couple in Georgia needed money to pay for medical expenses. They proposed to sell some timber from their property to raise the needed funds. But they were stopped by the FWS because the service found 17 trees with "possible" abandoned red cockaded woodpecker nests. No one had ever seen a woodpecker on the property, and the owners have lived there for 80 years. Even so, the timber sale was stopped.[19] And so it goes. . . .

The Endangered Species Act takes precedence over private property rights and ownership and the multiple-use mandates on federal lands. Once an area is designated as critical habitat, neither its private owners nor the general public can do anything that would in any way alter or destroy that habitat. To interfere with the habitat of the Alabama Beach Mouse or that of the Houston Toad or Desert Pup Fish or Puerto Rican Cave Cockroach (yes, cockroach!) or the Puritan Tiger Beetle or any of the 740 snails, rodents, and bugs that are listed, invites heavy fines and jail sentences. Penalties are far more likely to be imposed for environmental "crimes," even when committed unknowingly, than for unlawful acts like burglary or aggravated assault in the criminal justice system.

Where, oh where, are our priorities?

The Endangered Species Act actually *prevents us from setting priorities*. The legislation is so loosely drawn that it can be interpreted as a requirement to save *all* species and *all* subspecies and *all* geographically defined populations no matter what the cost. The Supreme Court of the United States has ruled that "the plain

---

* Not that this sort of behavior is unusual for government. Remember, the government also provides subsidies to tobacco farmers while simultaneously spending millions of dollars to discourage smoking.

intent of Congress" in passing the 1973 law was that *extinction be stopped in all cases, regardless of cost.*[20]

Make no mistake; the costs are enormous.

Here are some examples of what the FWS has spent to preserve and recover endangered and threatened species:

• Northern Spotted Owl	$9.7 million
• Least Bell's Vireo (bird)	9.2 million
• Grizzly Bear	5.9 million
• Red Cockaded Woodpecker	5.2 million
• Florida Panther	4.1 million
• Mojave Desert Tortoise	4.1 million
• Bald Eagle	3.5 million
• Ocelot	3.0 million
• Jaguarundi (type of wildcat)	2.9 million
• American Peregrine Falcon	2.9 million
• Highest-cost bug (the Valley Elderberry Longhorn Beetle)	$952,000
• Highest-cost plant (Northern Wild Monkshood)	$226,000[21]

At present, the protection of each listed "species" costs $2.6 million per year. If more Americans knew that the Puerto Rican Cave Cockroach and the American Burying Beetle (also known as the Dung Beetle) are among those being "protected" at this cost, would they approve?[22]

Are there perhaps more important problems on which to spend such sums?

The Department of the Interior has estimated that it will take 50 years and $114 million *just to list* the current candidates for protection, and billions more in recovery costs.

Although legally required by the Endangered Species Act to *recover* the listed species from the danger of extinction, by 1970 the FWS had reported only five such "recoveries." And it admitted that two of them happened without any action on the agency's part. The delisting of the alligator was called a recovery success by the FWS, even though Dennis David of the Florida Game and Fresh Water Commission surmised that the alligator should never have been placed on the list in the first place.[23]

More examples of spendthrift environmentalism are in the works, with billions upon billions of dollars being lobbied for protection of the California Gnatcatcher, the Sacramento Delta Smelt, and the Columbia River Salmon, whose protection will drastically impair hydro-electric power production, vast areas of agriculture irrigation, and freight and barge traffic on one of America's major rivers. As *The Wall Street Journal* editorialized: "The fact that much of the human species is hurting economically may not count for much with crusading ecologists for whom they [humans] are not the favorite fauna anyway. But these Homo sapiens do sometimes cast ballots, and we suspect the last word hasn't been heard yet on the environmental over-reaching."

Only a modification of the Endangered Species Act itself can rein in the "over-reaching" government agencies, but this will not be accomplished easily or soon, no matter how ridiculous the implementation of the law may become. As Donald Berry, vice president for lands at the World Wildlife Fund, notes, "If there is one event that causes the diverse environmental community to hyperventilate in unison, it is an assault on the ESA."

Given the recent history of congressional action, or lack of action, on environmental issues, neither the dismal state of the economy nor the property rights and economic survival of America's citizens counts for anything when weighed against the well-heeled activists of the environmental movement.

PART THREE

This Land Is Our Land

CHAPTER 8

Wetlands

The Land of the Free...?

In the name of wetlands protection, the EPA and the Army Corps of Engineers have punished a truck mechanic who cleaned up a tire dump in Pennsylvania, held up expansion of a homeless shelter in Alaska, penalized a farmer for plowing up a pasture in Missouri, required a forest to be levelled to compensate for wetlands lost when a highway was widened in Georgia, and temporarily stopped a Virginia county from providing clean drinking water to its residents. They have erected a system of national land-use regulation that brings minimal ecological benefits and substantial harm to the liberties of Americans.*

—RICHARD MINITER[1]

THE examples briefly alluded to in the quotation above are but a few of a growing list of injustices being inflicted on American citizens by an increasingly arrogant bureaucracy, all in the name of "saving the nation's wetlands." Is this a fair statement? Consider what follows:

To begin with, just how "wet" does a piece of property have to be in order to be classified as "wetland" and therefore brought under governmental jurisdiction? The answer, in many instances, is not very. Forget that it used to be easy for an ordinary citizen to tell the difference between swamps, marshes, bogs, and dry land.

---

* Emphasis added.

That's no longer possible now that environmental lawyers have gotten into the act. Now it takes a bureaucrat to make the determination.

This is true even though there isn't any law that either defines or regulates wetlands. Government authority in this area derives wholly from Section 404 of the 1972 Clean Water Act, which allows the Army Corps of Engineers to regulate "the discharge of dredged or fill material into the navigable waters of the United States." That's all. No mention of swamps or wetlands, no mention of any material other than "dredged and fill," no mention of water, other than "navigable waters."[2]

How, then, did Section 404 come to be used as authority to define wetlands and to regulate them? It is a saga of federal government agencies constantly seeking to expand their power, eagerly accepting new missions, and perpetually bowing to the pressure of special interests. The wetlands issue arose at just the right time for the Army Corps of Engineers. Building dams is no longer in style, nor are flood-control projects or the channeling of rivers. The Corps needed a new mission that would provide some job security. In February 1990, Lieutenant General Henry Hatch, Corps commander, officially endorsed President Bush's "no net loss" of wetlands policy and declared that the Corps should become the "nation's environmental cops."[3] So it has.

By defining any body of water to be "navigable," even if only by ducks, the Corps expanded its reach to all "wet" land. This meant that for any landowner to do anything with his property, a Corps permit is required that makes the land "jurisdictional wetland." All this started in the early days of President Jimmy Carter's administration.

For many years, significant segments of the environmental community—in this instance, led by the Audubon Society—have pressed for greater protection and preservation of the nation's dwindling marshy areas. During the first year of the Carter administration, several federal agencies were asked to define uniformly what kind of land should be protected. The Departments of Interior and Agriculture and the Environmental Protection Agency jointly identified "wetlands" as "areas flooded or saturated with ground water often enough that under normal circumstances they would support vegetation typically adapted for life in saturated soil conditions." The definition obviously applied to aquatic areas—that is, marshes, swamps, and bogs.

By 1987, this broad guideline evolved into a *Federal Manual for Identifying and Delineating Jurisdictional Wetlands*—"jurisdictional" meaning those lands that require a government permit if they are to be disturbed, used, altered, or changed in any way. The 1987 manual added to the earlier statement technical factors with respect to the soil, including its hydrology (wetness), its chemical properties (whether with or without oxygen; i.e. anerobic), and the many varieties of plants that could grow there. Theoretically, land is supposed to meet all three criteria before it's declared a wetland, but the burden of proof is on the property owners. Before long, the federal agencies, joined by the Soil Conservation Service, came out with a revised version.[4]

As Bernard Goode, who was the Corps of Engineers' representative on this project, pointed out, President Bush's campaign promise of "no net loss" of wetlands and the 1988 Wetlands Forum Report, which originated the "no net loss" idea, stimulated the agencies to expand the reach and geographic scope for wetlands delineation and to adopt the "no net loss" policy. Goode is now retired and works as a consultant to help communities and individuals deal with and avoid some of the worst consequences of the manual that he helped to write.[5]

And so, what *is* a wetland—legally?

According to the 1987 Corps Manual, a wetland is any ground that is inundated or saturated with water within 12 inches of the surface, during the growing season, and is dominated by vegetation that thrives or can survive only in a wet habitat. But according to the far more restrictive 1989 Federal Manual, drafted to meet President Bush's promise of "no net loss" of wetlands, a wetland is ground that is inundated or saturated to within 6 to 18 inches of the surface for *seven consecutive days* during the growing season.

The 1989 manual ran into a storm of protest, so the EPA drafted an alternative proposal that raised the inundation period to ten consecutive days. And EPA Director William Reilly and Vice President Quayle offered yet another revision that upped the inundation period to 15 consecutive days.

To deflect his critics, Reilly has also proposed that the whole question be referred to the National Academy of Science for a one-year study. In government, delay is the bureaucratic tactic of choice to support the status quo.

Goode, who helped write the 1989 manual, has admitted that "In our efforts to not miss any important wetlands, we built in many capture provisions to encompass that one wetland that was special in the mind of the negotiators. But in the process, we captured many other areas that should never be called wetlands. In addition, we constructed a technique far more complicated and expansive than it ought to be."

Nevertheless, all efforts to correct the excesses of the 1989 manual have been met with stubborn resistance from the activists, who take the position that *any* change is tantamount to gutting the regulations completely.[6]

The 1989 manual needs revision for many reasons, not the least of which is that it extended federal jurisdiction to more than 100 million additional acres of property, mostly privately owned. What concerns many people is that the newly restricted land has only the remotest connection with water, and of the 100 million new acres encompassed, 70 million are existing farmland. In Rochester County, Maryland, before adoption of the 1989 manual, there were 275,000 acres of identified wetlands privately owned; with the 1989 revisions, the "wet" area grew to 740,000 acres. There are many similar cases of large areas redefined as "wet" and therefore rendered useless.[7]

By official declaration, "wetlands" may now include (besides the obvious swamps) virtually every piece of ground touched by water. According to Goode, the federal government regulates as "wetland" corn, wheat, and alfalfa fields in active production; abandoned or fallow farm fields and pastures; dry woods above the 100-year floodplain; weed-covered vacant lots; depressions in sanitary landfills; dredged material disposal areas; moist tundra; pine-palmetto flatlands, and dry desert swashes. *The National Law Journal* adds, "woody areas, dry desert furrows, corn fields that were once marshy, all have been judged to qualify as wetlands. Prairie potholes are wetlands. Pools of spring rain or melting snow are wetlands. Arctic tundra are wetlands. . . ."[8]

Under federal wetlands determinations, as much as 60 percent of the total U.S. land area is "wet," as is 40 percent of the state of California and 90 percent of Alaska. On the other hand, an area as small as a coffee table and dry for all but one week out of the year can be declared a protected wetland.

Fifteen years ago, Congress mandated taxes on coal production for the reclamation of sediment ponds in abandoned coal mines. These water-filled pits were considered a hazard that had to be eliminated. Today these very same water-filled pits are considered open-water wetlands, as are farm ponds and drainage ditches. It is now impossible to reclaim them.[9]

A recent Army Corps of Engineers ruling warns property owners that if, in dragging a tree stump from their land, chunks of moist dirt should fall off, that might constitute filling a wetland! Such expansive government wetlands policy not only infringes on the rights of property owners; it goes against common sense, as well.

A growing problem in the regulation of wetlands is that everything is treated the same—as if the Florida Everglades and other long established cypress swamps and sphagnum bogs and potholes and estuarine areas at the mouths of rivers were all of the same value and importance and on a par with drainage ditches and farm ponds. Nor is any distinction made between naturally occurring swamps and marshes and wet areas created by human activity. There are no priorities. Some wetlands provide many benefits to man and nature. They offer breeding grounds for a great variety of birds, fish, and insects; habitat for an enormous variety of plant and animal life; flood control through water retention, and purification of water through filtration. But not all lands designated "wet" by government agencies do this. Some "wetlands" are merely stagnant ditches or worse.[10]

It is widely acknowledged that many swamps have been drained, often to provide land for agriculture and for housing. Washington, D.C., for example, is built on land that was drained and filled; it was once a malarial swamp. New Orleans was built on wetland and must be protected from flooding by dikes. Most of the Mississippi Valley and perhaps as much as 100 million acres of Midwest farmland have been drained and tiled so that water flows from the soil into the river. Enthusiasts for wetlands protection point to nearly 200 years of land recovery for purely human uses. They claim that more than 50 percent of the nation's original wetlands have been "lost," as though we should apologize for turning wetlands into bustling cities, sleepy small towns, and the farmland that feeds the world.

The fact is, no one really knows how much "original" wetland existed in the 1700s. There is no record of any coast-to-coast survey detailing the extent of swamps and marshes. The Lewis and Clark expedition didn't take place until 1804–05, and even then "wetlands" were not surveyed as such. All the claims about how much original wetland existed and consequently how much has been lost is purely subjective guesswork.[11]

Still, however much the radicals overstate their point, there is sufficient reason to protect much of the remaining swampy and estuarine areas, if it can be done without inflicting injustice and harm.

By and large, we must agree with Bernard Goode's observation that "Even when I was in government, the wetlands program seemed wrong. I've come to know just how unfair, outrageous, and abusive to landowners it really is." Surely we can do better.

But in the government wetland policy, the die has been cast. There are now vested interests in several agencies, not only to keep the present system, but to expand it, and this will not easily change.

The EPA has been especially zealous to establish its power and control over wetlands. It has brought criminal charges against landowners, has levied heavy fines, and has even caused the arrest and imprisonment of citizens whose "crime" was to improve their own property.

Among the growing number of horror stories were these reported by *Reason* magazine in its April 1991 issue:

In Missouri, when corn farmer Rick McGown repaired a sunken levee on his property, he was accused of illegally filling a wetland after an Army Corps official found a "cattail" growing on the land. McGown pointed out that the plant is a strain of sorghum he planted. If the corps wins its suit, the farmer will have to give the government one-third of his farm and pay a $7,500 fine. . . .[12]

After a normal spring thaw, the Idaho transportation department wanted to get rid of the mud-and-gravel mixture that collects on the sides of snowplowed dirt roads. Farmer Bud Koster allowed the department to dump this muck onto a part of his pasture. The Corps later ruled that Koster had illegally filled a wetland and told him to convert other property to a wetland, remove the dirt, or pay a fine. The case is still pending. . . .

In Nevada, a rancher who repaired irrigation ditches dug 75 years ago has been accused of "redirecting streams". . . .

Farmers in North Dakota have been charged with illegally destroying habitats for migrating birds when they drained potholes in their fields. . . .

In California and Maryland, regulators halted construction of low- and moderate-income housing projects after charging that the construction sites were functioning wetlands. . . .

In 1990, the EPA, together with the Corps of Engineers, issued a memorandum to all EPA regional administrators to produce a "cluster of new cases . . . to provide an early deterrent to potential violations which might otherwise occur. . . ."[13] These cases were intended for litigation to provide object lessons to landowners who might try to use their property.

The EPA also awarded a grant of $50,000 to the Chicago area's Sierra Club "Swamp Squad," whose sole purpose is unofficial policing of the environment. The Swamp Squad is a vigilante group that spies on developers and landowners to report what they believe to be wetland violations. In a press release about the grant, the EPA's Dale Bryson, regional director of the water division, stated, "This grant will allow them to continue their valuable work in a more vigorous way."[14]

In America? Paid spies?

Doubtless, the EPA took its direction from the land-use philosophy of administrator William Reilly. In 1973, Reilly was executive director for Laurence Rockefeller's Task Force on Land Use and Urban Growth.[15] In its report—which Reilly helped write—the task force laid out its premises for using biological diversity as a means to limit both single family housing and commercial farming. Reilly believes private ownership of land is a "quaint anachronism." He has called for a repeal of the Fifth Amendment to make it easier for the government to seize private land. And he has stated "a mere loss in land value is no justification for invalidating the regulation of land use." It is not surprising that the EPA pursues and prosecutes private landowners.[16]

Did Mr. Reilly really believe that his agency's rules and regulations should override the U.S. Constitution?

Fortunately, some relief from the highhanded federal bureaucracy may be coming. In April 1992, Judge Daniel Manion of the Seventh Circuit Court ruled that isolated bits of "wetland" that *might* be a stopping off point for migratory birds do not qualify as "navigable waters" of the United States.[17]

The case involved Hoffman Homes, a highly reputable property developer in Illinois, who in 1986 prepared a 43-acre site for much needed new housing in the Chicago area. On a small portion of the site—less than an acre—was a depression lined with clay that kept water from draining away. It would be known as "Area A" in the court battle that developed. The EPA fined the developer $100,000 for attempting to flatten its "wetland" and told Hoffman Homes it would be fined an additional $25,000 for each day it failed to remove its landfill—in other words, abandon the entire homesite. The EPA's contention was that migratory birds might use Area A as a stopping-off point en route to their flights south or north.

In his judgment against the EPA, Judge Manion said: "Birds obviously do not engage in commerce. Until they are watched, photographed, shot at, or otherwise impacted by people who do (or, we suppose, have the potential to) engage in interstate commerce, migratory birds do not ignite the Commerce Clause. The idea that the potential presence of migratory birds itself affects commerce is even more far-fetched."[18]

Bravo, Judge Manion! The agencies and the wetlands protection community have responded, predictably, that Judge Manion's opinion applies only to the Seventh District. It's time to test this critical point in other circuit courts.

One final but very important aspect of wetland preservation remains to be considered—human health. It would appear that sometimes, in their enthusiasm to protect and preserve ecological diversity, those who promote the retention of truly wet areas overlook significant risks to public health. Important diseases, of which malaria is a virulent and prime example, are transmitted by mosquitoes that breed in moist and marshy places.[19]

Since the preservation of wetlands became government policy, there has been an enormous increase in the population of mosquitoes, and, concomitantly and unfortunately, a resurgence of malaria and other mosquito-borne diseases. In the United States, malaria has increased ten times since the early 1970s. Worldwide there are now 400 million cases annually with a mortality of 1 percent, or 4 million deaths a year from a disease known since antiquity.

Although there is a tendency for people in America to dismiss malaria as a tropical African, Asian, or South European ailment, from colonial times until the 1940s malaria was *the* American disease.[20] One of the first expenditures of the Continental Congress was for $300 to buy quinine to protect General Washington's troops from malaria. During the Civil War, 50 percent of the white troops and four-fifths of the black soldiers of the Union Army suffered from malarial attacks every year. Some historians have concluded that the great western migration across the continental U.S. was as much due to an effort to escape malaria along the East Coast as for the promise of land to homestead.

Malaria has been contained, but not conquered or cured, by a combination of managing the swampy environment where mosquitoes breed, killing the larval and adult mosquito, and providing chemotherapy for the malarial patient. No one of these approaches by itself has or will eliminate malaria; all are essential parts of enlightened public health practice.

Now with draining wetlands out of the question, controlling mosquito breeding areas has become more difficult. With severe restrictions on the kind of pesticides available and further restrictions on their use to control mosquitoes, the tools to fight malaria have been severely curtailed. Sooner or later a choice must be made—preserve wetlands or protect public health. We can't have it both ways.[21]

The same situation exists with respect to encephalitis. This is a particularly vicious disease, endemic in many parts of the U.S.[22] Encephalitis is a neurological disease, caused by a virus transmitted by infected mosquitoes. There are three identified types—Western

Encephalitis, St. Louis Encephalitis, and Eastern Equine (Horse) Encephalitis. All have similar symptoms, which are difficult to distinguish from a bad case of flu, but they differ in their mortality rate. Western Encephalitis is especially hard on the young; during the 1952 epidemic in California, there were 420 cases with ten deaths; 28 percent of the cases were infants under one year of age. Extensive brain damage can occur with Western Encephalitis and, once infected, the human body is never free from the virus. St. Louis Encephalitis is particularly severe on older people. A variety of the Eastern Equine Encephalitis, known as the Venezuelan strain, broke out in Texas and the Gulf states in 1971, with 32,000 human cases and 190 fatalities. Earlier in 1967–68, Equine Encephalitis cases in humans were estimated to be between 250,000 to half a million; and 50,000 to 100,000 horses died. In 1990, there was an outbreak, largely unpublicized, of Eastern Equine Encephalitis in Massachusetts and New Jersey, spread by tideland marsh mosquitoes.

There is no medical treatment for encephalitis, either in humans or in horses, and no cure. The only protection is to prevent the transmission of this dreadful disease—by controlling mosquitoes. Wetlands preservation, coupled with restrictions on managing marshy areas, makes the future for insect-borne diseases either very dismal or very rosy, depending on whether one takes the human or the insect point of view.

And the news for humans can get worse.[23] Epidemics of yellow fever are possible; in America's South, they used to be devastating. Moreover, with recent, largely unrestricted immigration from Mexico, Southeast Asia, and the Caribbean, we now have a population that has introduced tropical parasitic diseases not encountered previously, such as River Blindness, dengue or bone-break fever, elephantiasis, schistosomiasis, and leishmaniasis—all ready to be carried to an unsuspecting and non-immune endemic population. Shouldn't there be *some* restraint on the total, governmental protection of mosquito-breeding spots?

As Bernard Goode has said, "wetlands are and will be whatever combination of soils and water that the government decides. The definition will always be determined politically." Isn't it time that some solid scientific facts are taken into account? Warren Brookes called wetlands regulation "the greatest war on private property rights in the history of the nation." It is probably also the greatest war on public health.

The preservation and protection of all wetlands is a fine example of good intentions gone wild; of our propensity to cure everything with legislation, and of our inability to see the ultimate consequences of ill-considered actions based more on sentiment and emotion than on sound science and logic.

Whatever happened to old-fashioned common sense?

CHAPTER 9

Of Forests—Public and Private

Which Is Better?

THE Pacific Northwest is quite properly known as timber country.[1] Much of the land is by nature better adapted to growing forest trees than any other kind of crop. But here, as in other parts of our country, the cutting of trees has become controversial—open to criticism, that is, if the trees are felled by human beings to fulfill human needs. If nature removes trees or destroys them, that is, well, different.

When Mount St. Helens erupted with explosive force on May 18, 1980, the blast leveled trees as far as 15 miles to the north and over a 156-square-mile area. The force of the shock wave was so great that it stripped the branches and foliage from the lush old-growth trees and then toppled the bare trunks as if they were pickup sticks. The blast area was inundated with ash. More than a billion board feet of lumber was downed in a single moment; much of it was destroyed. Most animal life was wiped out.[2]

The enormous area of forest destruction included parts of the Gifford Pinchot National Forest, as well as both state-owned and private land. Nature is no respecter of property rights. For weeks after the big eruption, and amidst all that gray and lifeless landscape, the questions persisted: How long will it take for nature to recover? Will this area ever support a forest again? Most people, including many biologists, believed that years would pass, decades, or maybe even centuries before the land could recover.

How wrong they were. On the government land a National Volcanic Monument totalling more than 110,000 acres has been established where nature has been allowed to take its course, unperturbed and unaffected by human actions. On neighboring private land, however, the forest industry set to work immediately, salvaging the downed trees and planting new seedlings. Eight hundred fifty million board feet of timber was saved, enough to build 85,000 three-bedroom homes.[3]

The stage was thus set for a grand demonstration. On similar but separate parcels of land, side by side, one could observe and compare natural recovery with managed and assisted recovery. Within a year or two, the return of life, both plant and animal, was remarkable, and the differences between the natural and the managed areas are dramatic. Both are recovering, but the public lands, left undisturbed, lag far behind.

Nature proved to be far more resilient than most people expected. Within a year, bracken, ferns, thistle, fireweed, and pearly everlasting dotted the landscape. On the private land, within weeks of the eruption, experimental plantings of tree seedlings were made to determine the ability of young trees to survive on the ash-covered ground. It was found that, as long as the seedlings' roots could reach the soil under the ash, the trees would survive. Using this information and scraping away ash where necessary, 18.4 million trees were planted on 45,500 acres by 1987. Douglas Fir and Noble Fir predominated, with some Lodgepole Pine and Black Cottonwood.

Now, a dozen years later, these plantings have grown to a lush forest, with most trees between 25 and 30 feet tall. Undergrowth has moved in to carpet the ground and wildlife is abundant.

The reforested growth on private land is not significantly different from the original (pre-1980) forest below the slopes of Mount St. Helens. Before the eruption, there was an almost unbroken expanse of evergreens, including Douglas Fir (some of these were truly ancient giants of 400 years or so in age), Noble Fir, Pacific

Silver Fir, and Western Red Cedar. The undergrowth was also extensive and diverse. About four miles of forested land, a remnant of old growth, was shielded by a ridge from the volcanic blast and remains as a striking example of virgin Northwest forest. It can be compared to the public and private reforested recovery areas closer to the mountain.

When this is done, no one can say, except on a subjective, emotional basis, which forest is "better"—the old untouched one that evolved slowly over many decades or the newly replanted one? The human-assisted one or the one that takes nature many, many times longer to produce? Both have approximately the same complex of tree species and varied undergrowth, and the same wildlife, birds, and insects inhabit both. The main difference in animals is that the elk prefer the young growth. Deciding that one forest excels over the other is a value judgment heavily influenced by what one believes a forest is "for."

Of Forests and Deforestation

The issue of forest preservation versus management and use is one of the half-dozen or so "big, scary" environmental problems about which many people have strong opinions. An international treaty that would govern the cutting of trees and curb deforestation everywhere was considered at the June 1992, UN–sponsored "Earth Summit" in Rio de Janeiro, Brazil. It failed to gain acceptance, largely because of opposition from Third World countries to whom President Bush pledged $150 million to study their problems. The discussion was lively. Some believe that the world's remaining forests should never be cut. Others point to the commercial value of trees, man's need for wood and wood products, and the value wood products can produce in foreign exchange for Third World countries.

Obviously, the Earth should not be denuded of trees; healthy forests are an essential part of a healthy environment. But it is equally true that trees are not immortal. They grow, mature, decay, die, and grow again. When harvested in their prime, they provide many important products for human use.

Given the strong polarization between protectionism and use, how can a reasonable middle ground be achieved? On the one hand forests have always brought out some of the noblest sentiments of mankind. President Theodore Roosevelt, who was one of America's first environmentalists, wrote, after spending the night in Yosemite Valley in 1903, "It was like lying in a great solemn cathedral, far vaster and more beautiful than any built by the hand of man." Later, in a speech at Stanford University, he proclaimed:

> I feel most emphatically that we should not turn into shingles a tree [redwood] which was old when the first Egyptian conqueror penetrated to the valley of the Euphrates, which it has taken so many years to build up, and which can be put to better use. That, you may say, is not looking at the matter from the practical standpoint. There is nothing more practical than the preservation of beauty, than the preservation of anything that appeals to the higher emotions of mankind.[4]

Surely no one would disagree.

On the other hand, without the forest products industry, we would miss, not just the obvious things we get from trees, such as lumber, plywood, 2-by-4s, particle board, fencing, and so on, but paper and packaging materials, as well as photographic film and recording tapes and rayon and acetates and food stabilizers and fragrances and eyeglass frames and football helmets and medicines and cosmetics and many, many other materials that few people identify with trees.[5]

It is estimated every American uses, on average, 600 pounds of wood and paper products annually. That is equivalent to one tree, 100 feet tall, with a trunk 18 inches thick, for each citizen. There are in America about 230 billion such trees—about 1,000 for each person. And some four million new trees are being planted every day. So we're not likely to run out of trees any time soon.[6]

Still, even if America is in good shape, deforestation is undoubtedly a severe ecological problem in some places. But what is seldom, if ever, publicly mentioned is the fact that most of the deforestation worldwide is the result of wood being used for fuel. A United Nations study claims that 83 percent of all trees cut in the Third

World are used for firewood, and other trees in the Third World are cut to support slash-and-burn-type primitive agriculture. Ironically, the International Monetary Fund actually forces people to burn wood for fuel. The IMF insists that foreign exchange must be reserved to pay foreign debts. So rather than import fuel, many Third World people burn firewood. We also need to remember that the program for "sustainable energy," beloved by the activist Greens, calls for burning "biomass" (a politically correct word for wood, wood waste, and animal excrement), instead of fossil fuels.[7]

Cutting trees for fuel is not necessarily bad, and there are programs to grow trees for just this purpose. When private property is involved, and entrepreneurial, market incentives are allowed to operate, the results can be beneficial, both economically and environmentally. Take, for example, the situation in India. State governments there have allowed contract logging on government land but have been lax or negligent about replanting. The result is extensive deforestation; probably 3.7 million acres per year of forestland were lost during the 1970s.

But as trees became more scarce, prices for wood rose and this stimulated reforestation on private lands. Farmers quickly learned that forests of fast-growing Eucalyptus could be their most profitable cash crop, earning 2,400 rupees per acre annually, even on unirrigated land. Within five years, 2.5 million acres were planted outside of governmental land—with considerable ecological benefit.[8]

Similar results have been obtained in Africa, where in some countries up to 90 percent of all trees cut were used for fuel. In Benin, farm co-ops plant trees as a provision for old age; in Kenya, peasants plant exotic tree species to pay for school fees.

Finally, most projections of deforestation worldwide are based on results from government owned and managed lands. They ignore the "unofficial" forests in private hands; so the numbers are often misleading.[9]

In fact, commercial logging appears to account for only about 18 percent of trees cut in the Third World. Banning this income-producing activity would have only minimal effect on the world deforestation question.

Another problem with deforestation projections is that they are mostly based on the "if present trends continue" type of thinking, and they are generally wrong. For example, if one takes the rate of construction of racquet-ball courts in the U.S. during the 1980s, one could project that the entire Earth would be covered with racquet-ball courts by the year 2010. Silly, isn't it?

And nature is even less easily projected, and it is less linear. Projecting a person's height, based on the growth rate of a baby up to the age of two years, would anticipate a teen-ager 20 feet tall![10]

If one were to project deforestation in the U.S. based on the logging rate of the late 1800s, the last tree would have fallen years ago. But projections based on the logging and growth rates of the late 1900s would show forests covering every square inch of America in the next century. Obviously, "if present trends continue" is misleading; the current trends never do continue.

But the environmentalist Green's position remains firmly against logging. Opponents of commercial forestry continue to quote the *Global 2000* report: "By [the year] 2000 some 40 percent of the remaining forest cover, in less developed countries, will be gone." And "Significant losses of world forests will continue over the next 20 years." How do they know? They cite no evidence for these assertions and that includes the claims made by Vice President Albert Gore.[11]

UN studies of the total world forest area since the 1940s reveal that there is no recent downward trend. Certainly there is no evidence for "near catastrophic" losses. Scientists for the organization Resources for the Future, Drs. Sedjo and Clawson, conclude, "there is certainly nothing in the data to suggest that the world is experiencing significant net deforestation."[12] Nevertheless, *Global 2000* also proclaimed in its section on tropical forests, "The world's tropical forests are disappearing at alarming rates ... tropical deforestation is an urgent problem." If the authors of *Global 2000* supported their statements with evidence, they might be believable, but documented data are lacking.

What is the situation with respect to the forests of the world?

It is true that over the long course of history, many parts of the world have been deforested.[13] But that process can also be reversed, as Israel has shown. With appropriate human intervention, intelligent selection of appropriate species, and care of seedlings, trees will indeed grow in arid, once denuded lands.

Reforestation in many parts of the world has not taken place for two basic reasons. One, the application of human care and nurturing of young seedlings—in other words, proper forest management—has not until recently been exercised; and, two, the feeding habits of the predators, especially the ubiquitous goat, were uncurbed. The goat is very popular throughout the Middle East for its hardiness and because it is a "walking food factory." But goats feed voraciously on young trees and actually it is the Moorish goat that has been a major factor in the continued deforested state of the Middle East from Greece and Crete to Spain and Morocco. Unrestrained goats are responsible for creating more deserts than any other creature—save only humans when *they* behave irresponsibly.

Reforestation has long been practiced in Sweden, Switzerland, Germany, and Britain. And in China, a vast reforestation program has been under way for more than 15 years.

The important thing is not to dwell on lamenting about problems that grew from the practices of the past, but to concentrate on how they can be corrected and improved. With intelligent forest management, this is being done in many nations around the world.

There remain the questions about the Brazilian rain forests of the Amazon Valley. Are they serious enough to require international attention?

Now what is the situation with respect to America's forests—those for which we have direct responsibility? Are our forests disappearing? Many people appear to believe so—but are they right? To reach a dispassionate judgment, we should first look at the baseline. What were America's "original" forests like and how does that compare with today?

When the pilgrims began to colonize North America, the area now occupied by the 48 contiguous states was estimated to be about 45 percent covered with mature forest.[14] Today it is closer to one third. Of the total 3.6 million square miles that constitute the U.S., 1.13 million square miles, or 32 percent, are now wooded.

From analysis of tree rings and other evidence, research shows that temperate region forests, left alone for nature to take its course, are regularly destroyed and then slowly replaced every 250 to 450 years. This natural "harvesting" is caused by lightning-strike fires, by storm wind blowdowns, by insect infestation, and by old age decay. Remember, no tree lives forever, nor does any forest.[15]

In colonial times, much of the Eastern seaboard and west to the Mississippi River was forested, as was the stretch from the Rocky Mountains to the Pacific. But there were also many open areas, where trees were scattered; there were swamps and bogs and, of course, the Great Plains. Forests dominated the Upper Midwest, and arid lands prevailed in the Southwest. From areas like the Badlands of South Dakota to the potholes and scabland of eastern Washington, from the prairies of Oklahoma to the central valleys of California, trees were sparse. Additionally, there were deserts, notably in southern California and, surprisingly, in Eastern Oregon and Washington.

From colonial days to the mid-19th century, there was considerable deforestation; most of the once expansive Eastern hardwood forest was cut before 1900 as the settlers cleared land for agriculture.[16] Today the evergreen dominated forests of New England and the Old South have regrown.

In the Southeast, many managed forests and tree plantations have extensively reforested the land. Much of the wood used for papermaking comes from these tree crops, planted for that very purpose.

Reforestation in Maine makes that state our most heavily wooded; 90 percent of its surface area is covered with forests.

Traditional logging—that is, trees cut for their value as structural timber, lumber, furniture-making, plywood, particle board, and many other wood products—predominates in the north central and western states.[17]

No one denies that the logging practices of the 19th century and early years of the 20th were destructive, brutal, and wasteful. Environmental damage was extensive. Up to about 1920, the classical robber-baron "cut and run" philosophy dominated. But beginning early in this century, forestry started to change.

Today's forestry practices are a long way from the cut and run habits of years ago. New, less damaging equipment has been developed. A few examples include big "feller-bunches"—tank-like vehicles with enormous snippers resembling great garden shears mounted at the front end which can cut through marketable trees at the base and lay them down carefully without hurting nearby growth. Mechanized skidders are fitted with over-size tires to avoid ground damage, and under special circumstances some logs are helicopter-lifted.

Sawmills, too, have become more efficient, using computer-guided lasers, saws, and every bit of what used to be "waste." Procedures for the cutting, gathering, transporting, and utilization of wood as a building material are more energy-efficient than those for other common construction materials. Brick, for example, requires three times as much energy to produce and use; aluminum takes 70 times more energy.[18]

Even the much maligned practice of "clear-cutting," contrary to popular notion, does not leave the ground scraped bare. It is generally conducted on a checkerboard pattern, which leaves large nearby parcels of forest untouched until a future cycle of cutting. Critics of clear-cutting overlook the fact that some important forest tree species—Douglas Fir, for example—will neither germinate nor will the seedlings grow in shade.[19]

The devastated appearance of a recently clear-cut area raises strong emotions. But the condition is temporary. As pointed out in a recent Report of the President's Advisory Panel on Timber and the Environment: "If properly applied, clear-cutting does not lead to soil erosion, nutrient depletion, wildlife habitat damage, or stream sedimentation." And, according to the U.S. Forest Service: "Drastic as it may seem, clear-cutting plays a legitimate and prominent role in scientific forestry. Properly done, it paves the way for a new, unencumbered and hence, vigorously growing, forest."[20]

Clear-cutting is a time-honored practice used even by native American Indians, who regularly burned areas to provide a cleared space for the young growth favored by many animals, like bear, deer, and elk.

Senator Mark Hatfield of Oregon commented on clear-cutting in a recent interview reported in Ron Arnold's *The Ecology Wars*: "I recall the debate on a bill concerning clear-cutting. I reminded my colleagues that long before the white man came, the Indians used clear-cutting by fire to enhance the growing area for their food plants. Meanwhile, the wildfire created the forest openings so nec-essary to the regeneration of the Douglas Fir, which needs mineral soil and direct sunlight to reproduce properly. There is wisdom to be learned from history."[21] Maintaining prairie land and open areas by intentional burning is a special kind of clear-cutting.

Despite the advantages, and sometimes the necessity of clear-cutting, no one would argue that a recently logged parcel of land is pretty. But, then, neither is a field of corn or wheat stubble, or a cabbage patch from which the heads have just been removed.

The recent announcement from NASA that satellite images from space showed extensive deforestation in the Pacific Northwest is another example of that agency's predilection for influencing sci-ence policy by press release. "Pictures" taken from 570 miles in space are not photographs; they are computer enhanced simula-tions of different wavelengths of light reflection from the Earth's surface. They do not reveal the presence of 4-to-10-inch healthy growing tree seedlings, or even of robust 8-to-10-foot tall trees in a young forest, however much NASA scientists would like to present themselves as biologists or foresters.

Northwest forestry experts have been able to identify the specific areas shown in the NASA report which the government's space scientists claimed were barren. The geography depicted was in the Mount Hood National Forest in Oregon. Ground level photo-graphs of the very same areas clearly show healthy seedlings or young trees. Certainly the sections had been clear-cut, but they are now well along the way to becoming productive forest. Only 8 percent of the Mount Hood National Forest is available for har-vesting, and for every 83 trees that are cut, 400 are replanted.[22]

Joining Forest Service Chief Dale Robertson in pointing out the misinformation put out by NASA, Jim Geisinger of the Northwest Forestry Association accused NASA of "the biggest sham that has ever been perpetrated on the people of the Northwest."

Finally, for all those who oppose the practice of clear-cutting, it should be a requirement that they view the popular motion picture, "Last of the Mohicans." When the film's director, Michael Mann, combed America for an old-growth forest duplicating the book's site in upstate New York, he found and fell in love with just the "right old forest"—between Burke and McDowell Counties at

Lake James in North Carolina. What he didn't realize was that "the white pines nearest the fort were planted only 19 years ago. In fact, the oldest tree in the 7,000 acres within view of the fort is 30 years old."[23]

It would not be surprising if NASA joined the "our forests are disappearing" lobby to win funds for a vast new program to plant forests on the moon. Some bureaucrats will do anything to pad their budgets.

CHAPTER 10

Of Private Property

And the Right to Use It

No person shall . . . be deprived of life, liberty, or property, without due process of law; nor shall private property be taken for public use without just compensation.

—The Fifth Amendment to the U.S. Constitution

THIS excerpt from our Constitution should hang in the offices of all government employees from Washington, D.C., to every state and local agency. And they should be required to read it every day. Why? Because, despite this profound constitutional guarantee, agencies of the government are taking control of private property at an accelerating rate, often with neither due process nor compensation.

In the name of "protecting the environment," Congress has enacted laws that allow government regulators to confiscate private property, to prevent an owner from using his land, to levy fines for noncompliance of up to $25,000 per day (just increased in Oregon by state law to $100,000 per day), and to jail the landowner who may try to use his land for any purpose other than that prescribed by government—even if the citizen was unaware of the restrictions.

We used to be very cautious about granting police power to anyone in America. No more. Today the number of law enforcement personnel assigned to carry out the edicts of all the new environmental laws and regulations must rival the number of traditional police. In the name of "protecting the environment," we not only have officials scouring the country for violators of environmental regulations, but neighbor is being set against neighbor to spy upon and report any suspected breaking of the myriad environmental rules. In many instances, bounties are paid for bringing any regulatory infringement to the notice of the authorities. How does this differ from the busybodies and tattletales of a totalitarian police state? And why is it being tolerated in freedom-loving America?

In its rush to protect the environment, Congress has failed to protect the constitutional right of our citizens to own and control private property.

With the stroke of a pen, a bureaucrat can declare private property to be a wetland, the habitat for a protected species, or a possible roosting place for a passing migratory bird, and the landowner can be prevented by law from doing anything with his land, other than continue to pay taxes on it. The landowner has no recourse—save at enormous personal expense—to sue the government. Do people and constitutional guarantees no longer count?

Since the federal government has failed in its obligation to protect private property rights, the states should step into this void and follow the lead of Arizona. On June 1, 1992, Arizona Governor Fife Symington signed Senate Bill 1053, commenting, in part:

"Private property rights lie near the source of the liberty under which Americans are free to enjoy the God-given beauty of the Earth. It is the nature of government constantly to close in upon that liberty, to diminish it, to consume it. Indeed, one day the historians may put down our era as one where the gradual intrusion of the public upon the private came to deprive Americans of the liberty that was once the envy of most of the world. The right to property is a civil right, no less than the right to freedom of speech and worship, and the rights to due process and equal protection under the law."[1]

Remember, one-third of America's land is already owned by the federal government, most of it in the West. These are "public lands." They comprise about 40 percent of the state of Washington, nearly half of the land in Wyoming, Oregon, and California, 63.8 percent of Idaho, 63.6 percent of Utah, 86.1 percent of Nevada, and nearly 90 percent of Alaska, just to cite a few examples.[2] But for some environmentalist Greens, this is not enough, and they are urging the extension of the federal grasp by every available law or regulation.

A few months ago, the state of Wyoming sponsored a conference in Laramie at the University of Wyoming. A couple of professors named Popper—a husband-and-wife team—from Rutgers University in New Jersey attended the meeting to discuss a program they call the "Buffalo Commons." Their thesis is that mankind was never meant to live on the Great Plains.

They believe that sooner or later all the people now living in the prairie states will be gone, and that it ought to be sooner. So, the professors have proposed that the U.S. government embark on a program to "deprivatize" 110 counties in nine states in which 400,000 people live. They want to move those people out so that the buffalo can once more roam upon the land.[3]

We can laugh at their proposal, but in large parts of America, farmers, cattlemen, woolgrowers, miners, timbermen, water developers, ski resort operators, and oil and gas explorers are being forced out of their jobs and off the land by government regulation. And going with them are all the little towns and communities whose economies depend on the land.

In many areas, people are locked in a battle for economic survival, for the survival of our most precious rights, for the right to own and use property, for individual liberty and freedom. In this battle, governments are all too ready to accept environmentalist proddings to expand their own power.

Oftentimes, their efforts are well-meaning, but ludicrous. Recently the government decided to outlaw the poison 1080 that Wyoming woolgrowers were using to kill coyotes that were decimating their herds of sheep. The government decided that instead of the poison, the woolgrowers should put out a feed that would render the coyotes sterile. One bright young man from the Environmental Protection Agency traveled out to Wyoming to explain it. He found himself in front of a standing-room-only crowd at an elementary school in Gillette, Wyoming.

After he explained the new concept to everyone, a gnarled old fellow in the back stepped up to the microphone in the center of the aisle and said: "Sonny, I don't think you understand the nature of the problem. You see, the coyotes are killing and eating the sheep. They're not raping them."[4]

Of Snails and Men

Then there is the case of Brandt Child of Kanab, Utah, in Kane County. Kane County, although huge (it's just slightly smaller than Connecticut), is sparsely populated. Fewer than 5,000 people live there. In the midst of some very beautiful country, it lacks two things: economic activity and water. Brandt Child sought to utilize the latter to create the former.

Retired with a partial disability from the construction industry, Child moved to Kanab, bought 400 acres of land near a highway, purchased $75,000 worth of heavy equipment, and began to build a recreational park and tourist stop. Shortly after he began work, the Fish and Wildlife Service informed him that the three aquifer-fed ponds on his land, around which he planned to build his resort, were the home of the Kanab Ambersnail, which is "endangered." When Child objected to the intrusion upon his land by saying, "This is my land; I own it and I pay taxes on it," a government agent responded, "You may own it and you may pay taxes on it, but we control it."[5]

Are all our liberties merely on loan from the government to be revoked when bureaucrats get power-hungry enough? That wasn't the idea of the Founders, but it seems to be the idea of our new ruling class of lawyers, environmentalists, and media people.

Perhaps, if government were a good steward of the land and of wildlife, we could accept government control in good grace. But consider the case of a Wyoming rancher who lost his entire cattle herd to the disease brucellosis. Believing that the disease had come from infected elk and bison managed by the federal government, he sued.

Although it permitted 50 percent of the elk and 40 percent of the bison to carry the deadly disease, the government asserted it had no legal duty to Wyoming ranchers to prevent the spread of brucellosis and thus could not be held liable. The district court, however, rejected the notion that the government was above the law, which requires that livestock infected with brucellosis be destroyed.[6]

Although the court concluded that the rancher had failed to prove that the disease came from the elk or bison, the court did conclude that the government "acted negligently in managing the wildlife." The court also ruled against the government in its attempt to evade responsibility as a matter of law: "The federal government does not have the discretion to do nothing in the fight against a disease which it is perpetuating by its wildlife management practices. . . ."

It is important here to note that brucellosis in cattle is highly infectious and causes undulant fever in humans. But the government seems more on the side of pestilence than on the side of human beings *or* the environment.

People, Trees, and Grizzly Bears

Recently five tiny towns, two counties, a family-owned timber mill, and a grass-roots organization filed a lawsuit against the U.S. Forest Service. In the Kootenai National Forest in Northwestern Montana and Northern Idaho, the Forest Service decided to cut back the allowable timber harvest by 43 percent so as to achieve a one percent increase in grizzly bear habitat. In these timber-dependent communities—communities in which more than 60 percent of the county land is federally owned—such a cutback will have devastating economic consequences.

It will also have catastrophic environmental consequences, since, at the same time, the Forest Service has decided to leave standing millions of board feet of timber devastated by the Mountain Pine Beetle. These diseased trees not only serve as a source of infection for a healthy forest; it is these trees that will serve as the tinder for the next cataclysmic fire to sweep through the region.

When it does—not if, but when—it will destroy not just the dead trees but also the healthy forest and homes; not just the homes of people, but the habitat of the grizzly bear that the government is trying to help![7]

This lawsuit is unique because the plaintiffs are not timber companies but the people of a community banding together to fight for their own survival—not just for the economic viability of their communities but for the health of the forest that surrounds them and that they love.

Of Tortoises and Harassment

Then there is the strange situation with respect to the Desert Tortoise in Nevada. Why did the government settle a lawsuit with the Humane Society over the Desert Tortoise? And what happened as a result of that settlement?

Because the Humane Society that deprived the federal government of the only program that would have improved the lot of the Desert Tortoise (that is, a program to reduce raven depredation of the turtles), the feds felt compelled to take other action. So they limited the grazing rights of cattlemen and woolgrowers, canceled off-highway vehicle events, denied permits to mining companies, and shut down the building boom in the fastest growing city in the country, Las Vegas, Nevada.

The Desert Tortoise is listed as "endangered," even though it is common in the land surrounding Las Vegas. The city agreed to place 400,000 acres of surrounding Clark County in a Desert Tortoise Management Zone. In the zone there will be no grazing, no mining, no off-road vehicle events, no hunting, and no hiking. In exchange for being allowed to build downtown, Las Vegas surrendered a total of 1.4 million acres of Clark County and nearby Lincoln County to the Desert Tortoise Management Zone. But in a document announcing the new program, the Fish and Wildlife Service threatened further confiscations: "There are 50 other threatened or endangered species for which provisions also must be made." All this because the government did not have the courage to fight the Humane Society. If only the government were as solicitous of the rights of ranchers, miners, recreationalists, and the city of Las Vegas.[8]

Is there really a dearth of Desert Tortoises? Is there a likelihood that the species might not survive? No, they are abundant in Nevada, as well as the desert areas of California, where highway signs, "Warning: Tortoise Crossing," abound.

Whatever happened to common sense?

If we're not to lose our communities, our civil liberties, and our traditions of individual freedom and common sense, we're all going to have to band together to beat back the depredations of cynical environmentalists and bureaucrats who value their own power more than the Constitution.

CHAPTER 11

Government Ownership of Land and Forests

How Much Is Enough?

WHATEVER may have been the forestry practices of the past and whatever claims are made about logging today, there is considerably more forested land in America now than there was even a few decades ago. This has resulted from vigorous reforestation programs, and because marginal agricultural land has been abandoned and returned to wood lot and forest. The increase is estimated to be at least 450 million more acres of wooded land and 23 percent more standing forest trees than 40 years ago. The present, average annual wood growth is three-and-a-half times more than in 1920, and the annual increase in the size of forests exceeds logging by 37 percent per year. In 1989 alone, approximately 2.1 billion seedlings covering more than 3 million acres were planted in the U.S. In 1991 alone six new trees were planted for every American.[1]

When faced with such facts about the extent and growth of America's forests, opponents of managed logging and reforestation argue that a second growth forest or a tree farm is different—not to be compared with the "natural" stands they have replaced. Further, the Greens persist in calling tree farms "monoculture."

They are not. Many species invade planted areas to establish a varied undergrowth, and shade-tolerant trees associated with old growth forests soon return.[2]

Old growth forests, that is, forests that contain trees 200 years old and older, are claimed to have unique and irreplaceable virtues. It's also asserted that what remains of old growth is in imminent danger of total destruction. Is there evidence to support these claims? There are in the U.S. today 13.2 million acres of old growth, of which 8 million acres are totally protected in national parks and wilderness areas. These trees can never be cut. If we took this 8 million acres of protected old growth and imagined it to form a band five miles wide, it would extend from the Pacific Coast all across the country to the Atlantic Ocean.[3]

Where old growth is being logged—outside of national parks and wilderness, as for example in the Tongass National Forest in Alaska—it is cut at a rate of only 1 percent per year. The forest management plan for the Tongass dictates that no more than 10 percent of the trees will ever be harvested. And, of course, the seedlings already planted will one day become "old growth."

The current public debate about old growth forests and trees on public lands is really about what purpose the forest serves. A combination of recreation and preservation with the least possible human intervention is the underlying philosophy of the national parks: visit, look, enjoy, but don't take anything away. National forests, on the other hand, were meant to serve society's needs. They were established for multiple use. Their purpose has traditionally been to provide for recreation and resource uses. The national forests were intended to be used for a sustained supply of timber in a perpetual cycle of cutting and reforestation. But now, and increasingly in recent years, the trend of public opinion seems to be swinging away from all uses other than recreation, and even what kind of recreation is more and more rigidly controlled.

Many of the national forests have stands of quite old trees, some approaching one or two centuries in age. Sometimes these parcels of forest are misleadingly called "ancient forests," which seems to imply no impact by humans. But "original" forests do not really exist; nature takes care of that at intervals of from 200 to 450 years in cycles of forest fires and/or blowdown from fierce windstorms. A forest is a dynamic system going through a life cycle of growth, maturity, old age, and death. These cycles occur whether humans are present or not.[4]

Despite the biological fact that every tree will eventually age and die, the extent to which trees on public lands should be used continues to be unresolved. Unfortunately, government uncertainty, environmentalist-lobby pressure, and conflicting agency approaches to forest management have led to "management by neglect." This has brought our national forests to a condition where vast areas are being destroyed by bugs and disease, and large numbers of people and their communities that are dependent on the forest products industry are facing economic ruin.

While it might seem reasonable to believe that the two systems, National Parks and National Forests, could provide the framework to resolve the differences between preservation and use, it has not worked out that way. Instead, there is a long history of polarization and acrimony; it shows no sign of abating. There is also a lengthy trail of legislation, none of it really addressing the central problem: Should America's natural resources, including timber, be government-owned, government-managed, and government-controlled? Incidentally, isn't that what socialism and communism are all about?

The reality is that after 200 years of supporting individual freedom and the right to own private property, our country appears to be succumbing to an assault on both. How is it that, as we have moved from an agrarian nation of small independent farmers to a largely industrial nation, the central government has become by far the largest landowner and has taken over the dangerous, freedom-destroying role of central planning for the future of all of us?

History reveals that a consensus about what should be done with vast land holdings in the U.S. has never been reached.[5] By the year 1784, 220,000 square miles of real property had been acquired by the federal government. Who should administer them was a critical question. Several states laid claim to territory west of the Appalachian Mountains, but, one by one, beginning with New York and followed by Virginia, all the original states relinquished their claims to the U.S. government by 1802 and lands in the "public domain" were established.

This "public domain" was expanded by the Louisiana Purchase from France in 1803. In 1819, the U.S. bought Florida from Spain. In 1845, we annexed Texas and in 1846 acquired the Northwest Territory, now including Oregon, Washington, and Idaho by treaty with Great Britain. In 1848, following war with Mexico, we absorbed all the Southwest, including parts of New Mexico and Colorado, all of Nevada, Utah, California, and most of Arizona. The final act of U.S. expansion on the North American continent was the purchase of Alaska from Russia in 1867. This amounted to a lot of "public land."

What to do with it? Sentiment was divided between the Jeffersonian belief that the future of the republic rested in the hands of a large number of individual, independent land owners and the convictions of Alexander Hamilton, who placed his faith in transferring land to investors and stock companies. And so we got a bit of both.

The Homestead Act of 1862 provided title to blocks of 160 acres of land to individuals who settled on the land. Less well known were the Timber Culture Act of 1873 (the U.S. government was an early supporter of reforestation), the Desert Land Law of 1877, and the Timber and Stone Act of 1878. All of these congressional actions were clearly supportive of private property rights and of placing responsibility for natural resource development in the private sector.

Federal land grants also went to various industries—for example, railroads and timber companies. Between 1812 and 1934, 62 percent of the original 1.8 billion acres of public land owned by the federal government was disposed of, mostly through land sales and outright grants.

Meanwhile, some sentiment for retaining a large measure of federal ownership persisted, and in 1871 the American Association for the Advancement of Science petitioned Congress to pass legislation that would protect and provide management of America's forests.[6] This occurred at the height of the irresponsible, "cut and run" way in which logging was practiced at that time. Public outrage against the timber companies' practices grew, and the result was creation of the Forest Reserve Act of 1891, which authorized the President to establish forest reserves by proclamation. Thus, the National Forest system was born. Presidents Harrison and Cleveland set aside 33 million acres for National Forests and President Theodore Roosevelt added 132 million acres by 1908.

Then, in 1911, Congress passed the Weeks Act, which further authorized expansion of the National Forest system through acquisition of private forestlands. It was under this law that most of the national forests in the eastern half of the U.S. were established. While it is beyond the scope of this book to recount the full history of legislation governing land and natural resource ownership, it amounts to a tangled web of private-public rights. There have always been claims as to who does the better job of managing land—government bureaucrats or private owners.

This muddled situation persists to the present, with new laws and agency-promulgated regulations that are growing at an accelerating rate. The ultimate goal of the environmental movement appears to be to move as much land as possible into the public domain. As Warren Brookes said, cogently, "Even as the [nations of the former] Soviet Union moves to grant property rights to its citizens, Congress and the Greens are leading an assault on U.S. property rights."[7] No agency is more active in this assault than the National Park Service, and this merits careful scrutiny.

The important thing to remember about National Parks is that they are *preserves*, but where previously existing homes or other private enterprises were present within the parks' boundaries, these were frequently "grandfathered." Even so, this guarantee of private property rights of "inholders" has not always been honored.

Perhaps the most outlandish and incredible example of bureaucratic arrogance and duplicity on the part of the National Park Service was reported in a July 1991, issue of the *Land Rights Letter*.[8] A newly appointed and controversial superintendent of the Olympic National Park decided that a modest wilderness camp for disadvantaged young people that had operated with great success at Washington's Lake Quinault had to go because it was on federal land—despite the fact that the joint Kiwanis Club-YMCA operators had received approval years earlier by previous National Park administrators. So the main lodge of Kamp Kiwanis, which provided ideal wilderness experience for 300 youths each year, including disadvantaged and Native American children, was ordered burned to the ground!

In a classic case of government intimidation, government inspectors first issued a series of trumped up health and safety charges against the rustic camp, then put the "fix up" cost so high the camp's operators couldn't afford it. Then, in a final charade, the Olympic National Park characterized the burning of the lodge as a necessary "fire drill." It was arson, pure and simple, and at the behest of your government and mine.

When the incident was publicly reported, families and communities unleashed a barrage of protests against the Olympic National Park superintendent. Congress eventually reacted, over the protest of the National Park Service, to the citizen complaints and directed the superintendent of the ONP to issue a ten-year permit for continued operation of Kamp Kiwanis.

But who will pay to rebuild the camp? In all fairness, the funds for a new Kamp Kiwanis should come out of the superintendent's paycheck! But even more important is this question: If Congress can see the folly in the case of the ONP superintendent, why can't it address the even greater issue of rapid increase in the government's "takings" of private property all across the U.S.?

Again, history can tell us a lot about the origin of attitudes. It is revealing to read the point of view of Park Service officials, as set down in the Service's own publication, *The National Parks*:

In the national parks, there is no harvesting of timber, no hunting of wild animals, no extraction of minerals, and no grazing of domestic livestock. Trees are apt to be consumed by disease. Or by wildfire, left to run its course. Or blown down in a windstorm. By whatever cause, trees are left where they fall. This is nature's way. The dead or dying tree provides a home for insects, and these, in turn, draw birds to feed upon them. In time, the tree will decompose to enrich the earth from whence it sprang. The burned-over area will become the source of a new forest destined to fulfill its cycle in time.[9]

OK. That is the operational philosophy of the National Park Service. But should it govern the National Forests and *all* public lands?

The oldest federal set-aside land program in the National Park system, Yellowstone, was established by legislation in 1872. It became the first National Park "for the benefit and enjoyment of the people."

Interest in parks, however, dates from 40 years earlier. In 1832, the first such action by the U.S. Congress was a reservation established at Hot Springs, Arkansas. A big step was taken with the 1870 exploration of Yellowstone (Washburn-Lanford-Doane Expedition). Instead of laying claim to their discoveries, the explorers decided that Yellowstone is unique should be a permanent preserve for all people.[10] In 1872, it became our first designated "National Park." By 1907, there were eight; now there are 37 National Parks in the traditional sense of an unusual natural area preserved for all people and all time and the number continues to grow.

Beyond this, there are 16 new, full-scale National Parks planned, and recently the National Park Service has expanded to include archaeological sites, historical sites, and seashores and parkways and rivers and even national recreation areas like Lake Mead, created when the Hoover Dam was built. The 1.5 million acres of Lake Mead make a wonderful recreation site, but it hardly fits the nature-preserving "crown jewels of our natural heritage" image of the National Parks.

In a continuing program to expand its holdings, a fund-raising letter sent out by the National Park Service and the Conservation Association says that of 86 priority areas targeted for acquisition in 1988, ten had already been added. The 1988 recommendations include expansion of the NPS to more than 71 million acres, adding to 178 existing National Park units another 130 new areas! Under the new definitions, the NPS, as of Spring 1992, had 358 separate "national park" units encompassing 80 million acres.

Additionally, there is now the National Natural Landmarks Program, also administered by the NPS.[11] There are 587 designated landmarks and 3,000 potential landmarks encompassing more than another 60 million acres . . . so far. Landmark evaluation is a feeder program for parks. Internally in the NPS this program is called "Ladies in Waiting." It's used to justify acquisition, but there is no authorizing legislation, as yet.

How much land is enough? Or is this country headed toward becoming one gigantic park? Incredibly, something like that seems to have been suggested by EPA Administrator William Reilly in an article in 1985, in which he proposed "to extend the National Park tradition to land not owned by the federal government . . . to further the evolution of the park ideal." Brock Evans, the Audubon Society's Washington lobbyist, said at a "Growth Management Forum" of the New England Environmental Network at Tufts University in November 1990 that land "should *all* be in the public domain. Be unreasonable. You can do it. Let's take it *all* back."[12]

The main problems facing national parks today grow out of their popularity: too many visitors. Many of the parks are being "loved to death," and the Park Service is hard put to exercise proper management. The agency's answer is to add more and more land to its holdings. A plethora of new laws, beginning with the Wilderness Act of 1964, has made this possible. Now in addition to the Wilderness Act, we have the Wild and Scenic Rivers Act, Surface Management Control and Reclamation Act, National Forest Management Act, Federal Land Policy Management Act, National Environmental Policy Act, Endangered Species Act, Clean Water and Clean Air Acts, Multiple Use Sustained Yield Act, Oregon Wilderness Bill, Federal Water Pollution Control Act—and a variety of others dealing with Scenic Areas, Historic Places, National Monuments, etc., etc. . . . Where will it end?

As of the end of 1991, the already authorized NPS land acquisition backlog was estimated to cost anywhere from $3 billion to $10 billion! And this despite an NPS maintenance backlog cost of $2 billion and a major repairs backlog bill of $5 billion!

The fiscal 1993 federal budget includes $100 million to the Forest Service to purchase 126,933 acres, $84.4 million to the NPS for an additional 29,483 acres, $79.5 million to the Fish and Wildlife Service for 63,013 acres, and $42 million to the Bureau of Land Management for 66,325 acres—and these, of course, are in addition to all the private land the federal government is taking without compensation.

To repeat, how much land in the "public domain" is enough?

According to a 1990 report from the Bureau of Land Management, private use through leasing of public lands in the past 30 years has increased the population of elk on public lands by 800 percent, bighorn sheep by 435 percent, and moose by almost 500 percent. By any measure, private management excels. When will common sense prevail?

PART FOUR

Rules and More Rules

CHAPTER 12

All (Environmental) Issues—Great and Small

A Collection of False Alarms

REMEMBER the cranberry scare? It turned out to be a nothing, and just went away. Nobody was ever hurt from eating cranberries. The only casualties were a number of cranberry farmers who were ruined economically.

Remember Red Dye #2? And cyclamates? Remember the mercury-in-fish scare? That one went away when an enterprising investigator showed that marine fish, specifically tuna, caught decades ago and preserved at the Smithsonian Institution, had just as much mercury in their bodies as those caught today. It has always been so in the ocean.

Of course it's possible to pollute small bodies of water that have little circulation. There have been such instances. And most of them have been cleaned up. But the mercury-in-fish scare was directed at tuna fish—and they live in the open ocean.

An interesting thing took place at the height of the mercury scare. A conference was held at Williams College in July 1970 for the purpose of "examining a series of critical environmental problems, and thence producing a book that would be entitled *Man's Impact on the Global Environment: Assessments and Recommen-*

dations for Action." One of the sessions dealt with mercury pollution.[1] Dr. Ed Goldberg, a marine geochemist from the Scripps Institute of Oceanography, presented a paper in which he showed that human activities could not possibly influence the amount of mercury in the open ocean. He demonstrated that the entire amount of mercury mining was comparable to the mercury content of natural erosion—and also that there is no reason to suppose there is any threat to the ocean or to sea life from mercury mining, since the total flowing into the ocean, both from human activity and from natural causes, is no more than one eight-thousandth of what is already present.

When Dr. Goldberg finished his presentation, Professor Carroll Wilson of the Massachusetts Institute of Technology, who was chairman of the conference, thanked him. Then he said that, in his opinion, the subject of the mercury contamination of fish would continue to receive major attention from the press—and if the conference report included a paper that showed mercury pollution of the ocean was not an important human problem, then "we would run the risk of destroying the credibility of our entire report." Accordingly, he recommended that Dr. Goldberg's analysis be omitted. No one objected.[2]

Now the mercury-in-fish scare, like the cranberry hoax, did not hurt anyone. It only destroyed much of the U.S. tuna fishing fleet. But that episode ushered in a new destructive attitude in American science: the assumption that it's all right to ignore data if they don't support the predetermined conclusions. How pervasive this presumption has become in scientific research, that the "ends justify the means," will be illustrated as we examine some key issues in the field of environmental "science."

Superfund

America's awakening to the fact that human impacts on the natural environment can have serious consequences has led to a large number of corrective actions. For the most part, these programs involve governmental intervention, including laws, regulations, and penalties. Today, with more than 20 years' experience of governmental "command and control" environmentalism, it's appropriate to ask the question: How well has it worked?

Well, there's some good news and some bad news.

The good news is that the condition of the natural environment has indeed improved. The air is cleaner and the water purer than 20 years ago, and the land is treated with greater care.

The bad news is that billions of dollars have been wasted on precipitous actions that weren't necessary, instances where political action moved faster than scientific research justified, and where government bureaucrats and the public just plain overreacted.[3] It's one thing to clean up a mess to the point where it no longer presents a hazard; it's something else to try to eliminate every last molecule of an offending substance. Our society has not yet really faced up to the question: How clean is clean enough?

The perfect, it's been said, is the enemy of the good. In environmental matters, this seems to be true. Nothing illustrates the problem better than the program called Superfund.

The Superfund toxic waste program was created in 1980 in response to growing public concern about industry's handling of hazardous materials.[4] The belief grew, whether justified or not, that American business was engaged in cheap, easy, irresponsible dumping of poisonous waste products. Not only was this damaging the environment, but it was harmful to human health. Abandoned waste dumps were recognized as posing special problems.

Central to the growing antipathy to hazardous chemicals was the sensational episode with toxic wastes at Love Canal, where families were terrified at the threat seeping chemicals posed to the health of their children. Public pressure was overwhelming. Immediate measures were demanded to correct the situation. So the federal government passed a new law, the Comprehensive Environmental Response, Compensation, and Liability Act (CERCLA), better known as the Superfund.[5] Since the events at Love Canal played so important a role in establishing the Superfund law, they deserve a critical look.

Love Canal, a residential community near Niagara Falls, New York, was built near a chemical waste disposal site. Its name has become synonymous with irresponsible, careless, perhaps even criminal dumping of toxic chemicals.[6]

The roots of the Love Canal story go back to 1892, when William T. Love proposed an ambitious project. He sought to harness the water power of Niagara Falls to support an industrial town and model city of as many as 600,000 people.

By 1894, preliminary excavation for the canal had begun, but economic hard times foreclosed the project and eventually the partly dug canal was abandoned. In the early 1900s, the children of Niagara Falls used William Love's dream project as a swimming hole.

In 1941, the Hooker Chemical Company looked into using the unfinished excavation, now known as Love Canal, as a disposal site for potentially hazardous industrial wastes. Studies showed that the canal had been dug out of clay, through which there was no seepage, and hence it was determined to be a good place to contain the waste products.

The necessary permits were obtained. Disposal began in 1942 and continued until 1953. Ultimately, about 21,800 tons of waste went into the canal. All procedures conformed to the waste disposal requirements in force at that time.

In the meantime, the city of Niagara Falls grew and land for expansion was limited. The Love Canal dump site area, where land values were low, appealed to city officials as a good place to expand. The plan was especially popular with the Board of Education's Building and Grounds Committee, which was determined to build a school there.

The Hooker Chemical Company was not a willing seller, even though it was reasonable to consider the site safe. Love Canal was no longer used for waste disposal, it had been properly capped, and the company thought the land could safely be used, as long as the actual waste site was not penetrated or excavated.

Eventually, Hooker bowed to pressure from the city and to threats that the land might be seized under the doctrine of eminent domain to build a public school. The company deeded the property to the city for the token price of one dollar.

The record shows that Hooker went to great lengths to warn the city about the danger of disturbing the waste area. The deed of conveyance of the land, dated April 28, 1953, contains such specific language.

Once the land was acquired, the Board of Education ignored the company's warnings and soon permitted construction of storm sewers, roads, and utilities. In 1958, some of the canal's waste site covering was breached as homes and schools were built.

Such is the history of how the community of Love Canal began. Starting about 1976, Michael Brown, a reporter with *The Niagara Gazette*, wrote a series of articles about suspected cases of illness at Love Canal attributed to the presence of the wastes. ("Laying Waste: The Poisoning of America by Toxic Chemicals.") Some of the residents became hysterical and others were militant and resentful. By 1978, continued reporting of anecdotal "evidence" made Love Canal a national media event and the New York State Commissioner of Health issued a report entitled, *Love Canal: Public Health Time Bomb.*[7]

Much later, in a thoroughly researched and well documented study, Marc K. Landy of Boston College and the Gordon Center for Public Policy concluded that the commissioner's report was "not based on any evidence whatsoever concerning illness of people surrounding Love Canal but rather was dictated by legal and fiscal exigencies. In order to obtain funds for health studies, state law required a finding of 'grave and imminent peril.' Similarly, in order to make Love Canal eligible for federal disaster aid, the health department had to claim that an emergency existed."[8]

Two studies in 1979 of the health of residents contributed to the rising anxieties at Love Canal. The first, by Dr. Beverly Paigen, claimed that increases in asthma, urinary disorders, epilepsy, birth defects, cancer, and many other dreadful maladies were found among residents. Her research has been thoroughly discredited by analyses conducted by the National Cancer Institute, by the New York Department of Health, and in 1983 by the Centers for Disease Control.[9]

The other study, commissioned by the Environmental Protection Agency in 1980, claimed to find chromosome aberrations and nerve damage. This, too, has not been corroborated despite extensive peer review. Now, with the benefit of still more studies and the perspective of more than a decade, the final judgment is that, aside from some psychological distress brought on by hysteria, not even a single common cold can be accurately attributed to the chemical wastes at Love Canal.[10]

But such was the media's success in fanning fear at Love Canal that the government ordered an evacuation of the area. The cost to the public was more than $30 million.

In 1981, *The New York Times* reported: "From what is now known, Love Canal, perhaps the nation's most prominent symbol of chemical assaults on the environment, has had no detectable effect on the incidence of cancer. When all the results are in..., it may well turn out that the public suffered less from the chemicals there than from the hysteria generated by flimsy research, irresponsibly handled."[11]

In her definitive review of the Love Canal disaster, Dr. Elizabeth Whelan concluded: "Love Canal is dishonest science; it is a regulatory agency [the Environmental Protection Agency] that pursues its own motives and ambitions; it is a state health department exaggerating the truth to get federal funds. And finally, Love Canal is a chilling example of just how powerful a force media-generated hysteria is in our high-tech society."[12]

And Love Canal gave us CERCLA—the Superfund. (Cynically it's known as the Comprehensive Employment for Regulators, Consultants, and Lawyers Act.)

In the beginning, the Superfund was heralded as a great step forward in waste handling; it was expected to protect the public health and to do so at small cost to the taxpayer. Now, a dozen years later, the program has failed to achieve its goals and proved to be expensive beyond belief.

As early as June 1988, the Office of Technology Assessment concluded that the Superfund program is "an expensive, inefficient, and ineffective use of taxpayers' money."[13]

Marc K. Landy, who has made extensive analyses of the Superfund and other EPA programs, came to a similar conclusion: "Superfund has produced an enormous legal morass that constitutes a substantial drain on public and private resources; yet it has yielded very little in the way of environmental improvement...."[14]

Jane S. Shaw, senior associate with the Political and Economic Research Center in Bozeman, Montana, and formerly associate economics editor for *Business Week*, reported: "Sometimes, of course, the results of furor about supposed dangers are merely more government boondoggles, such as the $10 billion Superfund program that supposedly cleans up hazardous waste sites. Fear that places like the Love Canal dump in New York, Times Beach in Missouri, and the Stringfellow Acid Pits in California were causing birth defects and cancer created and bankrolled this program. But Superfund, a political pork barrel, has cleaned up only about 50 sites since it was enacted in 1980. Yet reputable studies have failed to confirm any serious health effects from such sites."[15]

Even the EPA's own study, *Unfinished Business*, suggested that the whole rationale for the Superfund might be suspect: "Total health impacts [of Superfund sites] do not appear to match public concerns in most areas." This study also admitted that the toxic waste site problem is overrated and that too much of the agency's resources are spent on it.[16]

Even so, and in the face of extensive criticism from health experts and other independent scientists, the EPA has been unwilling to undertake a program of public information to bring reason and reform to the Superfund program. Meanwhile, the costs continue to rise.

Accurate figures on how much has been spent on the Superfund are difficult to determine. In part, this is because the source of funds is both public and private. In 1988, the (Congressional) Office of Technology Assessment estimated that $5 billion in public money had been spent; by 1991, the cost was running at $10 billion per year. It is estimated that the bill for waste containment could run at $20 billion per year by 2000. Everyone acknowledges that a significant portion of these monies go to fund litigation and lawyers' fees and to waste management corporations. An extensive industry that depends for its survival on public funds has been created by the Superfund. It is not in the waste industry's interest to solve or correct the problems. In 1991, the waste management companies' income exceeded $15 billion.[17]

More than 1,000 Superfund sites have been identified; fewer than 70 have been cleaned up. The General Accounting Office says there may actually be as many as 400,000 waste sites yet to be characterized as such and that it would take $10 billion just to assess them. That, of course, is based upon the EPA's standards as to what makes a site eligible for Superfund status, and the criteria for determining when the site is "clean." A few examples will illustrate the difficulties.

In the little town of Holden, Missouri, an 11-acre site was used until 1986 by the Rose Chemical Company to store and process polychlorinated biphenyls (PCBs).[18] The barrels containing the chemicals were removed when the activities ceased, but small residues could be detected in the building and surrounding soil. Because of trace quantities of dioxin in the PCB residues, the area became a Superfund site. A comprehensive study showed that the building could be cleaned up and safely isolated from the community for a mere $71,000. But Superfund requirements demand removal of the building itself and the addition of uncontaminated soil with a 10-inch cap of clay on the site. This was estimated to cost $3.6 million. But even that might not be sufficient to satisfy EPA cleanup requirements; one alternative is that the site be returned to some imagined "pristine" condition, such as might have existed before humans occupied the region. This would cost from $13 to $40 million and is the preferred alternative.

Does any of this make sense? Is there really a public health hazard so great as to justify this type of expense? No, but as a result of years of publicity claiming that dioxin is the most toxic substance known, fear is firmly implanted in the public mind, and that tends to justify any expense to remove a possible danger, however unlikely it may be.

To be fair, there is evidence of dioxin's hazardous nature; very small amounts, in fact, are fatal to guinea pigs. But the very same doses—and even doses 1,000 times larger—have no deleterious effects on rats, mice, or any other laboratory animals on which dioxins have been tested, or, as far as we know, on man.[19] In July 1976, a tremendous explosion spread huge amounts of PCBs in Seveso, Italy, and contaminated large numbers of people, but no fatalities and no cancers resulted. The only effect was a number of cases of chloracne, a skin rash that is unpleasant, but treatable and curable.[20] As Dr. Vernon Houk of the Centers for Disease Control has said, "Over the past eight years [1981–89], the science base on human exposure to dioxin has expanded substantially. . . . We know for certain that dioxin can cause chloracne . . . but as yet, we have found no other adverse health effect."[21]

A study conducted by the National Institute of Occupational Safety and Health showed that 5,200 workers with dioxin levels up to 200 times greater than the average U.S. exposure suffered no increase in cancer rates or any other health problem, save the skin rash.

A few years ago, Times Beach, Missouri, was evacuated by order of the Centers for Disease Control. Investigators had found traces of dioxin in some of the town's unpaved dirt streets. But the evacuation has had an interesting aftermath. Dr. Houk of the CDC now admits that "Given what we now know about this chemical's toxicity, it looks as though the evacuation was unnecessary." That is small consolation to the inhabitants whose lives were uprooted unnecessarily, as it now turns out.[22]

Eight years of research at a cost of $400 million, proving that dioxin is not the frightening toxin that had been claimed, can now be added to the $138 million cost of the evacuation itself. What price can be put on human misery, inflicted for no good reason? Exposure to dioxin, once thought to be much more hazardous than chain smoking, is now considered to be no more risky than spending a week sunbathing. The difference between these two beliefs— less than ten years apart—is that the first one was based on unsubstantiated statements, hearsay, and hype with no data to back it up, while the second rests solidly on years of carefully gathered evidence corroborated by independent experts.

But it appears that learning from experience does not necessarily take place. The dioxin exposure studies conducted as a result of the fiasco at Times Beach have not led to any change in the regulations on permissible dioxin levels still being enforced by the EPA and state agencies. Paper companies are held to a discharge standard of fractions of a part *per quadrillion*. The fact that dioxin is found widespread in nature, is formed whenever organic material is burned (for example, during forest fires), and is broken down chemically by microorganisms in the soil does not seem to faze the regulators. After all, as William Gough of the Office of Technology Assessment has acknowledged, there are 193 "toxic" air pollutants that are all substantially *less* dangerous than dioxin.[23] What would happen to them if dioxin exposure standards were relaxed? Would we put thousands of lawyers and bureaucrats out of business? Whatever happened to common sense?[24]

Another group of chemicals whose name has been associated with causing cancer are the polychlorinated biphenyls (PCBs). Introduced as a replacement for mineral oil in electric transformers, PCBs performed magnificently. Because they are not flammable—unlike the previously used mineral oil—they reduced dramatically the number of electrical fires in transformers. So effective were PCBs that many cities required utilities to use them in place of mineral oil. All that changed in the early 1970s.[25] For some reason, the EPA decided that PCBs could break down to form dioxin and that this would somehow emanate from the transformers and in some way be inhaled or eaten or otherwise absorbed by large numbers of people. No matter that workers in the chemical industries that produce PCB suffered no harmful effects; no matter that hundreds of electrical workers were in contact with PCBs, sometimes immersing their bare arms in the oily liquid—all without adverse health effects; no matter that no scientific evidence existed to support the notion that contact with PCB could cause cancer. No matter. The EPA banned the use of PCBs. The result was millions of dollars of replacement costs to utilities, thus raising everyone's bill for electricity on the one hand, while bringing a return of transformer fires, on the other. As Warren Brookes wrote: "The PCB experience, like that of dioxin, asbestos, Alar, and countless other false alarms, demonstrates that billions [of dollars] are being spent to rid substances from the environment whose actual exposure levels generate insignificant or nonexistent risks."[26]

Who can command so much money and spend it so wastefully? Only the EPA.

We have by no means reached the end of the litany of misrepresentation of the dangers of many commonly used chemicals and the resultant waste of taxpayer money. The EPA is now busy developing rules that will eliminate the use of methyl bromide, ethylene dibromide (EDB gas), and similar compounds.[27] Currently, they are used mainly to fumigate soil and stored grain. Simply put, if cereal grain is not fumigated, it will rot in storage very quickly. Bacterial and fungal spores are ubiquitous in nature, and are present in stored grain. Neither the EPA nor the Food and Drug Administration nor the Department of Agriculture can do away with these ever-present microorganisms. Methyl bromide prevents their growth. It also has some marvelous properties—for one thing, it stinks to high heaven, so if, by chance, it should be over-used, the workers would know instantly and take corrective action. Methyl bromide is not explosive or flammable or carcinogenic in any of the circumstances where it is actually used as a fumigant.

Oh, yes, it is possible to *force* tumor formation. This was done by the EPA using a process known as "gavage." Liquids containing methyl bromide were forced into a rat's stomach through a tube in such high concentration that the tissues were severely irritated with resultant cell damage and tumor formation. Such "research" procedures are irrational and so irrelevant and misleading as to be dishonest. What conceivable purpose is served in prohibiting the use of methyl bromide, other than to prevent protection of cereal grains against rot and thus diminish the world's food supply? Of course, there is an alternative—the process of food irradiation, using gamma rays, that has been proved safe and effective to protect stored grain—but the EPA is not about to support that!

Another program now being pursued by the EPA is to lower dramatically the permissible amount of lead in drinking water. If the agency's proposed new standards are adopted, the U.S. will have the lowest level of permissible lead, by ten times, of any industrialized country. The EPA's proposal is based on research that has been termed "flawed" by water quality experts.[28] It would also greatly increase the cost of drinking water by $5,000 to $20,000 per household, for a total estimated cost of between $200 billion to $500 billion.

Representative John Dingell, a liberal Democrat usually in favor of intrusive big government, pointed out, in an interview reported in *Insight* magazine (November 11, 1991), that: "Testing every child for lead levels [as is proposed] and remediating all houses and pipes where lead is present is unbelievably costly and will dissipate huge resources desperately needed for things we know will actually help children: prenatal care, Head Start, inoculations, and so forth. . . . But if it is a bad standard, if it is not founded on solid science, then they are wasting simply enormous public and private resources. Just wait until you see the lead-in-water bill!"

Congressman Dingell also said, in the same interview:

> It is increasingly apparent that there is something fundamentally wrong with much of the science underlying our environmental health regulations, as we have seen in recent episodes on asbestos, dioxin, and PCBs, where risks have been dramatically overstated at simply immense cost to the public. . . .
>
> You take the standard on CO [carbon monoxide]. That came out of the work of a VA [Veterans' Administration] scientist, who, it turns out, cooked the books. It was criminally fraudulent work. Yet today's clean air standards are still bottomed [based] on his work.[29]

We in the U.S. have only ourselves to blame when we permit government agencies to get away with such junk science. But it is something else when our public officials are directly (or indirectly) responsible for troubles elsewhere.

Case in point: Some bureaucrat functionary within the EPA produced an internal study in which it was claimed that chlorinated drinking water could, possibly, cause a minuscule number of cancers in the general population. The rationale was that the chlorine, under some circumstances, might lead to the formation of chloroform, and since chloroform is considered by some researchers to be a possible, but weak, carcinogen, then perhaps the widespread chlorination of drinking water should be reconsidered. The paper was largely ignored by public officials in the U.S. because they well understand that chlorinated public drinking water has been the greatest protection against water-borne diseases ever developed. There is no substitute for chlorination.

But in other countries, the public was not so fortunate.[30] In Peru, the authorities took the EPA study seriously and stopped chlorinating the drinking water in their cities. The result was a rapid spread of the water-borne disease cholera, which had just been introduced into Peru through contaminated seafood. More than 600,000 cases and 5,000 deaths have been recorded from the disease spreading throughout South America—wherever chlorination of water is not practiced. Twenty nations are now involved.[31]

And here at home, the EPA has begun to suggest that taking a hot shower *might* be carcinogenic, since the elevated water temperature *might* stimulate formation of chloroform from chlorine. There are no cases of asphyxiation or of cancer and certainly no cancer fatalities that can be traced to showering,[32] but one can imagine a series of "what ifs" and come up with a statistical model to predict . . . anything.

Perhaps it should be recalled that two very unpleasant diseases, leprosy and tuberculosis, both on the rise in the U.S., are associated with filth. But perhaps environmentalists at the EPA consider filth a more natural and healthy state of affairs than modern hot-water showering. We seem to have forgotten a great deal since the old days, when every school child learned that cleanliness is next to godliness . . . or at least our environmental lawyers and bureaucrats have.

Acid Rain

For many years, acid rain has been regarded as a scourge, an unpleasant and destructive byproduct of industrialization. Formed as a result of sulfur dioxide emissions from industry, primarily from burning coal to produce electricity, acid rain has been called "poison falling out of the sky, killing our forests and ravaging the countryside."

Throughout the 1970s, political environmentalists from the EPA, Sierra Club, Audubon Society, and other organizations promoted the idea that acid rain was causing an aquatic "silent spring" in the New England states. Thousands of lakes were claimed to be devoid of life, with thousands more doomed to become fishless.[33] The EPA announced in 1980 that the average acidity of northeast lakes had increased a hundredfold over the past 40 years, all due to acid rain. No evidence was cited to support this position. In 1981, the National Research Council joined in with a forecast that the number of acidified lakes would double by

1990.[34] This has not happened. For all the claims of disaster from acid rain, there was no scientific assessment on which to base them. It is now known that the "acidified lakes" have simply returned to their pre-Industrial Age condition. During the 19th century, extensive logging and slash burning had added quantities of alkaline ash to the watershed, countering the natural acidity of the surrounding soil and the water. With cessation of these activities, the lakes and rivers of the Northeast have simply reverted to their natural state.

But the conventional wisdom among scientists, environmentalists, politicians, and the public is to hold acid rain responsible for the decline of sport fishing in the Adirondacks and for damage to forests from Vermont to North Carolina. About 80 miles from Asheville, North Carolina, the trees are in terrible condition on Mount Mitchell, and Park Service people blame that on acid rain. But Dr. Patricia Irving, a scientist researching acid rain problems, said that such a claim was "deplorable," since the damage to the Mount Mitchell trees is known to be caused by an aphid-like insect called the balsam woolly adelgild.[35] Acid rain is also blamed for destroying trees along the Blue Ridge Parkway, but this devastation is due to gypsy moths.

Indeed, this issue has international overtones, since the government of Canada blames sulphide emissions from American utilities in the Ohio Valley for damage in Ontario. Acid rain has been blamed for the decline and loss of salmon from rivers in Nova Scotia, and President Carter's Council on Environmental Quality issued a report calling acid rain "one of the most serious environmental problems of the century."

By 1980, Congress responded to all this hype by authorizing a ten-year $500 million dollar study, which became known as the National Acid Precipitation Assessment Project (NAPAP).[36] Its purpose was to determine once and for all the effect of acid rain on the natural environment. Utilizing the talents of nearly 700 of the nation's top scientists in aquatic, soil, atmospheric, and related sciences and ultimately costing $537 million, the 28-volume report was completed by 1990. The report, issued after ten years of study, concluded "that acid rain should be 'viewed as a long-term problem' requiring pollution controls, but is *not the environmental crisis* some scientists have suggested."

This mild, well-documented conclusion was not accepted by environmentalists, and the report was ignored by Congress, which, by then, had already passed the 1990 Clean Air Act.[37]

The NAPAP study found that of more than 7,000 northeastern lakes, only 240 were acidic; the average lake has just about the same degree of acidity as before the Industrial Era. Most of the acidic lakes are in Florida, where 21 percent of the lakes are acidic and where there is the least acid rain in the eastern United States. For those lakes that are acidic, the report recommended adding lime to the surrounding watershed, at a combined cost for all acidic lakes of about $500,000 a year. When asked what would happen to lake and stream acidity if no actions were taken over the next 50 years, Dr. James Mahoney, the director of NAPAP from 1987 to 1990, said, "Nothing."[38]

As for forests, only the Red Spruce in the Adirondack Mountains, already growing under conditions of environmental stress— cold, wind, etc.—was found to be adversely affected. The NAPAP study found that, contrary to all the specious reports of "dying forests," acid rain has little or no deleterious effect on forest health.[39] Data from the U.S. Forest Service show that New England's forests are among the most robust in the country. It is also worth pointing out that many species of trees and bushes characteristic of the Northeast—Red and Black Spruce, oaks, balsam fir, eastern hemlock, rhododendrons, and blueberries—depend upon acidic soil for their survival. Even more important is what the public has *not* been told about the effect of acid rain on forests. NAPAP studies found that the nitrogen and sulfur that characterize acid rain really act as nutrients, essential for plant growth. "Acid rain" benefits trees; it is manna from heaven. Far from destroying forests, acid rain actually fertilizes the 300 million acres of eastern forest on which it falls. The same result was found in Sweden, where the world's first national acid rain program was carried out. The Swedish research determined that "the principal effect of acid rain is the improvement of crop yields and crop protein content."[40]

These results were already established by 1987 and recorded in an interim report. But the conclusions were unacceptable to the EPA and to the environmentalists whose reputations were at stake.

Dr. J. Laurence Kulp, the original director, was therefore removed and replaced by Dr. James Mahoney. Dr. Mahoney was directed, according to a report by Warren Brookes, to rewrite the report and repudiate its findings.[41]

Dr. Mahoney is too good a scientist to acquiesce to such political pressure and told economist-columnist Warren Brookes: "While I would challenge anyone who says acid rain has no effect on the environment, I would also challenge anyone who called it an environmental crisis. It's truly dismaying that the whole level of this debate has been reduced to cutting 10 million tons [of SO_2] now without reference to the science or the economics. I am very proud of the science that NAPAP performed and disappointed that it has been so largely ignored."

Ignored, indeed, it has been. As Dr. Edward Krug, one of NAPAP's key scientists, has recounted:

> Yes, there were political pressures, but they were to support, not oppose, the basis for the program's existence. *Acid rain had to be an environmental catastrophe, no matter what the facts revealed.**
>
> Since we could not support this claim . . . the EPA worked to keep us from fulfilling our goal of providing Congress and other decision-makers with our findings. Because EPA could not stop Congress from requesting a NAPAP hearing, EPA Administrator William Reilly resorted to altering the congressional testimony of NAPAP director James Mahoney—as was determined at NAPAP's Oversight Review Board meeting held on December 12, 1989. But EPA could, however, block the release of NAPAP's prepared Findings Document. This they did, and NAPAP's findings were not released until July 27, 1990, at which time they were of little relevance or interest to lawmakers.[42]

Congress did not even consider NAPAP's findings when it passed the 1990 Clean Air Act. And so, our nation is saddled with a $40 billion bill to reduce acid rain, a cost that will be borne mainly by the electric utilities and ratepayers of the Midwest— when the facts show that this is totally unnecessary and a waste of money.

* Emphasis added.

Asbestos

Breathing asbestos fibers can cause lung cancer. That statement is true. It is also grossly oversimplified. But believing it, without taking into account the importance of what *kind* of asbestos is involved and *how much* is inhaled, over *how long* a period of time, has led to the unnecessary, expensive, and possibly tragic ban on all uses of asbestos. Not only has the EPA issued such a ban (in 1989), it has also decreed that where asbestos has been used as insulation, as a fire retardant, or for sound-proofing in schools and other public buildings, it must be removed—at the owner's expense.[43]

The cost of compliance with the EPA's asbestos rules for schools and public buildings has been enormous—roughly $160 billion by the end of 1991. Most of that expense has been borne by school districts. Money spent to remove asbestos is, of course, not available to support better teaching, purchase school supplies, or fund school programs.[44]

If children's health *is* endangered by the incorporation of asbestos into the school building's structure, then no expense should be spared to remove it. But that is not the case. Let's take a look at the facts. First about asbestos itself. There are different kinds of asbestos; not all are equally hazardous.

Geologically, there are six forms of asbestos. Only three are used in commerce.[45] Of the three, the one known as "blue" asbestos—technically called crocidolite—causes serious lung problems, including lung cancer, mesothelioma (cancer of the chest and abdominal membranes), and asbestosis (a condition in which the lung tissue becomes fibrous and non-functional). Blue asbestos, however, has never been in general use in the U.S. Its only important application was in shipyards during World War II, where its highly non-corrosive properties were considered advantageous for wrapping pipes and for other applications in an environment with likely exposure to sea water.[46]

World War II shipyard workers—the most seriously affected of all exposed persons—deserve care and compensation, since they were neither properly warned about the hazards nor provided with proper protective gear. But we also know from their experience that the likelihood of contracting lung problems from breathing crocidolite fibers is greatly increased by smoking.

And that leads us to the results of an interesting study on crocidolite asbestos exposure and related lung diseases that was reported in the November 1989 issue of the *New England Journal of Medicine*.[47] Researchers from the Dana Farber Cancer Research Institute in Boston studied the 33 men employed by the Lorillard Tobacco Company between 1951 and 1957 to make "Micronite" filters for Kent cigarettes. Statistically, a maximum of eight out of the 33 could be expected to die in the ensuing years; 28, in fact, have died, or, to put it another way, the death rate is 325 percent higher than anticipated. More important, all but one of the 28 died from asbestos-related disease, 11 from lung cancer, five from mesothelioma, five from asbestosis, three from other cancers, and two from respiratory disease. The Micronite filter was made from crocidolite—blue asbestos.

Not only was the public never warned about the dangers of inhaling crocidolite asbestos fibers from the filters of Kent cigarettes; the tobacco company that made them has not been held accountable. That fact seems doubly ironic and unjust when we consider the harassment suffered by the entire asbestos industry that did not use crocidolite. In an impassioned report to *The Wall Street Journal* (July 15, 1992), Glenn W. Bailey, chairman of Keene Corporation in New York, complained bitterly of the "abusive litigation" that threatens the American asbestos industry.

In 1968, Keene acquired a thermal-insulation firm whose product contained 10 percent asbestos (probably chrysotile, not crocidolite). The asbestos was totally eliminated from the product four years later, and Keene closed the affiliate in 1972. Yet, because of the punitive, ad-hoc asbestos law, Keene has had to pay out $400 million in asbestos claims brought by workers who never even worked for Keene. Most of them had worked in Navy shipyards in World War II, 25 years before Keene was formed. Bailey said about $265 million of Keene's payments of $400 million went to lawyers, who, he added, have escalated the payouts by recruiting still more claimants to pad their income. In all, Bailey estimated the asbestos litigation, which he characterized as "legalized extortion," has already cost American firms $9 billion—with $6 billion of the total going to attorneys.

A second type of amphibole asbestos is brown asbestos or amosite. Like blue asbestos, it is imported from Africa and has never had many applications in the U.S. But it was used in a factory in Patterson, New Jersey, where workers were found to have elevated incidences of lung disease, 18.4 percent being cancer mortality (117 cases), 2.8 percent mesothelioma (8 cases), and 4.2 percent asbestosis mortality (27 cases).[48]

Both blue and brown asbestos belong to the general category called amphibole asbestos, which has been used in less than 5 percent of all asbestos applications in the U.S. And neither blue asbestos nor brown asbestos has ever been used in schools or other buildings.

Soft white asbestos, called chrysotile, is by far the most important form of asbestos, since it is used in 95 percent of all asbestos applications.[49]

Soft white asbestos is common in many localities. In the San Francisco Bay area, for example, there are widespread outcroppings of serpentine rock, which weathers, releasing chrysotile asbestos fibers to the atmosphere and water supplies. There is no evidence of elevated rates of asbestos-related lung disease in California.

Lifetime exposures to chrysotile fibers in Quebec, where soft white asbestos is mined, show no statistically significant increase in lung disease among miners or their families.[50]

The EPA's own data on the asbestos (chrysotile) content of water supplies in the U.S. show that millions of people are exposed to millions of fibers per liter of water. Consider that these people drink the water, cook with it, water lawns and gardens, wash their clothes and cars, and maybe even take hot showers in it. Their daily exposure to asbestos fibers is enormous. The record measurement of asbestos in water is from the Klamath River in California and Oregon, where 300 billion fibers per liter were found. Imagine the asbestos spread over the ground when the river floods. Remember, all this exposure is to the *chrysotile* type of asbestos.

The average exposure of miners and other chrysotile asbestos workers in the workplace is about two fibers per cubic centimeter of air.

In schools and other buildings, where the asbestos is entirely the chrysotile type, its fibers typically occur in air concentrations of 0.001 fiber per cubic centimeter. *After* many removal operations— actually *because* of them (removal procedures release the fibers into the air)—the fiber content of the air inside the building has been measured at 20 to 40 fibers per cubic centimeter. This is an improvement?

To sum up the properties and uses of asbestos: the amphiboles— blue and brown asbestos—have sharp needle-like fibers that, when inhaled, penetrate lung tissue and are very difficult to remove. They are hazardous and are responsible for causing lung diseases, but their use is minimal.

The chrysotile or soft-white asbestos has fibers that can either dissolve or be removed from the lungs by normal physiological responses. Even lifetime exposures to concentrations as high as two fibers per cubic centimeter of air have failed to show any significant hazard.

Besides serving as insulation, soft white asbestos has many other uses, in firefighting equipment and fire hoses, brake linings and clutch facings, tiles, and cement water pipes. It also appears that removing chrysotile asbestos from the putty that held the O-rings in place was the probable cause of their failure in the space shuttle Challenger, which resulted in the disastrous crash and deaths of all seven astronauts.[51] Since asbestos is no longer permitted in brake linings, the number of car and truck accidents due to brake failure has skyrocketed.

Should all commercial uses of asbestos be banned because of health problems with the rare, and discontinued, use of the amphibole type? Of course not; that is overkill. Why did the EPA impose the ban? In a speech delivered on June 12, 1990, to the American Enterprise Institute, the EPA's Reilly said: "Most recently, the unusually compelling medical evidence on asbestos *led to my decision* last year to phase out virtually *all remaining uses* of asbestos in consumer products in order to prevent the addition of additional asbestos into the environment."*[52]

It could be that Reilly was referring only to the medical problems

* Emphasis added.

of the World War II shipyard workers and others who were exposed to blue crocidotile asbestos, but he extended the ban to all chrysotile use, as well. Referring to asbestos other than the blue or brown amphiboles, EPA officials have been quoted as saying that there were "some studies that give a hint that some of these fiber types are less likely to cause cancer" but that given scientific uncertainties, "we treat them all as of equal concern."[53]

Why?

Mr. Reilly could not have been referring to the 1984 report of the Royal Commission on Matters of Health and Safety Arising from the Use of Asbestos in Ontario (remember that Ontario is the home of nearly all soft-white asbestos mining and the source of supply for most chrysotile used in the U.S.). The report states: "Even a building whose air has a fiber level up to ten times greater than that found in typical outdoor air would create a risk of fatality that was less than one-fiftieth of the risk of having a fatal automobile accident while driving to and from the building. . . . Asbestos in building air will almost never pose a health hazard to building occupants."[54]

There is ample evidence that the EPA and other regulatory agencies are guilty of jumping to conclusions about asbestos based not only on over-simplifying the diverse properties of this ubiquitous and useful mineral fiber, but on poor data, slanted research, and an overzealous attitude. The stage for this was probably set by the EPA's first administrator, William Ruckelshaus, who admitted that the agency's original policy on asbestos was designed to "get mothers to form a vigilante mob to storm the school committee . . . because otherwise . . . the federal government would have to pay for it [asbestos removal] and the cost would be astronomical."[55]

And so it has been—for what benefit?

Even in those instances where pipe wrappings have become friable with the asbestos crumbling and releasing fibers to the air, the affected parts could be covered up at little cost. Acoustic ceilings and other exposed areas could be stabilized with a good coat of paint. Why, then, the expensive and dangerous removal programs? Especially given that Mr. Reilly also said in June 1990 that the mere presence of asbestos in school buildings "poses no risk of harm to public health"? And "millions of dollars have been wasted on unnecessary asbestos removal operations. In-place management can protect public health, reduce costs and guard against liability."

Which William Reilly was in charge? Which one do we believe?

Why not rescind the ban and the orders to remove asbestos? One important reason is that now there is a whole industry dependent on asbestos cleanup jobs whose earnings in 1989 exceeded $5 billion and with a self-interest in removal costs of $200 billion by the year 2000.[56]

The saddest commentary of all is that the ban on asbestos *has been* lifted—by the U.S. 5th Circuit Court of Appeals in New Orleans. This occurred October 21, 1991 ... and the EPA has succeeded in ignoring the court's ruling![57]

Electro-Magnetic Fields: An Important Health Hazard?

The idea that the electromagnetic field (EMF) created by electric power lines has adverse health effects is as old as the power lines themselves. It has been investigated for decades, both in Europe and in North America. Is it harmful or is it not? Has any health effect been established?[58]

Those scientists who are involved in the research are far from ready to draw conclusions about whether EMF exposure could play a role in causing cancer. Note that whenever the term, "health effects," is used, it generally means some kind of positive association with cancer. So our question probably should be, does exposure to EMF cause cancer? There is a suggestion—nothing really definitive, but a suggestion only—from some of the most comprehensive epidemiological investigations to date of a possible relationship between magnetic fields and childhood leukemia.[59] Inconclusive though this research result may be, it is enough to raise doubts and even to cause some people to express fear. Fortunately, there are now extensive programs under way to obtain practical measurements of EMF exposures outdoors, in the workplace, and in the laboratory. We can expect a much better understanding to emerge in a few years' time.[60]

Meanwhile, it's important to appreciate what is already known about EMFs and their relation to human well-being, especially since we live in a world that is full of electric grids and appliances. Sadly, most people are ignorant of what reactions occur when electricity is transmitted and delivered. Utility companies in a sense have been too successful with their extraordinary capacity to avoid "outages" or quickly repair them; they have relieved most citizens from even having to think about the reliability of supply, or even about the commodity itself. And given the widespread failure to teach our young people physics, we have a public that is ill-informed about even the most basic physical principles and engineering procedures involving electricity. This has tended to make people either accept the technology without question or to distrust it without reason. Both of these attitudes are deeply flawed. When ignorance reigns, it can easily be turned into fear. With electromagnetic fields, we can see this happening. So here goes.

First, we should remember that electromagnetic fields are part of our normal environment. The Earth itself has a huge magnetic field that encompasses it (geomagnetism) and additional fields are created, temporarily, by the discharge of lightning. Solar flares also affect the Earth's field. Activity in both muscles and nerves generates small EMFs within the body; this is what is measured when taking an electrocardiogram or an electroencephalogram. But the fields created by the flow of commercial electric current through a wire or appliance are in addition to those of the normal internal and external environment. Hence the question whether they upset or otherwise affect bodily function.

Every wire or appliance that carries electric current produces electric and magnetic fields. These lines of force radiate outward, and their intensity falls off sharply with distance from the source. An electric field makes the electric charges move, and a magnetic field curves the path of these charges when they are in motion. Extensive laboratory research has established that it is the magnetic field, not the electric field, that might have an effect on living cells. This is probably related to the fact that natural electric fields occur across the membranes of cells, and these are about 100 times higher than any that can be induced by common power fields. So external electric fields alone are unlikely to have any effect. This conclusion is also borne out by measurements of both electric and magnetic fields in the vicinity of power lines and appliances.[61]

With the magnetic field, its strength is proportional to the current; voltage is not involved. It follows, therefore, that since the current is lower for the same power in the extra high voltage line, the magnetic field is not so strong there as it is for the standard 3.6 kV distribution line. Further, since magnetic fields are proportional to the current and inversely proportional to the distance away from it, these fields are stronger in the average home than near power lines.

Here are some typical fields, measured in milligauss (mG). Compare the magnetic field measured at the edge of a right-of-way under a 3.6 kV line; typically, 3–20 mG, with:[62]

- Clothes dryer, typical 1–24 mG; maximum 93 mG.
- TV, typical 1–3 mG; maximum 100 mG.
- Refrigerator, typical 1–8 mG; maximum 167 mG.
- Kitchen stove, typical 1–80 mG; maximum 625 mG.
- Dishwasher, typical 1–15 mG; maximum 712 mG.
- Stereo, typical 4–100 mG; maximum 500 mG.
- Blow dryer, typical 1–75 mG; maximum 2175 mG.
- Shaver, typical 50–300 mG; maximum 6875 mG.
- Electric alarm clock, typical 1–12; maximum 450 mG.
- Computer, typical 1–25 mG; maximum 1875 mG.
- Microwave oven, typical 3–40 mG; maximum 812 mG.

All the available evidence shows clearly that there is *no significant* risk from exposure to any or all of these sources; but neither does the evidence permit the conclusion of no risk at all. And there is another factor to consider—ground loops. Recall that when the current from the source and back flows through parallel wires, as it does in leads to an appliance, the conductors carry equal currents in opposite directions, and their magnetic fields almost cancel, falling off very rapidly with distance from the two conductors. But if the current forms a loop, then inside this loop the magnetic fields of the current elements reinforce each other and give rise to a comparatively strong field. There is very often just such a loop in the typical American house, which uses a three-phase current and grounds the system by connecting it to the water plumbing. The loads on the phases are seldom exactly equal, and the resistance from the plumbing to the ground wire differs from house to house. The result is a loop with a magnetic field in which people live all the time. And this field is about three times larger than that from either appliances or power lines. Is it dangerous? Is it harmless? Only further research will tell.[63]

Should the research reveal that there really is a problem, then the response is simple. No, it is not to put power lines underground. That would not reduce by a single milligauss the magnetic field linked to the ground current. The remedy would be to use plastic inserts in the plumbing, and direct grounding for a direct return current. This is both relatively easy to do and inexpensive.

Now, coming back to the epidemiological studies that cause the most worry, those that suggest a linkage between childhood leukemia and EMFs, the evidence is far from conclusive. Scientists from the University of Southern California found that children with leukemia were about twice as likely to live in homes with high-current wiring configurations (loops) as were children who did not have leukemia.[64] But no clear association was found when the same researchers used actual indoor measurements (instead of calculations from wire codes) to characterize exposure.

Dr. Stephanie London, a member of the USC team, explained that "if the association with wiring configuration is real, we are talking about a relatively weak effect, about a doubling in the risk of a very rare cancer." Childhood leukemia, though tragic, occurs in only about 1 in 20,000 youngsters. Dr. London continues: "With a weak association and an exposure that is difficult to measure, as we have here, a number of high quality studies will be needed before we feel confident to conclude that electric and magnetic fields do or do not cause childhood leukemia."

Now, this does not mean that we can dismiss from consideration the electromagnetic field produced by transmission lines. But before conclusions are drawn that require change in contemporary practice, all possible sources of exposure must be taken into account. Moreover, when claims are made, all data should be reported; recall the much publicized report of a higher cancer rate in

New York City among male telephone line workers—a report that failed to add that the cancer rate for all male line-related workers was less than that for all New York City males!

Fortunately, better designed and more definitive studies are now under way. These involve epidemiology of large populations in both high and low magnetic field homes with long-term exposures; controlled laboratory experiments with cells, tissues, and whole animals as diverse as insects, fish, and mammals; and direct measurements of exposure with improved instrumentation. If effects can be shown, then the mechanism of action must also be elucidated, whether it is the production of melanoma by the pineal gland, as has been suggested, or some other mode of action.

Finally, there is the problem of conveying accurate information to the public at large. In the absence of reasonable understanding about electromagnetic fields, this is difficult to do. But it is important, because if the public becomes convinced that EMFs are a health hazard—even if the evidence is trivial or contrived—it will be nearly impossible to change their belief with logic and facts. Once again, the media environmentalists, regulatory bureaucrats, and environmental lawyers will gain the public eye and raid the public purse, and good science will merely gather dust in reports stacked on library shelves.

CHAPTER 13

Governing by Regulation

At What Cost?

ALMOST without our realizing it, a whole new level of government has emerged in America. It is composed of a combination of lawyers and bureaucrats who have come to dominate federal, state, and local government. Nobody likes it, except its practitioners. It is government by regulation. It is now the fourth branch of government. It functions as law maker; though unelected, its rules and regulations have the force of law. It functions also as both judge and jury in cases involving its own rules. The accumulation of legislative, executive, and judicial power in the same hands is the real definition of tyranny. And it has become the essence of environmental overkill.

Since 1954 the number of federal regulations has increased from 16,502 to 200,000.[1] Add to that the proliferation of state and local regulations. Who benefits? Well, lawyers do, expert consultants on environmental law do, and special interests that can manipulate the regulations do. Consider these examples:

1. New federal rules require the closing of most community garbage dumps and increase the cost of opening a new landfill to $10 million or more, up five times from what it cost in 1975. The revenues of big waste management companies will soar, while their

competitors, the small companies, fold. Adding to the problem are the mountains of mandated "recyclables" that cannot be sold in a glutted market. New York City has already suspended its recycling program because of the high cost—$300 per ton, compared to the average landfill fee of $28 per ton.[2]

2. Three billion dollars have been spent to protect housewives from labels that proclaim spaghetti sauce to be "fresh."[3]

3. The rehabilitation of 222 sea otters was mandated after the Exxon Valdez oil spill at a cost of more than $80,000 per animal. At the same time, the population of more than 500 sea otters within Valdez harbor itself was untouched by the spill, and thousands of sea otters occupy Alaskan waters.[4]

4. The Stevens Kangaroo rat recently received exclusive rights to land worth $100 million (and the rats didn't even ask for it!).[5]

5. The regulatory bureaucracy drains $13.5 million from the economy for each premature death averted by a rule governing arsenic emissions from glass plants, or $5.76 trillion per premature death averted by a regulation covering wood-preserving chemicals. Never mind; it's only your money.[6]

6. Dr. J. Laurence Kulp calculates the cost of the acid rain requirements of the 1990 Clean Air Act at $4 billion a year. The benefits come in at just $100 million. This is one of the few regulated areas where a cost-versus-benefit study has been conducted. Most environmentalists maintain that it is unlawful to take possible benefits into account![7]

Enough. Just remember that regulations have required $1.4 trillion to be spent since 1970 on cleaning up roughly 90 percent of industrial air and water pollution; the next 5 percent will cost an additional $1.6 trillion, amounting to another $25,000 per family of four.

In a carefully documented study for the National Chamber Foundation entitled *The Cost of Federal Regulation*, Thomas D. Hopkins, former deputy administrator for the Office of Management and Budget's Office of Information and Regulatory Affairs (now at the Rochester Institute of Technology), wrote:

Regulation is an essential but costly tool of government policy. Complying with federal regulatory requirements, however well-designed they may be, creates costs that mostly do not show up in the federal budget. . . . While it is not possible to provide definitive cost estimates at this point, available evidence exists, however incomplete it may be, to suggest that regulatory costs are substantial and growing. . . . The fastest growing regulatory costs are in the environmental protection area.[8]

The Joint Economic Committee for the U.S. Congress revealed in 1992 that the costs of administering and policing all federal regulations had reached about $500 billion dollars annually. The committee broke it down in the following categories: environmental regulations, $115 billion; safety regulations, $29 billion; economic regulations, $256 billion, and paperwork (reporting) costs, $100 billion. The federal budget for fiscal year 1993 includes $562 billion for implementing federal regulations. That is double the 1992 defense budget! These costs, even without new rules or added laws, are expected to reach an *annual outpouring* of $688 billion by the end of the century.[9]

In the meantime, regulations keep coming. In October 1991, the *Unified Agenda of Federal Regulations* lists 707 pending regulatory actions that could affect state governments, and another 486 that affect local governments.

In an article for the *American Economic Review*, Wayne B. Gray estimated that 30 percent of the American drop in industrial productivity in the 1970s and 1980s could be traced to regulations imposed by the Environmental Protection Agency and the Occupational Safety and Health Administration.[10] Other economists agree.

Overall, it is the "growth of governmental regulation that is responsible for the shrinking of the private economy," says David Littman, senior economist at Manufacturers National Bank of Detroit. He points out that regulation forces private firms to increase staffing, work longer hours, and add to mail, paperwork, travel, and phone expenses. Further, he points out that the regulations force a "misallocation of time from productive work or research to government paperwork that boggles the mind." These are all hidden costs, and unproductive, as well. They also impact jobs.[11]

Since 1991, reports Littman, there have been more than 300 firms sufficiently well known to merit front page coverage in the *Wall Street Journal* that have made layoff announcements.[12] In one year, 1991-1992, private employment decreased by more than 800,000 workers. If we go back to January 1990, the loss is 1.5 million jobs. At the same time, the federal regulatory agencies were hiring; their employment increased by 6.8 percent. The size of the staff at EPA has increased 7.4 percent from 16,999 to 18,262 in just the past two years. Moreover, the total number of federal employees engaged in writing and implementing regulations now exceeds 123,000. The number of bureaucrats involved in the general policing of business alone totals more than 14,000. Somehow, somewhere, greater attention must be given to the burdens that regulations put on private business, the enterprise that generates America's wealth.[13]

Perhaps it would help if more of the lawmakers and regulation writers had experience in trying to make a living in the private economy. Recently, a sadder, wiser Senator George McGovern, after going through bankruptcy, has had to face the true cost of all those federal regulations he helped to pass.

"I wish," he said, "that during the years I was in public office I had had this firsthand experience about the difficulties business people face every day. That knowledge would have made me a better U.S. senator. . . . My business associates and I [have] lived with federal, state, and local rules that we all passed with the objective of helping employees, protecting the environment, raising tax dollars for schools, protecting our customers from fire hazards, etc., etc. While I have never doubted the worthiness of these goals, the concept that most often eludes legislators is: Can we make consumers pay the higher prices for the increased operating costs that accompany public regulation and government reporting requirements with reams of red tape?"[14]

The former senator from South Dakota found that his business, operating an inn in Connecticut, could not survive the regulations. He is not alone.

Some time ago, in 1974, Irving Kristol of New York University predicted, "If the EPA's concept of its mission is permitted to stand, it will be the single most powerful branch of government, having far greater control over our individual lives than Congress, or the Executive, or state, or local government."[15]

And what is the EPA's concept of its mission?

In a mostly overlooked and surprisingly candid article published in the March 1984, issue of *The Washington Monthly* by Jim Sibbison, a former press officer for the EPA, he boasted about how easy it was to use "gullible reporters to spread scare messages." Sibbison joined the EPA in 1970 under Administrator William Ruckelshaus and stayed with the agency through 1981.

"In those days," Sibbison wrote, "the idea was to get the media to help turn the EPA into an enforcer that struck fear into the heart of polluters."

Sibbison went on to say, "We [EPA press agents] routinely wrote scare stories about the hazards of chemicals, employing words like 'cancer' and 'birth defects' to splash a little cold water in reporters' faces. . . . Our press releases were more or less true; the air and water really were dirty and we really were out to make them cleaner. . . . Few handouts, however, can be completely honest, and ours were no exception. The deception lay in what we didn't say. The main thing was that we tended to omit that we weren't able to do as much about the problems we were complaining about as we implied. . . . We were out to whip the public into a frenzy about the environment."[16]

As Administrator Ruckelshaus put it, "We [EPA] couldn't even afford the appearance of being soft."[17]

That attitude about enforcement of environmental regulations still pervades the EPA, as communities all across the country have discovered. One, the city of Columbus, Ohio, decided to figure out just how much this was actually costing the municipal budget. Between 1988 and 1990, new federal and state environmental regulations arrived at Columbus' City Hall at the rate of one every two weeks. They totalled 67 for the period of nearly two years. The laws and the regulations to enforce them covered every imaginable use of land, air, and water; they were mandatory, with no local variances allowed. Of course, neither state nor federal funds were available for implementation. Note that every other U.S. city has been equally affected, but up to now, Columbus is the only municipality to prepare a thorough documentation of the problem.

Columbus' assistant health commissioner, Michael J. Pompili, was appointed to head a city task force to make the study. Both Pompili and the citizens of Columbus were shocked by the findings.

The Pompili task force identified more than one billion dollars (in 1991 dollars) in costs that were required to achieve compliance with the environmental regulations over the next ten years. They also determined that the city budget, which in 1991 was $591 million, would have to be increased by $100 million each year for a decade just to comply with the environmental regulations. As Pompili pointed out, "It will mean that fewer funds will be available to provide other city services, and that city leaders will have fewer choices and less freedom in budgeting." It also means a shift in control from local governments to Washington, D.C.[18]

Now, if all the environmental rules were reasonable and truly made needed improvements in the quality or safety of air, water, and/or land use, there would be little objection. But the evidence suggests that is not the case. According to Pompili, most of the added money will go for water—$770 million for compliance with the Clean Water Act and another $110 million for the Safe Drinking Water Act. The present average water bill in Columbus is $290 per year; this will increase to $550 a year within ten years. Now judge that increase in water bills against one of the rules that drives up the cost: a requirement for Columbus to spend $16 million to build a new treatment plant to use ozone to flush a farm chemical, atrazine, out of the water. The plant will have an annual operating cost of about $2.5 million. Is it really needed? Although atrazine is used in some nearby farms, it does not occur in the city drinking water in amounts exceeding one part per billion. EPA standards permit a level of 3 parts per billion—so the water is well within acceptable limits. Why, then, does the EPA insist upon the expense of a new treatment plant? Yet the EPA insists upon it.

Too often environmental mandates from the EPA are not based either on good, sound scientific data or on knowledge of local conditions. In Anchorage, Alaska, for example, the EPA, following to the letter the 1987 amendments to the Clean Water Act, requires the city sewage treatment plant to remove 30 percent of the organic material. The trouble is, Anchorage's sewage, which is heavily diluted with rain water, contains so little organic material that it is physically impossible to comply. The EPA demands were met by the officials in Anchorage in this manner: They invited three local fish processing plants to discharge 1,500 pounds of fish wastes daily into the municipal sewer. Then 30 percent of it could be removed, thus satisfying the bureaucrats![19]

The EPA also frequently underestimates both the cost and consequences of its rules. The city of Columbus was told that its November 1990 storm-water permit rule would cost the city $76,680. The lowest bid Columbus received from contractors to implement the storm-water permit requirements was $1.779 million! This is a common experience.[20]

These examples are, unfortunately, not unique and they add enormously to the size of municipal utility bills. An accurate estimate of how much the modern mania for ever more regulation really costs is hard to obtain. Says the nationally recognized economist, William J. Laffer, III:

> To be sure, the precise cost of regulation is extremely difficult to determine. Nonetheless, combining the estimates of different scholars suggests that the direct costs of regulation on the economy currently amount to at least some $636 billion to $857 billion per year, or between $6,565 and $8,869 annually per household. Even after subtracting the benefits of regulation, using the most generous estimates available, the net direct cost of regulation is some $364 billion to $538 billion per year, or between $3,762 and $5,561 annually per household.[21]

Then, echoing Hopkins, Gray, and others, Laffer commented:

> These figures include the costs to businesses and consumers of complying with environmental and other social regulations, the total cost to consumers in the form of higher prices and reduced choices due to economic regulations, the costs imposed by government paperwork requirements, administrative costs due to federal regulation of health

care, and the direct costs imposed by state tort law. . . . Most important, the cost estimates do not include any of the indirect, dynamic effects of regulation. In particular, the figures do not include any estimate of the reduction in productivity and output caused by the direct costs, or of the impact of regulation on technological innovation. While the productivity effects are difficult to quantify and the effect on innovation is impossible to quantify, a number of studies suggest that, taken together, the indirect costs due to reduced productivity and innovation probably are greater than the direct costs counted above.

Finally, Laffer concludes:

Assuming instead that the indirect costs only amount to somewhere between 50 percent and 100 percent of the direct costs, it appears that the total cost of regulation . . . could be anywhere between $811 billion and $1.656 trillion per year, or between $8,388 and $17,134 annually per household. . . . If transfers (of costs from one regulatory group to another) are not subtracted as benefits, then the total cost of regulation works out to somewhere between $1.056 trillion and $1.969 trillion per year, or between $10,922 and $20,376 per household. By way of comparison, Americans will pay an estimated $1.053 trillion in federal taxes in 1992, or about $10,897 per household. Although these estimates are subject to considerable uncertainty, it is quite possible that the total cost of regulation now exceeds the total cost of taxation.[22]

This is a trend that shows no sign of abating. When does environmental regulation become too expensive? And even too frivolous? Where does common sense come in? Of course, everyone wants to avoid pollution and to improve on what has occurred in the past. But standards must be set that are reasonable and achievable. The policies and procedures must be practical without consuming so high a portion of disposable income. Any other path leads to poverty—and poverty is truly the ultimate pollution. Wealthier is healthier, and excessive regulations can compromise the public health and safety that they are often designed to protect.

PART FIVE

Communications, Education, and Politics

CHAPTER 14

Who's Responsible for Overkill?

Why Do People Always Tend to Believe the Worst?

As the science editor at Time, *I would freely admit that on this issue (the environment) we have crossed the boundary from news reporting to advocacy.*

  —CHARLES ALEXANDER, *Time*[1]

I do have an axe to grind. . . . I want to be the little subversive person in television.

  —BARBARA PYLE, CNN environmental director[2]

There is no such thing as objective reporting. . . . I've become even more crafty about finding the voices to say the things I think are true. That's my subversive mission.

  —DIANNE DUMANOSKI, *Boston Globe* environmental
    reporter[3]

We in the press like to say we're honest brokers of information, and it's just not true. The press does have an agenda.

  —BERNARD GOLDBERG, CBS, "48 Hours"[4]

I'm not sure it is useful to include every single point of view.

—LINDA HARRAR, PBS producer[5]

It doesn't matter what is true; it only matters what people believe is true. . . . You are what the media define you to be. [Greenpeace] became a myth and a myth-generating machine.

—PAUL WATSON, co-founder of Greenpeace[6]

It is journalistically irresponsible to present both sides [of the greenhouse, global warming theory] as though it were a question of balance. Given the distribution of views . . . it is irresponsible to give equal time to a few people standing out in left field.

—STEPHEN SCHNEIDER, National Center for
Atmospheric Research (in *Boston Globe*, May 31,
1992)[7]

WITH attitudes like these shaping the news, is it any wonder that the public gets only the side that the media elite approve? It begs another crucial question: Having stated our case against "environmental overkill," we are obliged to ask ourselves, "Who is responsible for it?"

Is it the educational process? At least a measure of the responsibility belongs to the schools, mainly because they have been targeted by a barrage of "learning materials" from the extreme environmental organizations and because they have been influenced by media reports. For the most part, teachers and reporters and editors have neither the time nor the patience to challenge the assertions put forth by those who *appear* to have credentials or have been presented as "experts." The truth about the environment belongs in the classroom, of course. But *the whole truth* is not always what students get.

Jonathan H. Adler, environmental policy analyst at the Competitive Enterprise Institute, put it this way:

Most classroom environmental information, including most that is listed at the Environmental Protection Agency clearinghouse, comes from literature and teaching guides drafted and distributed by the major environmental groups. These materials include everything from the World Wildlife Fund's "Vanishing Rain Forests Education Kit" and the Chesapeake Bay Foundation's "What I Can Do to Save the Bay" to the Acid Rain Foundation's curriculum, "Air Pollutants and Trees," and the Sierra Club educational newsletter, "Sierraecology."[8]

We believe education's role in spreading the propaganda of the environmental extremists to the young and impressionable has been a large one. But we also believe that, without question, the primary culprits in misleading the public on environmental issues and producing the overkill—next to the environmental extremists, that is—are the electronic and print news media. Leading the way are the national television anchors and reporters and their local counterparts. They are the primary culprits because they have the largest audiences, by far, and thus the greatest influence.

Some examples:

1. From the beginning, the TV anchors and reporters adopted the line in news reports that the "Earth Summit" scheduled for Rio de Janeiro in June 1992, was a worldwide conference designed to "save the planet." Rarely, if ever, did a TV anchor or reporter question the nature of the United Nations Conference on the Environment and Development ("Earth Summit"), what the motives were behind it, who the planners were, and, most important of all, what the impact of the proposed treaties would be on the U.S. and other industrialized nations. Seldom has reportage on a single event been so one-sided.

As *Media Watch*, constant watchdog of all the American media, reported: "To reporters, the Earth Summit wasn't a forum for detailed reporting on the complexities of political and scientific debate on the environment. Instead, it was a laudable and idealistic gathering ruined by President Bush. The substance of the summit, the text of the treaties to be signed or rejected, took a back seat to style. Who was in favor of 'saving the planet'? And who was not?" Among the highlights of Rio bias:

Taking the position that the planet was in danger landed the media squarely in the liberal camp. In the days before the summit, anchors wallowed in the simplistic. On ABC's "World News Sunday" May 31 (1992), Forrest Sawyer stated: "The U.S. is under fire for standing in the way of efforts to protect the planet." CNN anchor Christiane Amanpour oozed like a U.N. press packet on June 3: "The Summit, with perhaps the loftiest goal ever, [seeks] to stop us from pushing our own planet toward environmental collapse."

The U.S. delegation was regularly described as "isolated" after it "watered down" a "global warming" treaty and refused to sign the biodiversity treaty, which was "designed to protect plants and animals." Almost every reporter, in print and broadcast, used this inaccurate shorthand. Few mentioned the actual text of the treaty, which demanded that the U.S. hand foreign aid to Third World countries *with no conditions*, meaning they could not designate the money to protect plants and animals.[9]

In another vein, the Alar episode referred to in an earlier chapter is a textbook example of how a major TV network, CBS, and its progeny, "60 Minutes," can be manipulated to serve the selfish interests of a large and unscrupulous environmental organization, in this case the Natural Resources Defense Council. In an astounding story of press agentry and propaganda, the NRDC managed to talk "60 Minutes" into airing its outlandish and unsubstantiated charges against Alar, claiming that the growth-regulating compound used to prevent premature falling of apples was a serious cancer risk to children. All the media played the charges prominently in newscasts or in newspaper columns. Horrified parents across the country quit buying apples. And scores of apple growers were launched on the road to bankruptcy.[10]

In time it was discovered that the NRDC had based its Alar warning on a totally discredited animal test back in 1977 by a researcher named Bela Toth, who found that feeding extraordinary amounts of daminozide (Alar) and its derivative to mice produced tumors. A similar study 11 years earlier had revealed *no* cancers in other laboratory animals, even in rats! Other subsequent studies by reliable scientists brought similar "no cancer" results. But the militant fringe in the EPA refused to accept the legitimate studies, demanding that dosages of Alar be stepped up until researchers finally produced "one lonely mouse tumor at 22,000 times the maximum exposure that children would receive." In other words, it was physically impossible for any child to eat enough Alar-treated apples at one time even (for 22,000 times the exposure?) to incur the risk of growing a tumor.[11]

If the media had cared or had given truth and the other side a chance to be heard, TV, newspapers, and news magazines should have been demanding a thorough investigation of the NRDC and its influence on EPA practices. And, for that matter, on the national media.

2. When the issue of censorship arises, all facets of the news media explode in defensive anger. And rightly so. Where, then, were the "indignation" and the investigative arms of the national TV networks in particular and the American news media in general when the Public Broadcasting Service refused to run a highly praised British TV documentary, "The Greenhouse Conspiracy"? The 55-minute production, which the *London Financial Times* called one of the best science documentaries made, was turned down because the educational network supported by U.S. tax dollars insisted it was "too one-sided."[12]

Utilizing the expertise of a large number of highly reputable scientists in the U.S. and Britain, "The Greenhouse Conspiracy" questions all the arguments for global warming and concludes that they are faulty and unsupported by reliable evidence.

While PBS was quick to reject "The Greenhouse Conspiracy," the broadcast network and its affiliated local stations had shown no qualms about running a large number of documentaries on the doom-and-gloom side of the environmental argument—among them a ten-part series, "The Race to Save the Planet"; "Crisis in the Atmosphere," and "After the Warming." All of them include many highly questionable conclusions that are fueled more by emotion and hysteria than scientific truth. One-sided?!

3. The Cable News Network matched the major TV networks' prejudice in favor of militant environmental action and frequently went them one better, probably because it hired an environmental director, Barbara Pyle, to manage its slanted, pro-environmental

broadcasts and documentaries. As CNN's vice president for environmental policy, she encouraged not only one-sided presentations on global warming, ozone "holes," and all the other scare stories in the environmental stable; she also targeted children through a special series of "eco-cartoon" programs under the label of "Captain Planet" and promoted "kiddie mail" to further CNN's doom-and-gloom agenda.

Here are a few among the many CNN pearls of "wisdom":

CNN anchor Bernard Shaw on global warming: "This is a story about human folly—mankind's attempt to engineer a better place to live, to improve upon nature with inventions such as refrigeration, foam packing, and electronics. But the man-made chemicals used in pursuit of the good life have all put life on earth in jeopardy. The chemicals have punched a hole in the sky. . . . Already there's a moral to the story, and that is: Nature may not always be able to recover from the abuses of modern civilization."[13]

Every one of these statements is wrong. And we were all under the impression that anchors, like other "news" reporters, were supposed to give us the news without opinion or prejudice!

CNN reporter Lucia Newman: "The problems are enormous and none of the solutions simple. But most are conscious that unless there's action, the planet may solve the problem—by simply making it impossible for people to live on it."[14]

CNN reporter Jill Dougherty: "Some environmentalists say that George Bush, the self-proclaimed 'environmental President,' should be called the extinction President."[15]

How else might one expect CNN newshands to behave with the likes of two militant Greens, Ted Turner and Jane Fonda, guiding the network's destiny?

4. But if you thought the TV reporters and anchors were alone in spooning out the one-sided opinions on environmental issues, try these from the news magazines:

Time, in its usual fashion of mixing news and opinion in giving advice on the Rio conference, suggested: "Put an international tax on emissions of carbon dioxide and other greenhouse gases. . . . Find a way to put the brakes on the world's spiraling population, which will otherwise double by the year 2050. . . . Give the U.N.

broad powers to create an environmental police force for the planet."[16]

Newsweek's Jerry Adler: "Almost alone among major nations, the United States retains a substantial constituency that is indifferent if not hostile toward environmental regulation—an attitude oddly shared by the GOP right wing and the leaders of the former Communist bloc. But this is increasingly a fringe position even among many of the business executives it is supposed to benefit."[17]

Newsweek reporter Sharon Begley: "When Bush shows up this week for a 40-hour appearance, even many of America's allies are going to greet him as the Grinch who stole the eco-summit. . . . America, in contrast, found itself in the role of cranky Uncle Scrooge."[18]

5. Another severe blot on the performance of America's news media came with the National Aeronautics and Space Administration's "ozone hole" reports late in 1991 and early in 1992. The first report—a press release proclaiming that the ozone "hole" had increased in size and would soon threaten the Northern Hemisphere in general and the U.S. in particular—became the No. 1 or No. 2 news item on TV news broadcasts across the U.S., from the networks to the local affiliates. It was front page news in virtually every newspaper in America and the main feature in the news magazines, as well. To say that Americans were frightened by the news-generated hysteria would be putting it mildly.

Then, a few weeks later, when a probing missile was sent up into the stratosphere to report back on what was really happening to the ozone layer, the next press release was issued quietly—and all but ignored by most of the media, except for *The Wall Street Journal* and a few columnists and commentators on the conservative side of things. Why? Because the new report was that the terrible "hole" hadn't materialized and the "danger" had passed! But the American public wasn't aware of NASA's duplicity, because it doesn't realize to this day that the news media had once again failed to do their job.[19]

6. The late Warren T. Brookes, courageous *Detroit News* columnist, whose investigations embarrassed many of the doomsaying environmentalists, pointed out several instances in which the

bulk of the news media, electronic and print, failed to report the misdeeds or outlandish claims of the radical fringe.

He was one of those who chronicled the serious misjudgment by the federal Centers for Disease Control when it finally "admitted it had made a mistake when it shut down Times Beach, Missouri, in 1982 because of the dangers of dioxin." The CDC and the EPA both acknowledged after the damage was done that the danger was overstated and that "tens of billions of dollars in cleanup costs" were wasted across the nation on other projects whose cleanup actions were instigated by the example of Times Beach. The confession by the two agencies was reported almost casually by a few newspapers and TV stations—but it certainly didn't get the same play on news broadcasts and TV reports that the first scary Times Beach report had been given.[20]

Brookes also called attention to the fact that the news media all but ignored "the fraud of asbestos hysteria" that had been uncovered by another *Detroit News* reporter, Michael J. Bennett, and detailed both in the newspaper and later in a hard-hitting book everyone should read, *The Asbestos Racket*. This is a case of still another dereliction of duty by the media in turning their gaze from a situation that has cost American taxpayers billions already and will cost them billions more as more lawsuits are filed.

The element in Bennett's work that should have caught the attention of every American but didn't because the media ignored the investigation was this report: Through painstaking research, Bennett discovered that the over-reaction of the EPA to the over-blown "danger" of asbestos may have been the cause of the Challenger Space Shuttle disaster that brought death to seven American astronauts.

Because of an EPA ban on the use of asbestos, a non-asbestos-containing putty was substituted which didn't have the insulating fire-retardant powers of asbestos. Bennett reported that the substitute putty used to seal the O-Rings was vulnerable to cracking in the extremely cold weather and led to the shuttle's crash on January 28, 1986.[21]

Why didn't the media follow up Bennett's investigation and question the EPA's panicky policy on asbestos? As Brookes pointed out, the finger should point to EPA Administrator William

Reilly and his flip-flops on the asbestos issue. Although he re-affirmed the EPA's asbestos-ban policy in 1989, he acknowledged a year later that "the mere presence of asbestos poses no risks of harm to human health" and that removing it "may actually pose a greater health risk than simply leaving (it) alone."

Even more extraordinary was Reilly's admission that solid scientific documentation of the relative lack of risk in white chrysotile asbestos (95 percent of all that is in use) was available since the 1970s but was relentlessly dismissed by the EPA. Which William Reilly can you believe?[22]

How much more evidence do all the media need to convey the truth to viewers and readers?

Remember, this is the same Reilly who tried to talk his "boss," President Bush, into agreeing to become the banker to all the imagined environmental ills of the Third World—and much of the Second World, as well. Why the President didn't ask for Reilly's resignation remains one of the unanswered political questions of 1992.

7. One more sobering example should be offered to indicate how complacent the news media have become when it comes to covering "the other side" of environmental issues. Because it wanted the facts on acid rain and on the environmentalist charges that acid rain was having a calamitous effect on lakes, rivers, forests, and even buildings and statues, Congress authorized a ten-year study, the National Acid Precipitation Assessment Program (NAPAP), by the most reputable scientists in America. More than half a billion dollars were spent on the massive scientific project.

The diligent NAPAP reported to Congress that it had found some acid-rain damage to some forests, lakes, and rivers—but that there was absolutely no "impending environmental disaster," as environmental groups had charged, and that "an expensive crash program to further accelerate the current rate of reduction of acid rain is not justified."[23]

Despite the well-researched report, Congress ignored it and passed the Clean Air Act of 1990, which will require the expenditure of $40 billion *needlessly* on projects designed to repair a crisis that doesn't exist! And yet the news media have chosen to ignore the effect of Congress' action, preferring instead to listen to the same political activists to whom the EPA listens.

Among the many reputable scientists who have tried in vain to break through the media's curtain of bias is Dr. Julian L. Simon, professor of business administration at the University of Maryland and the author of many books on demography and economics. Through years of painstaking research, he has provided convincing proof that the doomsday scenarios offered by government and the militant environmental groups—and dutifully reported by an obedient press—are without foundation.

Simon has methodically destroyed wild claims about disappearing agricultural land, soil erosion, diminishing natural resources, and the population "explosion." But, despite the compelling nature of his arguments, the news media have turned a deaf ear to his sound research.

"I come not in anger but in pain," Simon wrote. "Journalists take pride in their objectivity. But in reporting on population growth, natural resources, and the environment, objectivity goes out the window. The price in economic loss, misguided policies, and damage to national morale has yet to be calculated. But the costs may be fearfully high."[24]

Simon's compelling book dispelling environmental myths, *Population Matters*, should be required reading by all members of the media and, in fact, by every American who is sincerely interested in the environment and the nation's future.

Perhaps the most significant analysis of the media's love affair with the environmental extremists has been done by a doctoral threesome, S. Robert Lichter, Linda S. Lichter, and Stanley Rothman, in another book that should be on every media person's coffee table, *Watching America*.

Their profound, well-researched scientific study of the manner in which television has manipulated programs to suit the political and social beliefs of producers, editors, writers, and staff is an alarming revelation. The authors found, for example, that at least three-fourths of the creative leaders in TV acknowledge they are liberals and vote Democratic. Two-thirds of them believe the structure of American society is faulty and must be changed. Ninety-seven percent say women should have the right to decide whether they want to have an abortion, 80 percent believe there's nothing wrong with homosexual relations, and 51 percent see nothing wrong with adultery.[25]

Most significant, the TV people surveyed admit they work their ideas on social reform, mores, the environment, and other issues into the programs they create for their audiences. With that ultra-liberal background propelling TV programs, it's no surprise that so many television luminaries and staff people actively support the cause of the environmental extreme. Nor is it a surprise that Dr. Simon and all the other dedicated scientists who want to balance the environmental scales toward good science and logic are left out in the cold.

With the news media stacking the deck against common sense and scientific honesty in environmental affairs, it's little wonder, then, that polls indicate so many Americans believe "something must be done to protect the environment, no matter what the cost."

An August 1992 nationwide poll by the Wirthlin Group of McLean, Virginia, found that more Americans were "growing concerned about the environment and feel President Bush was not doing enough to protect it." Eighty percent said environmental improvements must be made regardless of the cost and that environmental standards cannot be too high. Sixty-seven percent said Bush was doing less than his share to reduce environmental problems. And 57 percent said environmental issues will be a "very important" factor in how they would vote in the 1992 presidential election.[26]

How can the electorate be expected to make truly intelligent decisions if the news media do not provide them with all the information on the environment, except what supports the most radical and outlandish environmentalist positions?

All of which brings us to some tips on what American TV watchers and newspaper and news-magazine readers should be alert to when they peruse the "news." To wit:

"Environmentalists say. . . ." Are the quoted "environmentalists" identified? If not, the article loses its validity and should not be taken seriously. If the environmentalists are identified, are they members of one of the militant environmental groups with a

political agenda and a treasury that needs a continuing infusion of members and donations? Or are they independent scientists with no axe to grind and a reputation for being dedicated scientists, not mouthpieces for some political cause? Remember, each of us is an environmentalist at heart because we care about the planet to one degree or another. John Doe may be an "environmentalist" to Reporter Smith, but he doesn't necessarily speak for us. Reporters should be more careful and define the expertise of every person they have been accustomed to identifying as "an environmentalist" and letting it go at that. Even "scientist" is too broad a term in many cases. A laboratory technician, for example, can be called a scientist in, say, the field of pharmaceuticals, but may know comparatively little about another science, say, atmospherics.

"*Critics say. . . .*" Ditto above. When a lazy reporter needs a hook for an opinion, he often borrows this time-worn and totally unreliable ploy—without identifying the "critics" or indicating the nature of their expertise.

"*Cancer-causing. . . .*" Beware of this hyphenated tiger, which is the irresponsible reporter's (and radical environmentalist's) favorite scare phrase in his attempt to grab attention. This overused and usually false description precedes what the activist—or the reporter—is trying to depict as dangerous, poisonous, deadly, or whatever, even if it isn't, which is most often the case. In the lexicon of the reporter/activist, "cancer-causing" precedes such items as PCBs, pesticides, insecticides, herbicides, chemicals, gases, anything he chooses to infect with terror or apprehension.

"*A commission or committee or group said. . . .*" Many reporters have a habit of failing or refusing to identify the source of an important decision or study or research. Or, worse yet, having identified the commission, or committee, or group, fail to list its members so the viewer, listener, or reader can gauge for himself the validity of the report. "The Committee to Redress Grievances," the reporter will say or write, "declared today that it is dangerous and could possibly be fatal to eat oysters after 8 o'clock in the evening on a cold day." Really? Just who sit on the Committee to Redress Grievances? Are they marine scientists? Or three garage mechanics who go fishing every Saturday?

"Analysis. . . ." This catchall word has become very popular, particularly in the print media, as a device to inject a highly opinionated piece into the news columns—a piece that belongs on the editorial or op-ed page of a newspaper, not on page 1, 2, or 3. But in recent years, reporters have more and more laced their "straight news" reports with hidden or obvious expressions of opinion. That is especially true in TV reporting today. Communications schools at colleges and universities are primarily responsible, because many of them tell and teach students that activist or participatory journalism is the order of the day. In "activist" or "participatory" journalism, the reporter becomes an adjunct of the news itself and includes his opinions—read that "prejudices"—into the event he's reporting. The line between fact and opinion in news reporting has, as a consequence, become blurred and confusing to the viewer/listener/reader who wants information, not a sermon.

"May. . . ." It's a simple word, but a lazy or incompetent reporter will use it often to mask a lack of definitive information or his or her own inability or unwillingness to get more information or be more specific. "Magnets in the brain may link cancer and electricity," writes the hedging reporter. If he had done his interviewing and research properly, he would have been able to say or write it in this fashion: "Researchers conducting experiments with electricity and its effects on the human body are tracking down the possibility that excessive amounts of electrical waves could affect a person's health. Some scientists in the study are suggesting the possibility that tumors might result, but no proof of it has been found. The research might, in fact, determine that electricity has no effect at all on the human body, several scientists have indicated." Just tell it like it is, as the saying goes; don't manufacture scare words for the sake of jarring the viewer or reader.

"Conventional wisdom. . . ." This phrase, rapidly growing in popularity with reporters, anchors, and editors, is acceptable—until it is used as an excuse for the reporter's not having done his homework. If his dispatch is based on official, statistical, or legal information, he should spell it out for the viewer or reader, not cover his faulty workmanship with such a generalized reference as "conventional wisdom says this or that is so."

All these—and many, many more not listed here—are common

devices that contribute heavily to environmental overkill in the news. Good reporters will avoid them. In fact, good reporters will refuse to be manipulated by anyone, let alone militant environmentalists.

In addition to such telltale words that should warn us of danger ahead in news reports, there are certain subtle techniques reporters use that are tipoffs to trouble ahead in their reports. For example:

The Second-Day Lead: In broadcast and print media, a "first-day lead" is a straightforward report of an event that has just happened. No frills. No extras. No interpretations. It might read: "Senator James Smith today said he would mount a campaign in the Senate to overturn the acid-rain provisions of the Clean Air Act because they will result in billions of dollars in unnecessary expense to taxpayers."

In the past, that report would ride out the day in the news just as is. The next day a lead devoted to reaction or rebuttal would be customary and proper. That is what's known in media as the second-day lead.

What some reporters frequently do—unintentionally or with subtle prejudice at work—is water down the impact of the first-day lead by introducing a counter or rebuttal immediately. For example: "Senator James Smith said today he intends to knock the acid-rain provisions out of the Clean Air Act, but environmentalists declared he's just grandstanding because he's thinking of entering the race for Governor and needs the publicity."

What has happened is that the reporter has punctured Senator Smith's balloon before it gets off the ground by twinning it immediately with a reaction that should have gone farther down in the story or used as a new lead the next day. In theater, it would be called upstaging. In journalism, it's sneaky and unfair. Watch for it; you'll hear and read the mechanism used frequently.

The Planted Paragraph: It's one of the most common devices in communications. An Associated Press reporter entered the following information after the first few paragraphs of a Washington report on a dispute between the Agriculture Department and the General Accounting Office on testing pesticides in fruits and vegetables:

"There are more than 60 pesticides that are known or suspected carcinogens used in foods," said Lawrie Mott, a senior scientist at the Natural Resources Defense Council specializing in pesticides and children's health. Ms. Mott said there is a special danger to children because they eat or drink some pesticide-laden foods—such as apple juice—in disproportionate amounts compared with adults.[27]

The unsubstantiated Mott statement was not only out of place in the report. It demonstrated the reporter's prejudice in favor of the NRDC position and his penchant for quoting a "scientist." He failed to mention her relevance to the report or to explain that the NRDC is a highly politicized environmental group with its own bias on pesticides, Alar, and similar subjects. Worst of all, Ms. Mott's statement stands alone, without presentation of the other side of the argument. Typical bad reporting.

The News that Isn't: Obviously, a great deal of news is not reported, which is a problem in itself. But what of the news that is unnecessary and "over-covered"—a report that suits a reporter's or editor's formula or prejudice about "what the public oughta know"? Here's a good example, known not only to many reporters and editors but to political environmentalists who include nuclear power on their hit lists, despite the fact that nuclear power is the friendliest energy to the environment:

PORTSMOUTH, N.H., Reuters—A fire broke out on the grounds of the Seabrook nuclear power plant Friday, officials said. The small blaze occurred about 50 feet from the plant's cooling tower and less than 500 feet from the core reactor building, said Rob Williams, spokesman for the plant's manager, North Atlantic Energy Service Core.

No radiation was released and the plant's operation was unaffected, Williams said. . . . The fire broke out in a portable diesel-driven air compressor being used for exterior sandblasting of the cooling tower building. Williams said the fire was a minor incident, which caused no injuries. The blaze was extinguished within 11 minutes by an on-site emergency team.[28]

The Reuter report was distributed nationwide. Why? Because anything that happens at a nuclear plant, no matter how minor or uninteresting, is reported, thanks to the media's "overkill" attitude about things nuclear. Let another fire happen in a coal mine and kill a dozen people and it won't get the national distribution of an insignificant incident at a nuclear plant.

The point here is that too many persons in the media treat anything nuclear with the same disdain and suspicion as they do other targets of the environmental lobby. Their personal prejudices dictate their reaction to the news.

Will the biased news coverage never end? Certainly no time soon. We can be sure the growing ranks of political environmentalists and pressure groups will think up new horror stories to replace those now in vogue. What can we expect in the future in the realm of environmental overkill? Here are a few issues that have begun to capture the fancy of the doom-and-gloom organizations:

Electromagnetic Fields (EMFs): We have detailed this issue in an earlier chapter, but it's important to stress the point that news media reports have frequently not told the whole story. The best science acknowledges that further research is needed but cautions that no serious danger is evident at this time. Still, the media can't resist sending out alarms and frightening people unnecessarily.[29]

The Chlorine "Peril": Despite the fact that chlorine in America's drinking water has undoubtedly saved millions of lives in the 20th century from a variety of once-waterborne diseases—like typhoid, cholera, gastroenteritis, and dysentery—we're now told that people who drink chlorinated water *may* be facing a 21 percent greater risk of developing bladder cancer and a 38 percent higher risk of rectal cancer. There's that word, "may," again, this time applied by a Dr. Robert Morris of the Medical College of Wisconsin to findings he and a research team came up with. Water officials everywhere remain skeptical and want to see more evidence before they propose any action on chlorine, which has been credited with saving more lives than perhaps any other single chemical. At least one water-quality manager has said that even if the risk of cancer should be supported by more research, that risk is far outweighed by the benefits provided by chlorine.[30] Is there a strong hint of environmental overkill here? Time will tell.

Lead Poisoning: One of the EPA's newest bogeymen is lead poisoning, which is reputed to be—by those who are ringing the alarm over it, that is—a growing danger to children particularly. Several scientists were at each other's legal throats in a developing donnybrook over research on lead poisoning. One faction says it's terribly dangerous if not controlled, while the other insists the problem has been seriously overblown and should be put back into proper perspective. At last reports, the EPA apparently wasn't waiting to find out who would win the lead poisoning battle. It was already using the work of the "terribly dangerous" advocates in writing regulations on the use of lead.[31] What could one expect, given the shoot-from-the-hip, environmental-overkill nature of the EPA?

In the meantime, it's appropriate to end this discussion of the role of education and media in overkill with this warning from Dr. Bernard Cohen, University of Pittsburgh physicist and one of America's most distinguished nuclear scientists:

> Our government's science and technology policy is now guided by uninformed and emotion-driven public opinion, rather than by sound scientific advice. Unless solutions can be found to this problem, the U.S. will enter the 21st century declining in wealth, power, and influence. . . . The coming debacle is not due to the problems the environmentalists describe, but to the policies they advocate.[32]

That should spell out the peril inherent in continued "environmental overkill."

CHAPTER 15

The Gospel According to Gore

Environmentalism Out of Control

Now that President Bill Clinton and Vice President Al Gore are running the nation, what can we expect from them as a national environmental policy? What measures will they espouse and recommend to Congress?

Because the new vice president, who was a key environmental policymaker in the Senate, chose to detail his philosophy in a recent book, *Earth in the Balance*, we do not need to guess. And since President Clinton indicated while campaigning that his environmental opinions coincided with those of his running mate, it should be quite clear what the nation can expect. And what we believe the nation will get can be characterized by the title of this book, a severe case of very expensive environmental overkill.

It's quite clear throughout Gore's book that despite his protestations to the contrary, he is an extremist on environmental issues. It is clear, too, that Al Gore came to his positions through narrow prejudice and partisan enthusiasm and has completely ignored scientific impartiality. Perhaps the clue to his one-sided view is his high regard for Rachel Carson's *Silent Spring*—an emotional, lyrical, and grossly unscientific and inaccurate book that became the

Bible of the militant environmental movement. Gore explains his devotion to Carson thus:

> I particularly remember my mother's troubled response to Rachel Carson's classic book about DDT and pesticide abuse, *Silent Spring*. ... My mother was one of many who read Carson's warnings and shared them with others. She emphasized to my sister and me that this book was different—and important. Those conversations made an impression, in part because they made me think about threats to the environment that are much more serious than washed-out gullies—but much harder to see.[1]

Gore apparently never went beyond Rachel Carson's hysterics to the scientific literature that would have told him that Carson had exaggerated the danger of pesticides. It was the abuse, not the use, of pesticides that was the problem. DDT, the most effective insecticide ever produced, could have saved millions of lives from malaria and other insect-borne diseases had not political pressure brought by environmentalists like Rachel Carson banned its use in the U.S. and reduced its use worldwide.

At least Gore is forthright about his environmentalist credentials: "I organized the first congressional hearings on toxic waste and focused on two sites, the small rural community of Toone, Tennessee, and one other recently discovered waste dump at a little place in upstate New York, Love Canal. Subsequently, of course, Love Canal became synonymous with the problem of hazardous chemical waste."[2]

It would be fair to state that a greater danger to the American people is a key senator and now a vice president who not only predicates his policies and actions on rumor, unsupported charges, and unscientific reports, but ignores the truth because it could counter his political aspirations. Love Canal was a "disaster" that never happened, but, because of its symbolic importance to the environmental extremism Gore and others practiced, its label as a "disaster" has been protected and extended.

Gore also acknowledged his leadership in the Senate on the issue of ozone depletion: "The day the scientific community confirmed that the dangerous hole in the sky above Antarctica was caused by

CFCs, I canceled my campaign schedule and gave a major speech outlining a comprehensive proposal to ban CFCs and take a number of other steps that would address the crisis of the global atmosphere. The entire campaign went into high gear, alerting the press, staging the speech, distributing advance copies of the text, and generally promoting the event."[3]

Gore's reference to the "scientific community" is typical of his pronouncements throughout the book. He cites the opinions of "many scientists" when pleading his case without identifying them or even providing some proof that they are scientists with expertise in the relevant branch of science. We suspect his "scientists" could be representatives from extreme environmental groups or whose disciplines don't qualify them as "experts." For example, a dental-lab technician might properly be called a "scientist," but his knowledge of atmospheric science or pesticides could be no greater than any layman's.

As columnist George Will indicated in a review of *Earth in the Balance*, "When Gore asserts . . . that 'the world scientific community' is in 'consensus' about global warming, he is being as cavalier about the truth as the Bush campaign has been about Clinton's tax increases. Gore knows that his former mentor at Harvard, Roger Revelle, who died last year, concluded: 'The scientific base for greenhouse warming is too uncertain to justify drastic action at this time. There is little risk in delaying policy responses.' "[4]

To this day, Gore has refused to acknowledge the wisdom of Revelle's words. It's another case of choosing to abide by only those beliefs that coincide with his own personal and political prejudices.

Columnist Will concluded that "Gore knows, or should know before pontificating, that a recent Gallup Poll of scientists concerned with global climate research shows that 53 percent do not believe warming has occurred, and another 30 percent are uncertain."

The Gallup Poll also makes ludicrous this statement by Gore: "When 98 percent of the scientists in a given field share one view and 2 percent disagree, both viewpoints are sometimes presented in a format in which each appears equally credible. . . . But the theory of global warming will not be disproved, and the skeptics are vastly outnumbered by former skeptics who now accept the overwhelming weight of the accumulated evidence."[5]

In a probing review of Gore's book, the eminent American atmospheric scientist, Dr. Hugh W. Ellsaesser, concluded that *Earth in the Balance* "proved the old adage: a little knowledge is a dangerous thing."

After examining Gore's plan to transfer money and technology from Western nations to the Third World, Dr. Ellsaesser made this astute observation: "Just how does he [Gore] hope to bring this detailed and integrated plan into existence, especially since he insists that he supports democracy and 'free market capitalist economics?' He sees the solution in successively more detailed and strengthened international agreements—treaties, patterned after the Montreal Protocol, under which we are now in the process of banning CFCs (freons, halons, etc.) because of their presumed threat to the ozone layer. Treaties take precedence over our Constitution and they require the support of only a few individuals in the executive branch and a majority of the Senate. While he does not spell this out, he apparently has recognized that treaties provide a mechanism for avoiding or circumventing a popular veto."[6]

In several instances, Gore the author sounds more like a woolly-minded dreamer who wants to use government power for un-proven and even fanatical ends than a dedicated public servant: "The more deeply I search for the roots of the global environmen-tal crisis, the more I am convinced that it is an outer manifestation of an inner crisis that is, for lack of a better word, spiritual."[7]

And, in a later chapter, this: "The cumulative impact of the changes brought by the scientific and technological revolution are potentially devastating to our sense of who are and what our purpose in life might be. Indeed, it may now be necessary to foster a new 'environmentalism of the spirit.'. . ."[8]

Gore's "environmentalism of the spirit" sounds in practice a good deal like an argument for, in his eyes, a benevolent dictator-ship:

This life change [he had just turned 40] has caused me to be increas-ingly impatient with the status quo, with conventional wisdom, with the lazy assumption that we can always muddle through. Such complacency has allowed many kinds of difficult problems to breed and grow, but now, facing a rapidly deteriorating global environment, it threatens absolute disaster. Now no one can afford to assume that the world will somehow solve its problems. We must all become partners in a bold effort to *change the very foundation of our civilization.**9

Do we want civilization reorganized by environmental evangelists like Gore, who approach vital issues from gross prejudice rather than real science? The prospect is frightening.

Gore repeats the unfounded contention that global warming will cause the seas to rise and drown millions: "The net effect of all the warming and melting is a steadily rising sea level, almost one inch per decade now, with collateral effects such as the invasion by salt water of freshwater aquifers in coastal areas and the loss of coastal wetland areas. . . ."

Then, borrowing from the Worldwatch Institute, another of the groups given to extremism, Gore adds: "In some coastal cities like Miami, the freshwater aquifer on which it relies for its drinking water actually floats on salt water, so that rising seas would push the water table up—in some cases, to the surface. . . . Bangkok, New Orleans, Taipei, and Venice are among the other major cities facing similar problems. Other large cities like Shanghai, Calcutta, Dacca, Hanoi, and Karachi, which are located on low-lying riverbanks, will be among the first heavily populated areas to be flooded out. . . ."10

Gore criticizes Earth First! and its "Deep Ecologists," who unabashedly state their preference for protecting animals, birds, and trees, even if it means sacrificing humans. But he gives his real feelings away with this comment on the Pacific Northwest's yew trees, which yield taxol, found to be helpful in combatting certain forms of cancer:

Most of the species unique to the rain forests are in imminent danger, partly because there is no one to speak up for them. . . . The

* Emphasis added.

Pacific yew can be cut down and processed to produce . . . taxol. . . .
It seems an easy choice—sacrifice the tree for a human life—until
one learns that three trees must be destroyed for each patient
treated. . . . Suddenly we must confront some tough questions. How
important are the medical needs of future generations? Are those of
us alive today entitled to cut down all of these trees to extend the
lives of a few of us, even if it means that this unique form of life will
disappear forever, thus making it impossible to save human lives in
the future?[11]

If he had tried, Gore would have discovered that other sources of
taxol are already being developed in the laboratory and in other
tree-growing areas. But, then, that would have squelched another
scary environmental scenario, wouldn't it?

Just as unhelpful is Gore's promise that he will work for more
federal legislation to force total recycling to get rid of solid wastes
and prohibit the sale of nonrecyclable products. Still more regulation for industry and a nation already groaning under tons of
restrictive laws and the regulations they spawn.

Recycling has already ballooned the cost of managing wastes to
taxpayers, and that cost continues to climb. Total recycling is not
only impossible but undesirable. Incineration and composting
were once accepted by cities and counties as companions to
recycling—until pressure from militant environmentalists caused
politicians to abandon them almost completely in favor of total
recycling programs. It has happened despite the fact that new
incineration techniques have virtually eliminated the problem of
controlling emissions and disposing of the resultant ash.

If people are alarmed by the actions Gore states without embar-
rassment, then they will certainly be doubly alarmed by those
chilling paragraphs that leave his intentions to the reader's imagination. As in this disturbing statement, for example:

The loss of one and a half acres of rain forest every second, the
sudden, thousandfold acceleration of the natural extinction rate for
living species, the ozone hole above Antarctica and the thinning of
the ozone layer at all latitudes, the possible destruction of the climate
balance that makes our earth livable—all these suggest the increas-

ingly violent collision between human civilization and the natural world. . . .[12]

Collision? What sort of collision? And how could such a collision ever take place? Gore's predicted catastrophes are without scientific foundation. But if he sincerely believes they can happen and he has the support of others in influential positions—for example, President Clinton—the result could be alarming.

To make matters worse, Gore indicates the same antipathy toward industrialization and corporate America that marks the statements of the radical environmental organizations.

Finally, he gathers all his beliefs and hopes into a massive proposal for action he calls a Global Marshall Plan, which it is assumed will become an important goal of the Clinton-Gore administration. For that reason, the "five strategic goals" of Gore's Global Marshall Plan deserve special attention.[13]

Target No. 1 is a strong belief that the first step taken "to save the global environment" should be to stabilize world population. Gore is correct that education and increased literacy and income levels can slow population growth in Third World nations. But then he makes the familiar error of suggesting that the answer to increasing population lies in forcibly holding down birth rates, rather than finding better ways to feed and care for populations with improved industrial, technological, scientific, and agricultural methods.

In Step 2, Gore unwittingly reverses himself by calling for "the rapid creation and development of environmentally appropriate technologies." In good conscience, one can't continually blame technology for a host of environmental "ills," then blithely call upon technology to provide a fix for those same ills. At the same time, Gore calls upon industrialized nations to transfer such technological capability to Third World nations so they are no longer dependent on the First World.

In Step 3, Gore asks for "a comprehensive and ubiquitous change in the economic 'rules of the road' by which we measure the impact of our decisions on the environment." Here he invites a jungle of global decisions that would be impossible to detail or to pay for, and a huge new bureaucracy to expand the already excessive and arbitrary regulatory powers of the state that unjustly deprives people of their property rights and their jobs.

In his fourth goal, Gore suggests "the negotiation and approval of a new generation of international agreements" that would stipulate global environmental regulations, along with means of enforcement, incentives to obey, and penalties for those who don't. It all sounds suspiciously like the rigid rules and Green-helmeted international cops proposed at the Earth Summit in Rio de Janeiro in June 1992, which drew Gore's admiration and praise.

The last step would be "the establishment of a cooperative plan for educating the world's citizens about our global environment." Gore doesn't explain who needs the educating and who should do it. Should the tutors come from Earth First! and Greenpeace, or from non-biased scientists? We all know the answer. What Gore really wants is global brainwashing.

How would Gore finance his gargantuan Global Marshall Plan? He insists that Japan, Europe, and the wealthy oil-producing nations should provide the money for the plan—but he also implies that the U.S. must play a major part. The odds are that the U.S. would wind up picking up the largest part of the tab in any global plan, as we almost always do. Japan, Europe, and the oil-rich countries would not ante up a dime unless the U.S. put its dollars on the table first.

In summary, then, the Gore plan is not only seriously flawed in its purpose. It would also drain billions from the U.S. for reasons that have nothing to do with science, but a great deal to do with political ambition. And the already heavily burdened American taxpayer would have to pick up the check for a meal he didn't order. Environmental overkill, indeed!

PART SIX

Conclusion

And that brir
only to have los
to accept the ne
that humanity's
ing to the Ear
human use of na
ronmentalism,
lieves in progres
is dedicated to "
condition of "st
industrializatio
"In living in
peasant or tribe
workers or tech
writes Wendell
cultural conserv
My, my. Sho
In the name o
kind to animals
According to t
(those who are l
nizations, such
ety, the Audubo
the Earth, Natu
cal groups, and
stewards of the
reduce human i
immediately by
tic, no matter he
is, unfortunatel
And there's t
provement in th
of the natural we
continue to spea
Consider anothe

Humankind ha
with the planet

CHAPTER 16

Epilogue

A Brief Look at Environmentalism, Backward and Forward

We cannot prove that those are in error who tell us that society has reached a turning point, that we have seen our best days. But so said all before us, and with just as much apparent reason. On what principle is it that, when we see nothing but improvement behind us, we are to expect nothing but deterioration before us?

—LORD THOMAS B. MACAULAY, 1830

IN the opening chapter of this book, we posed a question prompted by those environmental extremists who have stated candidly that the only way to "save the planet" appears to be to bring about the economic collapse of industrialized civilizations. We asked if that was what Americans wanted, whether our fellow citizens would surrender some of their independence and liberties for environmental causes, and whether we must destroy our own nation in the cause of "saving the Earth." In the main body of the book, we have tried to provide sufficient reason and data to refute destructive notions. We have emphasized throughout that it is necessary to

insist on scientil
there may be sev
facts and scienti
tion from our ne

"Modern indu
ing violently witl
assault on the Ea
are occurring so
them. . . . We m
organizing princ

And again, on
over the past 2
"undermine the
difficult actions

So much for s

As the end of
reflect upon two
back, we in the
privileged to live
use for the bette
experienced. Fro
health, expandeo
energy mainly fr
freedom from b
tronics, increase
we take it all for
basic human rigl

On the other l
subjected to a bi
what we eat, abc
our incredibly p
about how much
we handle the in
made to feel guilt
all that constitut

Perhaps we sh
wrote, "We are
wonders."

7. Lindzen, Richard S., 1992, "The Politics of Global Warming," *Ecologic*, May 1992, pp. 16–19.

   Ellsaesser, Hugh W., 1989, "The Politicizing of Climate Science," *21st Century Science and Technology*, May-June 1989, pp. 7,8.

   Hayward, Steven, *The Unholy Alliance of Good Politics and Bad Science in the Global Warming Debate*, Pacific Research Institute, FREE Perspectives, pp. 8–10.

8. All quotations remembering the scare of global cooling taken from the article, "The Ice Age Cometh," by Anne J. Bray, *Policy Review*, Fall 1991, pp. 81–84.

9. *Science and Environmental Policy Project, Issues Update: Greenhouse Warming*, Washington, DC, March 24, 1992.

10. Michaels, Patrick J. and David E. Stooksbury, "Global Warming: A Reduced Threat?" *Bulletin American Meteorological Society*, Vol. 73, No. 10, October 1992, pp. 1563–77.

11. Ellsaesser, Hugh W., Michael C. MacCracken, John J. Walton, and Stanley L. Grotch, 1986, "Global Climate Trends as Revealed by the Recorded Data," *Reviews of Geophysics*, Vol. 24, No. 4, November 1986, pp. 745–92.

12. Spencer, Roy W. and John R. Christy, "Precise Monitoring of Global Temperature Trends From Satellites," *Science*, Vol. 247, March 30, 1990, pp. 1558–62.

13. Weber, Gerd-Rainer, *Global Warming: The Rest of the Story*, Bottiger Verlags-Gmbtt, Wiesbaden, Germany.

14. Cathay, Marc, in interview with Warren T. Brookes, "Warnings More Hype Than Measurable Fact," *Washington Times*, 1990.

15. Ellsaesser, Hugh W., 1991, *Global Warming and the Doomsday Phenomenon*, CEO Conference on Global Warming, Minneapolis, Minnesota, October 1991.

16. Sanford, Richard F., 1990, *Environmentalism Versus Science*, Conceptual Conferences, July 1990.

17. Michaels, Patrick J., 1991, "Global Warming: Death of the 'Popular Vision'?" *New Scientist*, August 1991.

    Ellsaesser, Hugh W., 1985, *Do the Recorded Data of the Past Century Indicate a CO_2 Warming?*, Lawrence Livermore Laboratory Contract, W-7405, Eng.--48, pp. 87, 88.

18. Lindzen, Richard S., 1990, "Some Remarks on Global Warming," *Environmental Science and Technology*, Vol. 24, No. 4, 1990, pp. 424–26.

19. Op cit, Ellsaesser, Ref. 15.

20. Dyson, Freeman, 1992, "Carbon Dioxide in the Atmosphere and the Biosphere," Chapter 12 (1990) in the book *From Eros to Gaia*, Pantheon Books, New York 1992.

Jaworowski, Zbigniew, T. V. Segalstad, and Vidar Hisdal, 1990, *Atmospheric CO_2 and Global Warming: A Critical Review*, Norsk Polarinstitutt Rapportserie, NR. 59, Oslo 1990.

Ellsaesser, Hugh W., 1990, "Comments on the Jaworowski Paper," private communication, December 13, 1990.

21. Idso, Sherwood B., 1989, *Carbon Dioxide and Global Change: Earth in Transition*, IBR Press, 631 E. Laguna Drive, Tempe, Arizona, 85282.

    Idso, Sherwood B., B. A. Kimball, and S. G. Allen, 1991, "CO_2 Enrichment of Sour Orange Trees 2.5 Years Into a Long-Term Experiment," *Plant, Cell, and Environment*, pp. 351–53.

    Idso, Sherwood B., 1991, "Reply to Critics," *Bulletin American Meteorological Society*, Vol. 72, No. 12, December 1991, pp. 1910–13.

22. Drake, Bert G., 1991, "Rising Atmospheric CO_2 Concentration Increases Biomass Production and Carbon Accumulatin in Terrestrial Ecosystems," mimeo paper, Smithsonian Environmental Research Center.

23. Weber, Gerd, 1992, "Global Warming Theory Does Not Fit With Reality," *EIR Science and Technology*, January 14, 1992, pp. 18–25.

24. Handler, Paul and Karen Andsager, *The Effect of Volcanic Aerosols on Global Climate*, Symposium on Global Change Systems, American Meteorological Society, February 5–9, 1990, pp. 153–56.

25. Op cit, Dyson, Ref. 20.

26. Harris, D. M., Motoaki Sato, T. J. Casadevall, W. I. Rose, Jr., and T. J. Bornhorst, "Emission Rates of CO_2 From Plume Measurements, in *The Eruptions of Mount St. Helens, Washington, 1981*, Chapter on Gas Studies, pp. 201–7.

27. Revelle, Roger, 1991, also quoted by Gregg Easterbrook, "The Green Cassandras," 1992, *The New Republic*, July 6, pp. 23–25.

28. Friis-Christensen, E. and K. Lassen, 1991, "Length of Solar Cycle: An Indicator of Solar Activity Closely Associated With Climate," *Science*, Vol. 254, November 1, 1991, pp. 698–700.

    Kelly, P. M. and T. M. Wigley, 1992, "Solar Cycle Length, Greenhouse Forcing and Global Climate," *Nature*, Vol. 360, November 26, 1992, pp. 328–30.

    Schlesinger, Michael E. and Navin Ramankutty, "Implications for Global Warming of the Intercycle Solar Irradiance Variations," *Nature*, Vol. 360, November 26, 1992, pp. 330–33.

    Brookes, Warren T., "Sunspot Data Help Make Bush's Case," *Insight*, December 16, 1991, pp. 18–20.

29. Schneider, Stephen and N. Rasool, 1971, "Atmospheric Carbon Dioxide and Aerosols: Effects of Large Increases on Global Climate," *Science*, July 9, 1971 (also quoted by Daly in *The Greenhouse Trap*, p. 19.

Recommended Readings

Bryson, Reid Alan, 1989, "Will There Be a Global 'Greenhouse' Warming?", *Environmental Conservation*, Vol. 16, No.2, Summer 1989, pp. 97–99. (A thoughtful commentary by one of America's leading climatologists.)

Analysis and Critique of the Climate Change: Executive Summary. This document formed the basis for the Climate Change Treaty reached at the Earth Summit UNCED meeting in Rio de Janeiro, Brazil, June 1992. An analysis of it by S. Fred Singer will be found in *The Science and Environmental Policy Project*, Arlington, VA 22201, May 1992, pp. 2–10. The conclusions are significant:

"The Policymakers' Summary of the 1990 IPCC Report indulges in bold statements and predictions about future climate warming, not supported by current science nor indeed by the Report itself.

"The 1990 IPCC Report and the 1992 Supplement do not deal adequately with available scientific evidence, which throws doubt on the reality of any appreciable human-induced greenhouse warming, now or in the future.

"There is no scientific consensus backing the idea of an appreciable greenhouse warming. On the contrary, as shown by independent surveys, a majority of active climate specialists are skeptical about the importance and urgency of the greenhouse problem."

Rogers, Peter, 1990, "Climate Change and Global Warming," a new role for science in decision-making, *Environmental Science and Technology*, Vol. 24, No. 4, 1990, pp. 428–30.

Seitz, Russell, 1990, "A War Against Fire; the Uses of 'Global Warming' ", *The National Interest*, No. 20, Summer 1990, pp. 54–62.

Post, Wilfred M., et al, 1990, "The Global Carbon Cycle," *American Scientist*, Vol. 78, July-August, pp. 310–26.

Knoll, Andrew H., 1991, "End of the Proterozoic Era," *Scientific American*, October 1991, pp. 64–73. A fascinating discussion of ancient carbon dioxide isotopes.

Bogzaz, Fakhri A. and Eric D. Fajci, 1992, "Plant Life in a CO_2-Rich World," *Scientific American*, January 1992, pp. 68–74. This paper challenges the theory that increased atmospheric carbon dioxide benefits most plants.

SIGNIFICANT BOOKS ABOUT GLOBAL WARMING

Sound and Fury: The Science and Politics of Global Warming, by Patrick J. Michaels, CATO Institute, Washington, DC, 1992, 208 pages.

The Heated Debate: Greenhouse Predictions Versus Climate Reality, by Robert Balling, Jr., Pacific Research Institute for Public Policy, 1992, 177 Post Street, San Francisco, CA 94108.

Global Warming: The Rest of the Story, by Gerd R. Weber, Boettiger-Verlap-Gumb H., Wiesbaden, Germany, November 15, 1991, 250 pages.

These three volumes are the most current and most important books on the present state of information about "global warming."

Also very readable and of considerable interest are the following:

Chapter on Greenhouse/Global Warming in *Rational Readings on Environmental Concerns*, edited by Jay H. Lehr, Van Nostrand, Reinhold, 1992.

Carbon Dioxide and Global Change: Earth in Transition, by Sherwood B. Idso, 1989. This is probably the most complete and well documented book on carbon dioxide ever written.

Global Climate Change; Human and Natural Influences, 1989, S. Fred Singer, editor, Paragon House, New York. An enormous range of issues from mechanisms of climate change to Gaia and climate "religion." Valuable.

Lamb, H. H., *Climate History and the Modern World*, 1982, Methuen & Co. Ltd, London and New York. Invaluable; a classic.

The Greenhouse Trap; Why the Greenhouse Effect Will Not End Life on Earth, by John L. Daly, 1989, Bantam Book published in Australia by Transworld Publishers. Fascinating reading, excellent and understandable explanations of complex phenomena.

Green Hoax Effect; Greenhouse and Other Myths From the Multi-National Corporations, by Peter Sawyer, 1990, published by Groupacumen Australia, Victoria, Australia, also by permission, Fraser Publishing Co., Burlington, VT 05402. Very irreverent, but good!

Climate and the Affairs of Men, by Winkless, Nels III, and Ibn Browning, 1975, Fraser Publishing, Box 494, Burlington, VT 05402. A different approach. Contains much information that is controversial but thought-provoking. Definitely not P.C.!

Additionally, two videotapes are informative and worthwhile:

The Greenhouse Conspiracy, produced by Hilary Lawson, British Independent TV, available in the U.S. from Accuracy in Media, 1275 K Street, Washington, DC 20005.

The Greening of Planet Earth; The Effects of Carbon Dioxide on the Biosphere, Western Fuels Association, Inc., MacGruder Building, 1625 M Street NW, Washington, DC 20077.

APPENDIX

The following is from *National Review*, October 5, 1992:

Regarding the environmentalists' concern over CO_2, here are some facts nobody argues with:

1. Atmospheric pressure is about 15 psi (pounds/in./in.).
2. Earth's radius is about 4,000 miles.
3. CO_2 constituted about 0.04 per cent of the atmosphere in 1950....
4. CO_2 now constitutes more like 0.06 per cent of the atmosphere.

From #2 we calculate that Earth's surface area is 0.8 billion billion square inches. And from #1 that the atmosphere weighs 11.9 billion billion pounds. This is 6 million billion tons. Now take fact #3; 0.04 per cent is 2,400 billion tons of CO_2. Half (the change since 1950) is 1,200 billion tons. Let's call this fact #5:

5. There were 2,400 billion tons of CO_2 in the atmosphere in 1950; 3,600 billion tons now, give or take a sigh or two....
6. Human activity currently releases 6 billion tons of CO_2 per year.
7. Non-human activity (oceans, trees, Pinatubo, Mauna Loa, etc.) releases 200 billion tons of CO_2 per year. . . .

Now compare fact #5 with fact #6. Simple division tells you that if every molecule of human-released CO_2 at the current rate of production stayed in the atmosphere, it would take another 200 years for the post-1950 change to be matched. Or looking backward, since minus 200 years takes us back to before the Industrial Revolution, it means that if every CO_2 molecule from every factory, car, steam engine, barbecue, campfire, and weenie roast that ever was since the first liberal climbed down out of a tree right up until today was still in the atmosphere, it still wouldn't account for the change in CO_2 since 1950.

Fact #7 has been going on for a long time, a lot longer than any piddling 200 years. Comparing #5 and #7 means it takes about 12 years for the average CO_2 molecule to be recycled back out of the atmosphere.

Given the above, here are some conclusions that nobody can argue with and still claim to be a reasoning creature:

8. Human activity, carried out at the present rate indefinitely (more than 12 years) cannot possibly account for more than 6 per cent of the observed change in CO_2 levels.
9. Entirely shutting off civilization—or even killing everybody—could only have a tiny effect on global warming, if there is any such thing. . . .

That leaves two questions that no one knows how to answer:

Q-1. Why do all these supposedly educated, supposedly sane people want to end civilization?
Q-2. Since humanity can't possibly be causing the CO_2 level to go up, isn't it time to start wondering about what *is*?

—S/L. L. VAN ZANDT, Professor of Physics,
Purdue University, West Lafayette, Indiana

CHAPTER 3:   STRATOSPHERIC OZONE AND THE "HOLE"

1. Lemonick, Micheal D., 1992, "The Ozone Vanishes," cover story, *Time*, February 17, 1992, pp. 60–68.
2. Morrison, Micah, 1992, *The Ozone Scare*, "Insight on the News: Vanish-

ing Facts, NASA, the Media, and the Ozone Hype," April 6, 1992, pp. 7–13, 34–35.

3. Bailey, Ronald, 1992, "The Hole Story; The Science Behind the Scare," *Reason*, June 1992, pp. 25–31.

4. "Two Environmental Issues: 1. Ozone, 2. The Greenhouse Problem," a report to the World Affairs Council, Pittsburgh, George C. Marshall Institute, Washington, DC., "Ozone," December 1991, pp. 1–7.

   Ellsaesser, Hugh W., 1991, "The Holes in the Ozone Hole II," Cato Institute Conference, Washington, DC, June 5–6, 1991.

5. Ellsaesser, Hugh W., 1992, "Is Stratospheric Ozone Really Under Chemical Attack? Back to the Drawing Board," *21st Century Science and Technology*, Winter, 1992, pp. 23–27, 79.

   Zingaro, Ralph A., 1992, "Lots of Scientists Aren't Falling for the Ozone Scare," *Houston Chronicle*, December 7, 1992.

   "The Heidelberg Appeal," 1992.

6. Ellsaesser, Hugh W., 1982, "Should We Trust Models or Observations?", *Atmospheric Environment*, Vol. 16, No. 2, 1982, pp. 197–205.

   Perbac, Ralph M., 1989, "A Critical Look at Global Climate and Greenhouse Gases," *Power Engineering*, September 1989, pp. 41–44.

   Singer, S. Fred, 1992, "Global Change—Greenhouse Warming and Ozone Trends," AAAS Annual Meeting, Chicago, February 11, 1992.

   Maduro, Roger A. and Ralf Schauerhammer, 1992, "The Holes in the Ozone Scare; Experimentalists vs. Modelers," *21st Century Science Associates*, Washington, DC, 1992, pp. 73–75.

7. Rowland, F. Sherwood, 1989, "Chlorofluorocarbons, Stratospheric Ozone, and the Antarctic 'Ozone Hole'," Chapter 7 in *Global Climate Change*, edited by S. Fred Singer, Paragon House, NY, pp. 118–19.

8. Lee, Robert W., 1991, "Punching Holes in the Ozone Myth," *New American*, June 4, 1991, p. 42.

   Dunn, Michael J., 1992, "Looking Harder at What's Up With the Ozone Hole Debate," Letters to the Editor Dialog in *Insight*, April 27, 1992, p. 3.

   Beckmann, Petr, 1992, "The Sky's Not Falling," *New American*, April 6, 1992, pp. 13, 14.

9. Op cit, Ellsaesser, Reference 5.

10. Dobson, G. M. B., 1968, *Ozone in the Atmosphere*, Oxford University Press, reprinted in Appendix.

    Op cit, Maduro and Schauerhammer, Reference 6.

    Rigaud, P. and B. Leroy, 1990, "Presumptive Evidence for a Low Value of Total Ozone Content Above Antarctica in September, 1958," *Annales de Geophysique*, 1990, Vol. 8 (11), pp. 791–94.

Op cit, Reference 6, Maduro, 1992, "Scientists Poke Holes in Ozone Hoax."

11. "Press Release: Ozone Hole," editorial in *Wall Street Journal*, February 28, 1992, p.A-14.

Singer, S. Fred, 1991, "Policy by Press Release," *Washington Times*, November 20, 1991.

12. "Issues Update: Stratospheric Ozone," *Science and Environmental Policy Project*, February 19, 1992.

Op cit, Singer, Reference 11.

Science and Environmental Policy Project, Candace C. Crandell, executive director. Comments on Bromley (Dr. D. Allan, the President's Science Advisor) response to questions from Congressman John Dingell regarding ozone "hole" over North America.

Singer, S. Fred, 1991, "Is the Ozone Doomsday Scenario Based on Hype?", *San Diego Union*, July 7, 1991.

"U.S. Study Enhances Concern for Northern Ozone Depletion," *NASA News*, April 30, 1992.

"Hole in Ozone Didn't Develop, NASA Reports," *Wall Street Journal*, May 1, 1992.

Monastersky, R., 1992, "Northern Ozone Hole Deemed Likely," *Science News of the Week*, Vol. 141, p. 84.

" 'Ozone Hole' Fails to Materialize as Feared, NASA Says," *Washington Times*, May 1, 1992.

Maduro, Roger A., 1992, "There Is No Ozone Hole Over the Northern Hemisphere," *EIR Science and Technology*, March 27, 1992, pp. 16–27.

Krug, Edward C., 1992, "Taking a Reality Check on Depletion of Ozone," *Indianapolis Star*, January 21, 1992.

"There's a Hole in the [Ozone] Propaganda," 1992, publisher's page, *New American*, March 23, 1992, p. 44.

13. Penndorf, R., 1950, "The Annual Variation of the Amount of Ozone Over Northern Norway," *Annales de Geophysique*, Vol. 6, No. 1, January-March, 1950.

Henriksen, K, T. Svense, and E. Larsen, 1991, "On the Stability of the Ozone Layer at Tromso," *Journal of Atmospheric and Terrestrial Physics*, Permagon Press, Vol. 54, No. 9, pp. 1113–17, 1992.

Larsen, Soren H. and Thormod Henrickson, 1990, "Persistent Arctic Ozone Layer," *Nature*, January 11, 1990, p. 124.

14. Op cit, Maduro, Reference 6, "Antartic Chlorine and the Ozone Hole," pp. 13–16.

15. Ibid, Chapter 1, "Natural Sources of Chlorine Are Much Greater Than CFC's," pp. 11–40.

16. Ibid, Chapter 4, "Do CFC's Rise to the Upper Stratosphere?", pp. 99ff.

17. Johnston, David A., 1980, "Volcanic Contribution of Chlorine to the Stratosphere: More Significant to Ozone Than Previously Estimated?", *Science*, Vol. 209, July 25, 1980, pp. 491–93.

18. Op cit, Maduro, Reference 14, "Seasonal Values of Sunspot Number With Variations in Total Global Ozone," p. 78.

    Op cit, Reference 4, Marshall Institute, "Two Environmental Issues," p. 3.

    Friis-Christensen, E. and K. Larsen, 1991, "Length of the Solar Cycle: An Indicator of Solar Activity Closely Associated With Climate," *Science*, Vol. 254, November 1, 1991, pp. 698–700.

    Angell, J. K., 1989, "On the Relation Between Atmospheric Ozone and Sunspot Number," *Journal of Climate*, Vol. 2, pp. 1404–16, 1989.

19. Op cit, Reference 4, Marshall Institute, "Two Environmental Issues," p. 2.

20. Op cit, Reference 13, Larsen and Henricksen, p. 124.

21. Op cit, Reference 5, Ellsaesser.

22. Op cit, Reference 6, Perbac, p. 43.

    Op cit, Reference 6, Singer.

23. Op cit, Reference 10, Dobson.

24. Op cit, Reference 10, Rigaud and Leroy.

25. Chubachi, Shigeru, 1985, "A Special Ozone Depletion at Syowa Station, Antarctica, From February 1982 to January 1983," proceedings of the Quadrennial Ozone Symposium held in Halkidiki, Greece, September 3–7, 1984, D. Reidel Publishing Co., Boston.

    Chubachi, Shigeru and Ryoichi Kajiwara, 1986, "Total Ozone Variations at Syowa," *Geophysical Research Letters*, Vol. 13 (November supplement), pp. 1197–98.

CHAPTER 4:   THE OZONE AND ULTRAVIOLET RAYS

1. Penkett, Stuart A., 1989, "Ultraviolet Levels Down Not Up," *Nature*, Vol. 3431, September 28, 1989, p. 283.

   Scotto, Joseph, Gerald Cotton, Frederick Urback, et al, 1988, "Biologically Effective Ultraviolet Radiation: Surface Measurements in the United States, 1974–1985," *Science*, Vol. 239, February 12, 1988, pp. 762–64.

2. Liu, S. C. (NOAA), S. A. McKeen (University of Colorado), S. Madronich (NCAR), 1991, "UV Radiation Decreases Observed in Industrialized Nations," *American Geophysical News*, December 24, 1991.

De Muer, D. and H. De Backer, 1992, "Revision of 20 Years of Dobson Total Ozone Data at Uccle (Belgium): Fictitious Dobson Total Ozone Trends Induced by Sulfur Dioxide Trends," *Journal of Geophysical Research*, Vol. 97, No. 5, April 20, 1992, pp. 5921–37.

Baker, C. Bruce, William R. Kuhn, H. Jeffries, H. Briggs, unpublished manuscript from NOAA/ARL Research Triangle Park, *Variation of Surface UV Irradiance Associated With Atmospheric Aerosols and Ozone*, 6 pages.

3. Maduro, Roger A., 1992, "The Ultraviolet Radiation: Friend or Foe?", Chapter 6 in *The Holes in the Ozone Scare*, 21st Century Science Associates, Washington, DC, see especially p. 153.

4. See "The Ozone Scare," by Micah Morrison in *Insight*, April 6, 1992, for many such statements by officials.

Ellsaesser, Hugh W., 1991, *The Holes in the Ozone Hole II*, Cato Institute Conference, "Global Environmental Crises: Science or Politics?", June 5–6, 1991, p. 7, "The Significance of the Ozone Layer to Health."

Pool, Robert, 1991, "Ozone Loss Worse Than Expected," quotes Reilly claims, *Nature*, 350, p. 451, 1991.

5. Op cit, Ellsaesser, Reference 4.

Armstrong, Bruce K., 1988, "Epidemiology of Malignant Melanoma: Intermittent or Total Accumulated Exposure to the Sun?", *Dermatology Surgical Oncology*, Vol. 14, No. 8, August 1988, pp. 835–49.

6. Ellsaesser, Hugh W., 1978, "A Reassessment of Stratospheric Ozone: Credibility of the Threat," *Climate Change 1*, (1978), pp. 257–66, D. Reidel Publishing Co., Dordrecht, Holland.

7. Ellsaesser, Hugh W., 1992, in Chapter 6, "Ultraviolet Radiation: Friend or Foe?", *The Holes in the Ozone Scare*, p. 176; also in *21st Century Science and Technology Magazine*, Summer 1990.

8. Op cit, Maduro, Reference 3, pp. 3–5.

9. Ibid.

10. Op cit, Shapiro, *Insight*, Reference 4, "The Ozone Scare.

11. Op cit, Reference 3, Robert Watson, p. 188.

12. Ibid, William Reilly, p. 189.

13. In Benedick, Richard Elliot, 1991, *Ozone Diplomacy*, Harvard University Press, p. 190.

14. Ibid, preface.

15. Ibid, pp. 1, 2.

16. Khalil, Aslam and R. A. Rasmussen, 1989, "The Potential of Soils as a Sink of Chlorofluorocarbons and Other Man-Made Chlorocarbons," *Geophysical Research Letters*, Vol. 16, No. 7, July 1989, pp. 679–82.

Khalil and Rasmussen, 1990, "The Influence of Termites on Atmospheric Trace Gases," *Journal of Geophysical Research*, Vol. 95, No. D-4, March 20, 1990, pp. 3619–34.

Khalil and Rasmussen and M. Y. French, 1989, "Emissions of Trace Gases From Chinese Rice Fields and Biogas Generators," *Chemosphere*, 1989, Vol. 20, No. 1–2, pp. 207–66.

17. Hegg, Dean A., Lawrence F. Radke, Peter V. Hobbs, et al, 1990, "Emissions of Some Trace Gases From Biomass Fires," *Journal of Geophysical Research*, Vol. 95, No. D-5, April 20, 1990, pp. 5669–75.

18. Singh, H. B., L. J. Salas, and R. E. Stiles, 1983, "Methyl Halides In and Over the Eastern Pacific," *Journal of Geophysical Research*, Vol. 88, No. C-6, April 20, 1983, pp. 3684–90.

19. Michaels, Patrick J., 1992, "Following the Sheep Over the Edge," *Cleveland Plain Dealer*, August 10, 1992.

20. Op cit, Benedick, Reference 13, Chapter 13, "Strong Decisions in London."

21. Ibid, p. 189.

22. Op cit, Reference 3, Robert Watson, p. 189.

23. Op cit, Reference 13, Benedick, "Ozone Diplomacy."

24. Op cit, Reference 2, De Muer and De Backer (Belgium).

25. Reported by Hugh W. Ellsaesser at Lawrence Livermore National Laboratory, July 7, 1992.

CHAPTER 5:   URBAN AIR POLLUTION AND SMOG

1. Henderson, Rick, 1992, "Insufficient Data," *Reason*, June 1992, pp. 55–57.

Brookes, Warren T., "Is the Nation Headed for 'Greenouts'?", *Washington Times*, July 29, 1991, p.D-1.

2. Ellsaesser, Hugh W., 1978, "Air Pollution: A Different View," *Water, Air, and Soil Pollution 11*, 1979, D. Reidel Publishing Co. Dordrecht, Holland and Boston, pp. 115–27.

3. Brock, David, 1992, "Everybody's Watching L. A. Law," *Insight*, February 10, 1992, pp. 6–10.

4. Jones, K. H., 1992, "The Truth About Ozone and Urban Smog," *Policy Analysis No. 168*, Cato Institute, Washington, DC, pp. 1–27.

5. *National Academy of Sciences Report, 1992*. Also reviewed in the *New York Times* and by Warren T. Brookes, *Insight*, January 13, 1992, pp. 22–23.

6. Scott, John A., 1953, "Fog and Deaths in London, December 1952," *Public Health Reports 68*, pp. 474–79, 1953.

Wilkins, E.T., 1954, "Air Pollution and the London Fog of December 1954," *Journal of the Royal Sanitary Institute*, Vol. 74, pp. 2–15, 1954.

Ibid, "Air Pollution Aspects of the London Fog of December 1952," *Quarterly Journal of the Royal Meteorological Society*, Vol. 80, pp. 267–71, 1954.

Ellsaesser, Hugh W., 1989, "Global 2000 Revisited the Environmentalists' Errors," *Executive Intelligence Review, Science and Technology*, July 28, 1989, pp. 22–29 (covers aspects of the London "Killer Fog" not found in most reports).

Battigelli, M. C., 1968, "Sulfur Dioxide and the Acute Effects of Air Pollution," *Journal of Occupational Medicine*, Vol. 10, pp. 500–11, 1968. "The obvious discrepancy between the alleged disastrous effect of air pollution on health and the inconspicuous concentrations of sulfur dioxide measured in the air have taxed the imagination of toxicologists for the past 20 years," said Battigelli in 1968. Now it's more than 40 years!

7. Ellsaesser, Hugh W., 1975, "Where We Are Now in Air Pollution," *Proceedings of the 12th Space Congress, Technology Today for Tomorrow*, Cocoa Beach, Florida, April 9–11, 1975, pp. 2–5 to 2–17.

8. Goldsmith, John R., 1968, *Air Pollution*, Vol. 1, p. 573, Academic Press, 1968. Included in Ellsaesser, Hugh W., 1975 "Historical Development of Our Air Quality Standards or How to Guarantee Failure," *Environmental Sciences Seminar*, Laurence Livermore Laboratory, July 25, 1972 and American Meteorological Society, November 16, 1973, pp. 1–20.

9. Miniter, Richard, 1992, "Environmentalism Smothers New York," *Wall Street Journal*, op ed, March 31, 1992.

10. Beard, Wertheim, 1967, *American Journal of Public Health*, Vol. 57, p. 2012, 1967, discussed in Ellsaesser report, Reference 8.

Lawther, P. J., 1963, "Compliance With the Clean Air Act: Medical Aspects," *Journal of the Institute of Fuels*, No. 36, pp. 341–344.

Ibid, "Looking Forward and Backward," Symposium on Environmental Effects of Sulfur Dioxide and Related Particulates," *New York Academy of Medicine*, 1978, pp. 1199–1208.

11. Nader, Ralph, 1991, *Public Interest Research Group*, November 1991, quoted in "Politicians Lost in Ozone Smog," Natalie's Corner, *Citizen News*, December 4, 1991.

12. Linvill, Dale E., W. J. Hooker, and Brian Olson, "Mother Nature: 'The Source of Ozone Pollution'," *21st Century Science and Technology*, September-October 1989, p. 22.

13. U.S. National Research Council, 1991, *Rethinking the Ozone Problem in Urban and Regional Air Pollution*, Committee on Tropospheric Ozone Formation and Measurement, 489 pages, December 1991.

Stone, R., 1992, "NRC Faults Science Behind Ozone Regulations," *Science*, January 3, 1992, p. 26.

Ellsaesser, Hugh W., 1989, "Global 2000 Revisited: The Environmentalists' Errors," *EIR Science and Technology*, July 28, 1989, pp. 22–29.

14. Ellsaesser, Hugh W., 1989, "President Bush's New Clean Air Bill: Lots of Money and Hot Air," *21st Century Science and Technology*, September-October 1989, pp. 19–23.

Sirkin, Gerald and Natalie, 1991, "Politicians Lost in Ozone Smog," *Citizen News*, December 4, 1991.

15. Abelson, Philip, 1989, "Rural and Urban Ozone," *Science*, 241:1569, 1989.

16. *EPA Study: Battling Smog: A Plan for Action, No.93*, Center for the Study of American Business at Washington University, St. Louis, MO, September 1989.

17. Jones, K. H., 1992, "The Truth About Ozone and Urban Smog," *Policy Analysis*, Cato Institute, No. 168, February 19, 1992.

18. Ray, Dixy Lee, 1989, "A Breath of Fresh Air," *Eco-Logic; Econ Update*, April 1989, p. 2, and *Washington Institute for Policy Studies*, No. 6, February 13, 1989.

CHAPTER 6:   OF FOOD AND POPULATION

1. Dowswell, C., 1989, Interview With Dr. Norman Borlaug, Nobel Laureate, *Africa Fertilizer Review I*, (1):12–15.

2. Avery, Dennis T., *Technologies for a Changing World Economy*, paper presented at IMC World Food Production Conference, Kuala Lumpur, Malaysia, October 8, 1992.

3. Avery, Dennis T., "Global Food Progress," Hudson Institute, Indianapolis, IN, July 1991.

Avery, Dennis T., "Mother Earth Can Feed Billions More," *Wall Street Journal*, September 19, 1991.

4. Borlaug, Norman E., 1985, Foreword in *Toxic Terror*, by Elizabeth Whelan, Jameson Books, Inc., Ottawa, IL, 1985.

5. Simon, Julian L., 1990, *Population Matters*, see especially "Part 2, Natural Resources," Transaction Publishers, New Brunswick, U.S., 1990.

Simon, Julian L. and Herman Kahn, *The Resourceful Earth*, Basil Blackwell, Inc., 432 Park Avenue South, Suite 1505, New York 10016, 1984.

6. Op cit, Avery, Ref. 2, and Simon/Kahn, Ref. 5.

7. Dibb, David W., 1990, *Sustainable Agriculture: The World Scene*, paper presented at New Zealand Fertilizer Manufacturer's Research Association meeting November 20–22, November 1990.

8. Op cit, Avery, Ref. 2.

9. Ibid, Avery, and op cit, Avery, Ref. 3.

10. Culp, Christopher L., 1992, "The Anti-Biotech Coalition," *Competitive Enterprise Institute Update*, August 21, 1992.

    "Those Terrifying Cows," editorial, *Wall Street Journal*, January 7, 1991.

11. Simon, Julian L., 1990, *Population Matters*, see especially Chapter 7, "Global Food Prospects: Good News," p. 106.

12. Op cit, Avery, Ref. 2, p. 10.

13. Ibid, p. 8.

14. *Alternative Agriculture, National Research Council*, 1989, published by the National Academy Press. The author (authors) of this highly biased report do not identify themselves, preferring apparently the anonymity of a Committee of the Board on Agriculture, NRC.

    Alternative Agriculture: Scientists' Review, 1990, published by CAST (Council for Agricultural Science and Technology), a nonprofit consortium of professional scientific societies. Also reviewed by Richard S. Fawcett in *Plant Protection*, pp. 145–149.

15. Op cit, Avery, Ref. 2, p. 8.

16. Jukes, Thomas H., 1991, "Organic Deception," *California Farmer*, Vol. 274, pp. 44, 45, April 6, 1991.

    Larkin, Marilynn, 1991, "'Organic' Foods: Feeding the Frenzy," *Priorities*, pp. 21–23, Summer 1991. *Priorities* is a publication of the American Council on Science and Health.

17. Jukes, Thomas H., 1984, "Garden of Eden Revisited," reprinted in *Environmental Action*, newsletter of the National Council for Environmental Balance, Inc., Louisville, KY 40207, Summer 1984, p. 2.

18. Quoted in "Why Banning Pesticides Would Be a Costly Mistake," by Warren T. Brookes, *San Francisco Chronicle*, June 12, 1990.

19. Koop, C. Everett, 1991, testimony before the Subcommittee on Health and the Environment, Committee on Energy and Commerce, U.S. House of Representatives, June 19, 1991. Under consideration was HR 2342, the "Safety of Pesticides in Food Act of 1991."

20. Op cit, Brookes, Ref. 18.

21. Francis, F. J., *Public Perception of Food Safety Priorities*, Summer 1991, pp. 29–32.

    Knote, Charles, *The Amazing Truth About Pesticide's Safety*, 1989, update data collected by Dr. Paul Slovic, Decision Research, Eugene, OR; also printed in *Scientific American*, February 1982.

    Jukes, Thomas H., 1990, "Environmentalists Would Destroy Agriculture," EIR Commentary, May 7, 1990.

Ibid, "People and Pesticides," *American Scientist*, Vol. 51, No. 3, September 1963, pp. 355–61.

Ames, Bruce, 1990, "Heresy in the Cancer Lab," *Business Week*, October 15, 1990.

Barrons, Keith C., *Are Pesticides Really Necessary?*, Regnery Gateway, Washington, DC.

22. Scheuplein, Robert, director of the Office of Toxicological Sciences, U.S. Food and Drug Administration, "Those Who Eat Run a Calculated Risk," 1990, *Health and Environment Digest*, Vol. 4, No. 7, August-September 1990, p. 5.

23. Ames, Bruce N. and Lois Swirsky Gold, "Environmental Pollution and Cancer: Some Misconceptions," in *Rational Readings on Environmental Concerns*, edited by Jay H. Lehr, Van Nostrand Reinhold, New York, 1992, pp. 151–67.

24. Ibid, Orient, Jane M., 1992, "Worried About TCE? Have Another Cup of Coffee," in *Rational Readings*, pp. 186–88, reprinted from *Tucson Citizen*, December 6, 1985.

25. French, John R., 1990, "Stalking Celery," *Priorities*, publication of ACSH, Summer 1990, pp. 15, 16.

26. "Food Safety and Toxicology," 1990, a Digest Special Report in *Health and Environmental Digest*, publication of the Freshwater Foundation, Vol. 4, No. 7, August-September 1990, pp. 1–11.

Koop, C. Everett, ibid (13).

Knote, Charles, 1985, "U.S. Urban Pest Control Research Affects Disease and Human Dignity," *Pest Management*, January 1985, pp. 14–16.

Op cit, Koop, Ref. 19.

27. Maduro, Roger, 1992, "Methyl Bromide Ban Will Hasten World Depopulation," *EIR Science and Technology*, December 4, 1992.

28. Whelan, Elizabeth M., *Toxic Terror*, 1985, Jameson Books, Inc., Ottawa, IL 61350, Chapter 2, "The DDT Debate and the Birth of Environmentalism," see p. 67.

29. Hearings before the Committee on Agriculture, House of Representatives, 92nd Congress on the Federal Pesticide Control Act of 1971. Quoted in questions by Mr. Rarick, pp. 266, 267.

30. Op cit, Whelan, Ref. 28.

31. De Toledano, Ralph, *National Review*, June 11, 1990.

32. Press, Frank and Sir Michael Atiyah, 1992, joint statement: *Population Growth, Resource Consumption, and a Sustainable World*, February 26, 1992.

33. Ehrlich, Paul R., 1992, *Population Ecosystem Services and the Human*

Food Supply, paper presented at annual meeting of AAAS, Chicago, February 7, 1992.

Simon, Julian L., 1990, "Part 6, Failed Prophecies and the Doomsday Establishment," in *Population Matters*, Transaction Publishers, New Brunswick, USA.

34. United Nations Population Fund (UNFPA), 1991; see also Ben Wattenberg, columnist, "World Fertility Rates Decline Dramatically," *Washington Times*, May 28, 1992.

35. Simon, J. L., 1981, *The Ultimate Resource*, University of Princeton Press.

Beckmann, Petr, *Access to Energy*, "The Mysterious Roller Coaster (Population)," Vol. 20, No. 3, November 1992, p. 2.

36. Turner, Ted, in *Audubon* magazine interview, also quoted in *CFACT Citizen Outlook*, Vol. 7, No. 4, p. 3, July-August 1992.

37. Turner, Ted, *CFACT Citizen Outlook*, Vol. 7, No. 4, p. 3, July-August 1992.

Hardin, Garrett, quoted: "Every time we send food to save lives in the present, we are destroying lives in the future," from interview on "Living Within Limits," Oxford University Press, 1992, and from interview in *Omni Magazine*, June 1992, pp. 55–63.

Chapter 7: Endangered Species

1. Both quotations cited from Global 2000 in *Rational Readings on Environmental Concerns*, edited by Jay H. Lehr, 1992, and *Disappearing Species Deforestation and Data*, by Julian L. Simon, pp. 741, 742.

2. Train, Russell, 1992, fund-raising letter for World Wildlife Fund and the Conservation Foundation, opening sentence, July 18, 1992.

3. Lovejoy, Thomas, 1992, included in Norman Meyer's *The Sinking Ark*, ibid (1) above, pp. 742–45.

4. Simon, Julian L., ibid (1).

5. The Endangered Species Act, enacted December 28, 1973, published by the Bureau of National Affairs, Inc., Washington, DC, Sec. 2 (b), *Purposes*.

6. Hatfield, Mark O., 1992, "Can't See the Forests for the Endangered Species," *Washington Post*, June 12, 1992.

7. Endangered Species Act of 1973, Sec. 3, paragraphs 16, 14, 8.

8. Gordon, Robert, 1992, *What's in a Name? The Subspecies Question*, Special Report on Endangered Species, National Wildlife Institute Resource, a voice of reason on the environment, Vol. III, Issue 1, Spring 1992, p. 5.

Gordon, Robert E., Jr., 1991, *One of these two owls is considered threatened by the federal government: Can you tell which one?* National Wildlife Institute Resources, Vol. II, Issue 1, February-March, 1991, pp. 1--, 9–10.

Oliver, Charles, 1992, "All Creatures Great and Small Species Preservation Out of Control," *Reason*, April 1992, pp. 23–27.

Felton, Eric, 1990, "Species Listing a Can of Worms?", *Insight*, August 27, 1990, pp. 24–25.

Pendley, William Perry, "The Great Sham of the Endangered Species Act," Fourth Annual Wilderness Conference and *ESA Issues for Consideration*, February 5, 1992, Mountain States Legal Fund.

9. Ibid, Pendley.

10. Rice, James Owen, 1992, "Where Many an Owl Is Spotted," *National Review*, March 2, 1992, pp. 41–43.

Petersen, Jim, "The Year of Discovery," *Our Land* magazine, pp. 61–63.

Moseley, Furman C., "Spotting the Reason for Mill Closures," *Seattle Times*, June 10, 1992.

"The Spotted Owl Controversy," *American Loggers Solidarity*, Forks, Washington; also *WoodBox*, September 1991.

Bradford, R. W., 1991, "The Owls Are Not What They Seem," *Liberty*, July 1991.

11. Stahl, Andy, Sierra Legal Defense Fund, National Wilderness Institute, Spring 1992.

12. Harris, Darryl, 1991, "Spotted Owl Debate: What Can the Public Believe?", *Our Land*, Vol. 3, No. 1, Summer 1991, pp. 5–7.

Ibid, "Commonly Asked Questions About the Northern Spotted Owl," pp. 8–11.

Ibid, Petersen, Jim, "The Soft Underbelly of the Environmental Movement," an interview with Alston Chase, pp. 13–15.

13. Op cit, Rice, James Owen, Reference 10, *National Review*.

Durbin, Kathie, 1991, "New Surveys Chart Favored Nesting Spots," *Oregonian*, July 11, 1991, pp.D1,2.

14. Mader, T. R., "ESA: Flawed Law, Few Species Saved, Millions Spent; Thousands of Jobs Lost," *Abundant Wildlife Society of North America*.

"Fresh Tracks: Environmental News You Can Use," *National Wilderness Institute*, April 1992, p. 3.

15. Gordon, Robert et al, 1992, "An Endangered Species Blueprint," Vol. III, Issue 3, *Some Case Studies: Spotted Owl*, p. 15.

16. *The Spotted Owl Controversy*, publication of American Loggers Solidarity, PO Box 2141, Forks, Washington, May 19, 1991, p. 2.

17. Ibid, "Costs: Economic Impact of Lockup," p. 7.

18. Pendley, William Perry, 1992, "Wither the West? A Call to Action," manuscript from the Mountain States Legal Foundation.

19. Ibid.

20. "Species Act, Endangered," 1992, *Wall Street Journal*, editorial, January 15, 1992.

21. "Snails, Dung Beetles, Frogs, Spiders, and Clams," 1992, *Alliance News*, Putting People Back Into the Environmental Equation, Vol. 1, Issue 6, Alliance for America, August 1992, p. 2.

22. Gordon, Robert E., Jr., 1990, *The Art of Statistics*, Species Recovery Program Critique of Fish and Wildlife Report, reprint from National Wildlife Institute.

23. Donald Berry, World Wildlife Fund, in *NHLA Greenspeak*, January 1992, Issue 28, p. 4.

CHAPTER 8:   WETLANDS

1. Miniter, Richard, 1991, "Muddy Waters: The Quagmire of Wetlands Regulation," *Policy Review*, Spring 1991, pp. 70–77.

2. Adler, Jonathan H., 1991, "Wetlands: It's Time to Lose 'No Net Loss'," *Update: Competitive Enterprise Institute*, September 1991, p. 6.

3. Henderson, Rick, 1992, "The Swamp Thing," in *Rational Readings on Environmental Concerns*, edited by Jay H. Lehr, Van Nostrand Reinhold, New York, p. 797 for Corps of Engineers comment.

   Henderson, Rick, 1991, "The Wetlands Policy Muddle," in the *Sacramento Bee*, April 13, 1991, *New York Times*, and many other newspapers.

   "Citizens' Revolt Against EPA 'Wetlands' Dictates"; see also Law: Wetlands Preservation and Restoration Act, March 20, 1989, which gave EPA precedence in wetlands issues over the Corps of Engineers.

   Brookes, Warren T., 1991, "The Strange Case of the Glancing Geese," *Forbes*, September 2, 1991, pp. 104–12.

4. "What Is a Jurisdictional Wetland?", 1991, *National Wetlands Newsletter*, Vol. 13, No. 5, September-October 1991, p. 5.

5. Goode, Bernard N., 1990, *Practical Solutions to Alaska's Wetland Dilemma*, manuscript text of speech delivered December 5, 1990 in Anchorage, Alaska, 5 pages. See also congressional testimony and Federal Register, June 16, 1992.

6. Lehr, Jay H., 1992, "Wetlands: A Threatening Issue," *Rational Readings on Environmental Concerns*, Van Nostrand Reinhold, pp. 799–806.

7. Op cit, Reference 3, Brookes, Warren T., 1991, *Forbes*.

8. Miniter, Richard, "Drowning Property Rights," *Update: Competitive Enterprise Institute*, 1992.

9. Ercole, Antony J., 1992, "Wetlands and Coal," *Perspective: Eco-Logic*, June 1992, pp. 4, 5; reprinted from *Pennsylvania Coal Quarterly*, Vol. 8, No. 2, June 1991.

10. Albrecht, Virginia S., 1991, "Are All Wetlands Created Equal? Bring Standards Back to Reality," *National Wetlands Newsletter*, Vol. 13, No. 5, September-October 1991, pp. 6, 7.

11. Most estimates of the "original" extent of wetlands are based on guesses made by the Audubon Society — hardly a disinterested organization. The assumption that 50 percent of America is wetlands is also a guess. See discussion in *CFACT, Citizen Outlook*, "Wetland Policy Soaks U.S. Property Owners," Vol. 7, No. 2, March-April 1992, pp. 1, 2.

12. Laffer, William G., 1991, "Bogged Down in Wetlands," *Ludwig von Mises Institute Freemarket*, November 1991.

13. Op cit, Reference 3, Brookes, Warren T., 1991, *Forbes*, p. 109.

    Ibid, p. 112.

    Ibid, p. 106

    In a 1991 article titled "Bankrupted by EPA," Peter Samuel, director of *Greentrack International*, a Washington, DC-based news service concerning environmental issues from a skeptical position, wrote this: "Last month the Environmental Protection Agency put out a thick 'Note to Correspondents' and staged a press conference on what it called its 'record-breaking enforcement accomplishments for clean water in 1991.' It was a 'banner year for enforcement,' with 3,109 prosecutions, $28 million in penalties, and 346 months of incarceration for the polluters. 'The 1991 numbers [of prosecutions] are more than all previous years combined,' said the EPA. But does this mean justice is being done? Take the case of Lewis 'Chuck' Law, 54, of Charleston, WV. Mr. Law was sentenced in U.S. District Court to $160,000 in fines and two years in jail for breaches of the Federal Clean Water Act.... The prosecution did not argue that the discharges from the springs [on his property] constituted any health hazard. They just didn't meet EPA clean-water standards. And in what appears to be a complete perversion of the principles of common law, the U.S. Attorney prosecuting the case argued that it is immaterial under the Clean Water Act whether the property owner is the cause of the pollution. He argued that under the act the defendant could be found guilty simply on the basis that polluted water was emerging fromhis property, regardless of its source." This is justice?

14. Ibid.

15. Ibid.

16. Reilly, William, 1991, in a *Human Events* article by Warren T. Brookes, "EPA's Reilly Continues His War on Private Property," August 3, 1991, p. 11. See also Brookes, "War on Property Rights," *Washington Times*, July 18, 1991.

17. Judge Daniel Manion, U.S. Court of Appeals for 7th Circuit, April 20, 1992, *National Hardwood Lumber Association Weekly Update*, April 27, 1992.

    Wall Street Journal editorial, "Wetlands," May 26, 1992.

    Ivester, David, 1992, "New Wetland Precedent Isolated Wetlands Exempted Under Clean Water Act," *Eco-Logic*, July 1992, pp. 9, 10.

18. Op cit, Manion, Ref. 17.

19. Testimony of William Hazeltine, American Mosquito Control Association, at hearings on wetland protection before the Water Resources Subcommittee of the House Public Works and Transportation Committee, together with submitted materials, October 31, 1991.

20. Desowitz, Robert S., 1991, *The Malarial Capers*, W. W. Norton & Co., New York and London, p. 145.

21. "Saving the Ecosystem...for the Mosquitoes," *Doctors for Disaster Preparedness Newsletter*, Vol. VIII, No. 6, November 1991.

    Ibid, "Malarial Miasma From Washington," Vol. IX, No. 3, May 1992.

    Ibid, "Wetlands: A Public Health Hazard," Vol. IX, No. 4, July 1992.

    Dorman, Thomas A., MD, "Malaria," *Newsletter*, San Luis Obispo, September 1992. Especially important for bibliography that contains significant references to international literature not easily available.

22. "Defenses Break Down, Diseases Proliferate," 1992, *Physicians for Civil Defense Newsletter*, Tucson, Arizona, *Civil Defense Perspectives*, Vol. 8, No. 6, September 1992.

    Eckert, Toby, 1991, "Third Youth Infected With Encephalitis," *Journal Star*, Peoria, IL, September 10, 1991.

23. Holzman, David, 1990, "Old Viruses With a New Virulence," *Insight*, November 26, 1990, pp. 52, 53.

CHAPTER 9:   OF FORESTS—PUBLIC AND PRIVATE

1. "Timber Country Revisited," by Earl Roberge, *Managing Our Renewable Resource*, 1991, published by Washington Contract Loggers' Association, Olympia, WA, 185 pages.

2. *The 1980 Eruptions of Mount St. Helens, Washington*, Peter W. Lipman and Donal R. Mullineaux, editors, U.S. Geological Survey Professional Paper 1250.

3. *Mount St. Helens; Weyerhaeuser's Reforestation*, 1991, Weyerhaeuser Co., Tacoma, WA 98477.

   Rochelle, James A., Richard L. Ford, and Thomas A. Terry, 1992, "The Reforestation Challenge," *Journal of Forestry*, 1992, pp. 20–25.

   Rochelle, James A., 1990, *Natural Resource Recovery Following the 1980 Mount St. Helens Eruption: Lessons in Ecological Resilience*, transcript, 25th North American Wildlife and Natural Resources Conference,

Wildlife Management Institute, Washington, DC, pp. 210–215, 1990.

Winjum, J. K., et al, 1986, "Regenerating the Blast Zone of Mount St. Helens," *Journal of Forestry*, 1986, Vol. 84(5), pp. 28–35.

Roberge, Earl, 1992, "Logging the Blast Zone," *Newsletter of the Carbide Processors*, November 1992, pp. 1–3.

4. Roosevelt, President Theodore, 1903, "The Search for Meaning," *The National Parks*, by Michael Frome, photos by David Muench, Rand McNally & Co., 1977, p. 6.

5. *Newsletter*, Weyerhaeuser Co., 1992.

6. "Answers to Some Frequently Asked Questions About America's Forest Products Industry," *America's Forests: A Commitment to Balance*, American Forest Council, National Forest Products Week, October 18–24, 1992, pp. 7, 19, 23.

"NHLA Greenspeak," *Forest Facts*, December 1992, pp. 3, 4.

"Forest Facts," 1992, Weyerhaeuser Co.

Forest Resource Fact Book, American Forest Resource Alliance, Washington, DC.

7. *Eco-92 Must Be Stopped*, 1992, Section III, "The Scientific Hoaxes, No. 6, Deforestation," Schiller Institute, Inc., p. 5.

8. "Prices, Trade, and Forest Economics," 1989, *Economic Update*, April 1989, pp. 5, 6.

9. Ibid, p. 5. See also *Beyond the Woodfuel Crisis*, reviewed in *The Economist*, March 4, 1989.

10. Maurice, Charles and Charles Smithson, 1987, "Projections Without Prices Don't Come True," *The Doomsday Myth*, Hoover Press, 1987, p.XVI.

11. Gore, Senator Albert, 1992, *Earth in the Balance*, Chapter 6, "Skin Deep," pp. 115–125, Houghton Mifflin Co., New York.

Dunn, James R., "America the Beautiful," essay for National Council for Environmental Balance, Inc., August 8, 1992. Also in *National Review*, June 6, 1992.

"Global 2000 Report," analyzed by Julian L. Simon, 1992, "Disappearing Species, Deforestation, and Data," *Rational Readings on Environmental Concerns*, Van Nostrand Rheinhold, edited by Jay Lehr, 1992, p. 741.

12. Sedjo, Roger and Marion Clawson, op cit, pp. 745–46.

Sedjo, Roger and Marion Clawson, 1984, *Global Forests in the Resourceful Earth*, by Julian L. Simon and Herman Kahn: "A Response to 'Global 2000,'" Basil Blackwell, Inc., New York, p. 128.

13. Dunn and Simon, op cit, Ref. 11.

14. Ibid, "The History of U.S. Forests," pp. 138–43.

15. Fahenstock, G. R. and J. K. Agee, 1983, "Biomass Consumption and

Smoke Production by Prehistoric and Modern Forest Fires in Washington," *Journal of Forestry*, Vol. 81, pp. 653–657.

16. Op cit, Sedjo and Clawson, Reference 13.

17. *The American Forest: Facts and Figures*, 1991, American Forest Council publication, 1991, 23 pages.

18. Bowver, Jim, 1991, *Study Shows Wood to Be Energy-Efficient Building Material*, American Forest Council publication, February 15, 1991.

19. "Why Clearcut?", 1992, *Managing Our Forest Resources*, Weyerhaeuser Publication Update, 1992.

20. Reported in "From the Trenches: Spotted Owl of Ohio," Washington Report from *Putting People First*, August 26, 1992, Kathleen Magnardt, chairman.

21. Arnold, Ron, 1987, *The Ecology Wars*, Chapter 4, "History: The Unconventional Weapon," Free Enterprise Press, Bellevue, WA, 1987, p. 67.

22. Draper, John, 1992, "The Eye in the Sky; Does It Lie?", *Forests Forever*, Headquarters Report, Weyerhaeuser Co., July 1992.

    Associated Press, 1992, "Forest Chief Disputes NASA Photos of Northwest Logging," June 16, 1992, by Scott Sonner, AP writer.

    Washington Times, 1992, "Chides NASA for Misleading the Public," National Hardwood Lumber Association, August 30, 1992.

    "Satellite Forestry, A Closer Look Shows New Forests," commentary of Christopher I. West, Northwest Forestry Association Loggers' World, August 1992, pp. 25–27.

23. Smith, Doug, 1992, "Ah, Nature—and Crescent Resources; Mohicans' Ancient Forest, A Crescent Created Youngster, *Charlotte Observer*. Other portions of Smith's article are enlightening. For example: "[George] Moyers (forest manager overseeing the film site), who has kept photographic records of the area for 30 years, says that when he told members of the film crew they were standing on land that had been clear-cut and replanted, 'They just about dropped their teeth.'

    "Ron Bost, vice president of forestry for Crescent, Duke Power Company's land management subsidiary, believes the movie could clear up what he believes are misconceptions about clear-cutting. . . .

    "'We take a different view of clear-cutting,' Bost says. 'When someone cuts it down, walks away and leaves, it looks awful for now and for a long time to come. To us, clear-cutting is not only a harvesting technique but a regenerating technique. We've taken the timber off that land and reforested it.'

    "In another 20 years, Moyers says, the trees around Lake James will mature, 'and then we'll start the process all over again.'"

Recommended Reading

For an excellent discussion of the relative merits of public versus private ownership and management see *Protecting the Environment: Old Rheto-*

ric, New Imperatives, by Jo Kwong Eckard, Capital Research Center, 1990, Section 7, "The Free Market Alternative," especially p. 93, "The Myth of Government Efficiency."

CHAPTER 10:   OF PRIVATE PROPERTY

1. Letter from Governor Fife Symington to the president of the Arizona State Senate re: Senate Bill 1053, excerpted in *News From the FLOC*, Cambridge, MD, November 1991, p. 7.

2. Arbogast, Nicole, 1991, "Public Vs. Private Land Management," *CEI Update*, December 1991, p. 4.

3. Pendley, William Perry, 1992, "Whither the West? A Call to Action," manuscript from the Mountain States Legal Foundation.

4. Ibid.

5. Ibid.

6. Reported in *The Litigator*, publication of the Mountain States Legal Foundation, Summer 1992, p. 4.

7. Op cit, Perry, Reference 3.

8. Ibid.

CHAPTER 11:   GOVERNMENT OWNERSHIP OF LAND AND FORESTS

1. "NHLA Greenspeak," Elizabeth Pease, editor, *Forest Facts*, Issue 39, December 1992, p. 3.

   "The American Forest: Facts and Figures, 1991," American Forest Council, Washington, DC, 1992, 23 pages.

   "Managing Our Forest Resources," *Update*, 1992, Weyerhaeuser Co., Tacoma, WA.

2. Ibid, "The American Forest: Tree Farm System," pp. 13, 14.

3. Ibid.

4. Sedjo, Roger A. and Marion Clawson, 1984, "The History of U.S. Forests," in *The Resourceful Earth*, by Julian Simon and Herman Kahn, Basil Blackwell, Inc., 1984, pp. 138–43.

5. Eckard, Jo Kwong, 1990, "Protecting the Environment; Old Rhetoric, New Imperatives," Section 1, *Creating a "Public Domain"*, pp. 1–14.

6. Ibid, American Association for the Advancement of Science, p. 7.

7. Brookes, Warren T., 1991, "Greenlining: An Assault on U.S. Property Rights," *Detroit News*, January 21, 1991.

8. Christian, George L., 1991, "Outrage at Olympic," in *Land Rights Letter*, July 1991, p. 4.

9. Frome, Michael, 1977, "The Search for Meaning," *The National Parks*, p. 6, Rand, McNally & Co.

10. Ibid, p. 7.

11. "The National Park Service Natural Landmarks Program," 1992, "Fact Sheet," *Land Rights Letter*, Sharpburg, MD, February 1992.

    Ibid, "Parks Without Boundaries," by Erich Veghl, August 1991.

    Chase, Alston, 1991, "Landmark Lassitude?", *Washington Times*, December 14, 1991.

    "Greengate," by Alston Chase in *Washington Times*, March 1990.

12. Brock Evans, quoted by Warren T. Brookes in a commentary in *Washington Times*, Wednesday, October 16, 1991.

CHAPTER 12:   ALL (ENVIRONMENTAL) ISSUES—GREAT AND SMALL

1. Brown, John F., Jr., 1981, "Environmental Theology," Paxton Lecture for 1981, *Torch* magazine, Vol. 54, No. 3, Summer 1981, 4 pages.

2. Ibid.

3. Courtney, Phoebe, 1991, "The Phony Claims of the Environmental Lobby," Tax Fax No. 234, *Independent American*, July 1991, 16 pages.

4. Eckard, Jo Kwong, 1990, "Protecting the Environment; Old Rhetoric, New Imperatives," Section 7, *The Free-Market Alternative*, p. 94.

    Landy, Mark and Mary Hague, 1992, in *Environmental Politics, Public Costs, Private Rewards*, Chapter 4, "The Coalition for Waste: Private Interests and Superfund," edited by Michael S. Greve and Fred L. Smith, Jr., p. 71, "Origin of Superfund."

5. Orme, Thomas W., 1992, "Superfund: Is It Bulldozing Our Public Health Dollars?", *Priorities*, Summer 1992, pp. 7–10.

6. Wildavsky, Aaron, 1991, in *Health Lifestyle and Environment Countering the Panic*, Chapter 10, "If Claims of Harm From Technology Are False, Mostly False, or Unproven, What Does That Tell Us About Science?", pp. 111–45.

7. Ibid, p. 112.

8. Landy, Marc K., 1986, "Cleaning Up Superfund," *The Public Interest*, No. 85, Fall 1986, pp. 58–71.

9. Paigen, Dr. Beverly in Wildavsky, op cit, Reference 6, p. 113; see also her original paper presented October 21, 1980, American Public Health Association meeting, Detroit, MI.

    Paigen, Dr. Beverly, research reviewed in *Toxic Terror*, 1985, by Elizabeth M. Whelan, Chapter 3, "'Disaster' of Love Canal, pp. 99ff.

10. Op cit, Wildavsky, Reference 6.

11. Op cit, Whelan, *Toxic Terror*, Reference 9, p. 104.

12. Ibid, p. 105.

13. OTA Special Report, U.S. Congress, 1988, *Are We Cleaning Up?*, "Ten Superfund Case Studies," OTA-ITE-362, June 1988, p. 1.

14. Op cit, Landy and Hague, Reference 4, p. 67.

15. Shaw, Jane S., "The Costly Policies They Blithely Propose," in *Rational Readings on Environmental Concerns*, edited by Jay H. Lehr, Van Nostrand Reinhold, 1992, chapter entitled "Is Environmental Press Coverage Biased?", pp. 475–476.

16. *U.S. EPA, Unfinished Business: A Comparative Assessment of Environmental Problems*, Washington, DC, EPA Office of Policy Analysis, February 19, 1987, pp. 128–134.

    Op cit, Wildavsky, Reference 6.

17. Op cit, Landy and Hague, Reference 4, p. 80 for extensive bibliography.

18. Passell, Peter, 1991, "Experts Question Staggering Costs of Toxic Cleanups," *Sunday New York Times*, September 1, 1991, pp. 1 and 12.

19. Op cit, Whelan, *Toxic Terror*, Reference 9, Chapter 8, "Deadly Dioxin?", pp. 171–92.

    AIM Report, Accuracy in Media, 1990, "Prime Time Poison," Reed Irvine, editor, Washington, DC, Nov-A 1990.

    Irvine, Reed, 1991, "The Dioxin Un-Scare—Where's the Press?", *Wall Street Journal*, August 6, 1991.

20. Tazieff, Haroun, 1992, in "The Holes in the Ozone Scare," by Roger Maduro, Foreword, p.IX, 21st Century Associates, Washington, DC.

21. Janson, David J., 1991, "Dioxin Toxicity: New Studies Prompt Debate, Regulatory Action," *Chemistry and Engineering News*, August 12, 1991, pp. 7–14.

22. Ibid.

23. Op cit, Reed Irvine, "The Dioxin Un-Scare," Reference 19.

    Taylor, Rob, 1991, "Scientists Question the Peril From Dioxin," *Seattle Post-Intelligencer*, February 18, 1991.

24. Currie, Bob, 1991, "A Very Green Recession," *Eco-logue*, March 1992, p. 7.

25. Op cit, Haroun Tazieff, Reference 20.

    Abelson, Philip H., 1991, "Excessive Fear of PCBs," editorial in *Science*, Vol. 253, No. 5018, July 16, 1991, p. 3.

    "PCBs: New Hudson 'Headless Horseman'," *AIM Report, Accuracy in Media*, Feb-A 1992.

26. Brookes, Warren T., 1991, (1) "Debunking EPA's Radical Risk Model"; (2) PCBs, Like Dioxin, Another False Alarm,"; (3) Bad Science Creates a Toxic Superstar"; (4) "Studies Refute Link Between Lead and IQ," four-part series in *Detroit News*, 1991.

27. Maduro, Roger A., 1992, "Methyl Bromide Ban Will Hasten World Depopulation," *EIR Science and Technology*, December 4, 1992, pp. 22–28.

28. Adler, Jonathan H., 1991, "Is Lead the Next Environmental Hoax?", *CEI Update*, October 1991, pp. 2, 3.

Felten, Eric, 1991, "Lead Scare: Leftist Politics by Other Means," *Wall Street Journal*. *

"EPA Perpetuates Lead Fraud," 1991, *Washington Inquirer*, Vol. XI, No. 43, November 8, 1991.

Brookes, Warren T., 1991, op cit, Reference 26, on "Studies Refute Link Between Lead and IQ," and "Lead Level Scandal Escalates," *Detroit News*, September 23, 1991.

Putka, Gary, 1992, "Research in Lead Poisoning Is Questioned," *Wall Street Journal*, March 6, 1992.

"Memo for Media: Get the Lead Out," *AIM Report, Accuracy in Media*, 1992, XXI-6, March-B 1992.

29. Dingell, Congressman John, interview in *Insight*, November 11, 1991.

30. Anderson, Christopher, 1991, "Cholera Epidemic Traced to Risk Miscalculation," *Nature*, Vol. 354, November 28, 1991, p. 225.

31. "Environmentalism Kills Civil Defense Perspectives," *Newsletter*, Physicians for Civil Defense, Vol. 8, No. 6, September 1992.

Tucker, I. W., editor, 1992, "Environmentalism Kills," *Energy and Environment Alert*, National Council for Environmental Balance, Vol. 14, No. 4, Winter 1992.

Rush, Valerie, 1991, "Cholera Coverup Aids Contagion's Spread," *EIR Economics*, August 30, 1991, pp. 8, 9.

Solis, Diana and Bruce Ingersoll, 1991, "Spread of Cholera in Mexico Prompts Warning by U.S. to Areas Along Border," *Wall Street Journal*, August 16, 1991.

Golden, Tim, 1991, "Cholera Ambushes the Poor," *New York Times News Service* in *Colorado Springs Gazette Telegraph*, September 22, 1991, p.A-17.

32. "Worries Proliferate," *Civil Defense Perspectives*, 1992, Physicians for Civil Defense, Vol. 8, No. 4, May 1992.

33. Krug, Edward C., 1990, "Acid Rain and the Environmental 'Crisis'," Center for Constructive Alternatives Seminar Series, Hillsdale College, Hillsdale, MI, November 4–8, 1990, pp. 1–14.

34. Ibid, p. 1.
Anderson, William, 1992, "Acid Test," *Reason*, January 1992, pp. 20–26.
Krug, Edward C., 1992, "Acid Rain: A Case Example of Environmental Epistemology," *Mining Engineering*, 1992.

35. "Prime Time Poison," notes by Reed Irvine, *AIM Report, Accuracy in Media*, Nov-A 1990.

Op cit, Krug, Reference 34.

36. McKetta, John J., "Acid Rain: The Whole Story to Date," National Acid Precipitation Assessment Project, *Rational Readings on Environmental*

Concerns, Jay H. Lehr, editor, Van Nostrand Reinhold, 1992, pp. 44–58.

Kulp, J. Laurence, "Acid Rain Causes, Effects, and Control," *CATO Review of Business and Government*, 1992.

37. "NAPAP Report," quoted by Senator John Glenn, *Congressional Record*, March 27, 1990, S-3254. The NAPAP Report received only a one-hour hearing in the Senate and was never presented in the House. Senator Glenn said, "We spend over $500 million on the most definitive study of acid precipitation that has ever been done in the history of the world and then we do not want to listen to what [the experts] say."

Adler, Jonathan H., 1992, "Clean Fuels, Dirty Air," Chapter 2 in *Environmental Politics; Public Costs, Private Rewards*, edited by Michael S. Greve and Fred L. Smith, Jr., p. 41.

38. Brookes, Warren T., 1990, "Acid Rain: The $140 Billion Fraud?", *Consumer Alert Comments*, Barbara Keating-Edh, editor, Vol. 14, No. 6, November 1990.

Krug, Edward C., 1990, "The Great Acid Rain Flimflam," *Policy Review*, Heritage Foundation, Spring 1990, pp. 44–48.

39. "Requiem for Acid Rain," *AIM Report, Accuracy in Media*, Reed Irvine, editor, XIX-19, Oct-A 1990.

Op cit, Krug, Reference 33.

Op cit, Kulp, Reference 36.

40. Krug, Edward C., 1991, "America's Energy Battle: A Casualty Speaks Out," *CFACT Citizen Outlook*, Vol. 6, No. 2, July-August 1991.

Krug, Edward C., 1991, "A Casualty Left by the Greenies," *Cleveland Plain Dealer*, June 21, 1991.

Op cit, Krug, Reference 33.

41. Op cit, Brookes, Reference 38.

42. Op cit, Krug, Reference 38.

43. Bennett, Michael J., 1991, *The Asbestos Racket*, "An Environmental Parable," Free Enterprise Press, Bellevue, WA, 241 pages.

Asbestos in Public and Commercial Buildings; A Literature Review and Synthesis of Current Knowledge, 1991, Health Effects Institute, Asbestos Research, Archibald Cox, chairman of the board.

(These two books are essential to reach a full understanding of the asbestos problem. Both are thorough and well-documented. Bennett's book is the more popular and readable; the one by the Health Effects Institute is technical but sound.

44. "Asbestos Rip-out Is a Consumer Rip-off," *Consumer Alert Comments: Truth*, special edition, ISSN 0740–4964, June 1990.

45. Ross, Malcolm, 1992, "Minerals and Health: The Asbestos Problem," in *Rational Readings on Environmental Concerns*, Jay H. Lehr, editor, pp. 101–115.

Ross, Malcolm, 1987, proceedings of the 21st Forum on the Geology of

Industrial Minerals, Arizona Bureau of Geology and Mineral Technology, 1987.

Dunn, James R., "Asbestos—Let's Get the Facts Straight," *National Council for Environmental Balance*, Louisville, KY, 1992.

Kinney, John E., 1992, "The Asbestos Distortion," *Rational Readings*, op cit, above.

46. Efron, Edith, 1984, *The Apocalyptics; Epilogue*, Simon & Schuster, Inc. Review of paper (unpublished), "Estimates of the Fraction of Cancer Incidence in the United States Attributable to Occupational Factors," p. 437ff.

Irvine, Reed, 1990, "The Real Asbestos Horror Story," *AIM Report, Accuracy in Media*, XIX-17, Sept-A 1990.

Asbestos: Wonder Mineral or Health Hazard?, booklet of the American Council on Science and Health, 1992, ACSH publication, New York.

47. Dana Farber Cancer Research Institute, 1989, *New England Journal of Medicine*, November 1989.

Op cit, Bennett, Reference 43, p. 23.

48. Op cit, Malcolm Ross, Reference 45, "The Asbestos Problem: Amosite or 'Brown' Asbestos," p. 108.

49. Op cit, Dunn, Reference 45.

Beckmann, Petr, 1986, *Access to Energy*, Vol. 13, No. 6, February 1986, p. 1; see also Vol. 14, No. 4, December 1986, p. 2.

Bennett, Michael J., 1990, "EPA's Asbestos Farce," *Washington Times*, August 15, 1990.

50. Op cit, Ross, Reference 45, *Rational Readings*, pp. 106, 107, 109.

51. Brookes, Warren T., 1990, "EPA's Asbestos Disaster," commentary in *Washington Times*, March 6, 1990.

Brookes, Warren T., 1990, "The Asbestos Risk in Perspective," *Detroit News*, March 1, 1990, including this quotation from Malcolm Ross, U.S. Geological Survey: "There is no doubt in my mind that the Challenger disaster was caused by the EPA's asbestos paranoia."

52. Op cit, Wildavsky, Reference 6, Chapter 10, p. 133.

53. Ibid, p. 133.

54. Ibid, p. 134.

55. Op cit, Bennett, Reference 43, p. 14.

56. "The Asbestos Racket," editorial in *Detroit News*, October 28, 1991.

57. Kramer, "Fossil Bill," 1992, "Toothpicks More Dangerous Than Asbestos, Court Says," *Angry Environmentalist Newsletter*, February 1992, reprinted in *Eco-Logic*, including this significant comment: "The Court made the sardonic observation that using toothpicks is much more dangerous than using asbestos. Aproximately eight people will die between now and the year 2000 from swallowing toothpicks — twice as many as EPA expects to save by banning 'asbestos' pipe, shingles, and

roof coatings. Asked if they would accept the Court's finding, an EPA spokesman said, 'We've asked the Court to reconsider.' To date, the Court hasn't, and the EPA continues to ignore the ruling."

AIM Report, Accuracy in Media, "Notes From the Editor's Cuff," Reed Irvine, editor, Nov-A 1991.

"Fifth Circuit Court Overturns 1989 EPA Ban on Asbestos," *Environment Week*, 1991, Vol. 4, No. 42, October 24, 1991.

Bennett, Michael J., 1992, "Great Hoax on Asbestos Finally Ends," *Science and Environment Policy Project*, Washington, DC, 1992.

"EPA: One Life Worth $76 Million: EPA Didn't Follow Own Regulations," *Washington Inquirer*, Vol. XI, No. 41, October 25, 1991.

Op cit, Reference 56, *Detroit News* editorial.

58. Beckmann, Petr, 1989, "Power Lines and Magnetic Fields," *Access to Energy*, Vol. 17, No. 1, p. 3, September 1989.

59. Beckmann, Petr, 1991, *Electromagnetic Fields and VDT-itis*, Golem Press, "Effects of Non-Ionizing EM Fields," p. 5.

60. Douglas, John, 1992, "Taking the Measure of Magnetic Fields," *EPRI Journal*, Vol. 17, No. 3, April-May 1992, pp. 16, 17.

61. Moore, Taylor, 1990, "Exploring the Options for Magnetic Field Management," *EPRI Journal*, Vol. 15, No. 7, October-November 1990, pp. 5–19.
Florig, H. Keith, "Responding to the Potential Health Effects of Electric and Magnetic Fields," *Resources*, publication of Resources for the Future, Fall 1992, pp. 6–10.

62. Op cit, Beckmann, Reference 59, p. 9.

63. Beckmann, Petr, 1991, "No Ground for Loopholes," *Access to Energy*, Vol. 18, No. 7, March 1991, p. 3.

64. Moore, Taylor, 1992, "Sharpening the Focus in EMF Research, Health Effects," *EPRI Journal*, Vol. 17, No. 2, March 1992, pp. 5–13.

CHAPTER 13: GOVERNING BY REGULATION

1. "Regulatory Proliferation," *Alert*, newsletter of the National Council for Environmental Balance, Inc., Vol. 14, No. 1, Winter-Spring 1992.

2. through 6. Ibid.

7. Kulp, J. Laurence, "How Zealous Greens Hurt Growth," *Fortune*, March 23, 1992, p. 26.

8. Hopkins, Thomas D., "Whose Lands Are Wetlands?", *Journal of Regulation and Social Costs*, Vol. 2, No. 1, March 1992, pp. 5–31.

9. "Choked by Red Tape," *Reason* magazine, October 1992, p. 10.

10. Gray, Wayne B., "The Cost of Regulation: OSHA, EPA, and the Productivity Slowdown," *American Economic Review*, December 1987.

11. Quoted in *Wall Street Journal*, April 21, 1992.

12. Ibid.

13. Ibid.

14. "The True Cost of Federal Regulation," *Weekly Update*, National Hardwood Lumber Association, June 29, 1992.

15. Drummey, James J., quoting Irving Kristol in *The Establishment's Man*, p. 55.

16. Sibbison, Jim, "The Real Asbestos Horror Story," *AIM Report, Accuracy in Media*, XIX-17, Sept-A 1990; see also *Washington Monthly*, March 1984.

17. Ibid.

18. "EPA to Your Town: Drop Dead," *Aim Report*, publication of Accuracy in Media, Washington, DC, April 1992.

19. Op cit, *AIM Report, Accuracy in Media*, Reed Irvine, editor, XXI-8, April-B 1992, p. 4. See also "Officials See Groundswell Opposing EPA Mandates That Deny Local Priorities," *Inside EPA*, December 20, 1991.

20. *Inside EPA*, July 26, 1991.

21. Laffer, William G., 3rd, "George Bush's Hidden Tax: The Explosion in Regulation," *Backgrounder*, Heritage Foundation, Washington, DC, July 10, 1992.

22. Ibid.

CHAPTER 14:   WHO'S RESPONSIBLE FOR OVERKILL?

1. "Journalists and Others for Saving the Planet," David Brooks quoting Charles Alexander of *Time* at summer 1989 environmental conference, *Wall Street Journal*, October 5, 1989.

2. *American Spectator*, quoted by Micah Morrison, July 1991.

3. Ibid.

4. "The Media's Middle Name Is Not Objectivity," Harry Stein quoting Bernard Goldberg, *TV Guide*, June 13–19, 1992.

5. "Editor's Comment," by Chuck Diaz quoting Linda Harrar, *Speak Up America*, September 1, 1992.

6. Ibid.

7. *Boston Globe*, May 31, 1992.

8. "Little Green Lies: The Environmental Miseducation of America's Children," Jonathan H. Adler, *Policy Review*, summer 1992.

9. "Rio Reductionism," *Media Watch*, July 1992.

10. "How a PR Firm Executed the Alar Scare," *Wall Street Journal*, October 3, 1989.

11. "How the Media Launched the Hysteria About Alar," Warren T. Brookes, *Detroit News*, February 25, 1990.

12. *The Christian Science Monitor*, Richard Miniter, February 17, 1991.

13. *Media Watch*, June 8, 1992, referring to CNN News Telecast, Bernard Shaw, May 26.

14. Ibid, June 22, 1992, CNN "Agenda Earth" Telecast, Lucia Newman, June 3, 1992.

15. Ibid, CNN World News, Jill Dougherty, May 30.

16. Ibid, June 8, 1992, quoting *Time*, June 1, 1992.

17. Op. cit., quoting *Newsweek*, Jerry Adler, June 1, 1992.

18. Op. cit., quoting *Newsweek*, Sharon Begley, June 15 and June 22, 1992.

19. "Hole in Ozone Didn't Develop," *Wall Street Journal*, May 1, 1992. (Associated Press, Knight-Ridder News Service, Reuter, and other news services noted the development almost as a non-news event, most of them twinning the brief NASA press release with the disclaimer by NASA scientists that "the threat would return.")

20. Brookes, Warren T., *Detroit News*, December 23, 1991.

21. *The Asbestos Racket*, Michael J. Bennett, Free Enterprise Press, 1991.

22. *Access to Energy*, Dr. Petr Beckmann, December 1990.

23. "Save the Planet, Sacrifice the People: The Environmental Party's Bid for Power," Edward C. Krug, soil scientist, *Imprimis*, July 1991.

24. *Population Matters*, by Dr. Julian Simon, Transaction Publishers, 1990.

25. *Watching America: What Television Tells Us About Our Lives*, S. Robert Lichter, Linda S. Lichter, Stanley Rothman, 1992.

26. "Bush Not Doing Enough to Protect Environment, Poll Says," *Reuters*, August 6, 1992.

27. "GAO Recommends Suspending Pesticide Testing Program," Associated Press, December 19, 1991.

28. "Fire at Seabrook Nuclear Plant," Reuter, July 6, 1992.

29. *Access to Energy*, Dr. Petr Beckmann, July 1990 and May 1992.

30. "Chlorinated Water Holds Risk for Cancer, Researchers Find," *Seattle Times*, Junly 2, 1992.

31. "A Lack of Integrity Also Poisons the Air," Warren T. Brookes, *Detroit News*, November 11, 1991.

32. "The Global Warming Panic," Warren T. Brookes quoting Dr. Bernard Cohen, *Forbes*, December 25, 1989.

11. Quoted in *Wall Street Journal*, April 21, 1992.

12. Ibid.

13. Ibid.

14. "The True Cost of Federal Regulation," *Weekly Update*, National Hardwood Lumber Association, June 29, 1992.

15. Drummey, James J., quoting Irving Kristol in *The Establishment's Man*, p. 55.

16. Sibbison, Jim, "The Real Asbestos Horror Story," *AIM Report, Accuracy in Media*, XIX-17, Sept-A 1990; see also *Washington Monthly*, March 1984.

17. Ibid.

18. "EPA to Your Town: Drop Dead," *Aim Report*, publication of Accuracy in Media, Washington, DC, April 1992.

19. Op cit, *AIM Report, Accuracy in Media*, Reed Irvine, editor, XXI-8, April-B 1992, p. 4. See also "Officials See Groundswell Opposing EPA Mandates That Deny Local Priorities," *Inside EPA*, December 20, 1991.

20. *Inside EPA*, July 26, 1991.

21. Laffer, William G., 3rd, "George Bush's Hidden Tax: The Explosion in Regulation," *Backgrounder*, Heritage Foundation, Washington, DC, July 10, 1992.

22. Ibid.

CHAPTER 15:   THE GOSPEL ACCORDING TO GORE

1. *Earth in the Balance*, Senator Al Gore, Houghton Mifflin, 1992, p. 3.

2. Ibid, p. 4.

3. Ibid, p. 9.

4. "Gore's 'Earth' Worthy of Trash Barrel," George Will, column reproduced in *Seattle Post-Intelligencer*, September 3, 1992.

5. Gore, op cit, p. 38.

6. Review by Dr. Hugh W. Elsaesser, 1992, private communication.

7. Gore, op cit, p. 12.

8. Ibid, p. 242.

9. Ibid, p. 14.

10. Ibid, pp. 105–106.

11. Ibid, p. 119.

12. Ibid, p. 223.

13. Ibid, pp. 305–360.

CHAPTER 16: EPILOGUE

1. Gore, Albert, quoted by Steven Chapman, as reported in *Chicago Tribune*, October 8, 1992.

2. Postrel, Virginia I., Editor, *Reason*, "The Environmental Movement," reprints by Consumer Alert, Modesto, CA, 1991, p. 9.

3. Gore, Albert, 1992, in prepared remarks at the Earth Summit UNCED, typescript distributed June 1992, Rio de Janeiro.

4. Brown, Lester, 1972, *World Without Borders*, New York, Vintage Books, p. 308 ff.

   See also Lester Brown, 1991, "State of the World," issued by Worldwatch Institute, to wit: "...the battle to save the planet will replace the battle over ideology as the organizing theme of the new world order." W. W. Norton, p. 3.

   Hair, Jay D., 1991, president of National Wildlife Federation, who proposes nothing less than "an environmental revolution [which] will be socially disruptive, potentially violent — but will receive massive support." Publication of Capital Research Center, January 1991, p. 3.

5. Postel, Sandra, 1992, "Worldwatch Institute Calls for Launch of Global Environmental Revolution," *Chemical and Engineering News*, January 20, 1992, p. 18.

6. Op cit, French, Hilary F., p. 3.

7. Ibid, Renner, Michael, p. 4.

8. Bari, Judy, quoted by Walter Williams, columnist with Heritage Features Syndicate, *State Journal-Register*, June 25, 1992.

9. Bahro, Rudolf, 1992, "Building on Unlimited Future," *Imprimis*, January 1992, also excerpted in *The "Green Brick" of Socialism*, by Barry Asmus, National Center for Policy Analysis, *Abundant Wildlife*, Issue 5, 1992.

10. Porritt and Winner, quoted by Virginia I. Postrel, Editor, *Reason Magazine*; also editorial in *Chem Tech*, August 1991, p. 459.

11. Brower, David, ibid Reference 9.

12. Graber, David M., 1989, *Los Angeles Times Book Review*, October 22, 1989, p. 9; see also Virginia I. Postrel, ibid, Reference 10, p. 461.

13. Manes, Christopher, 1990, *Green Rage*, see p. 34, Little, Brown & Co., Boston, Toronto, London, 1990.

14. Club of Rome, Alexander King and Bertrand Schneider, 1991, *The First Global Revolution*, Pantheon Books, New York, p. 115.

15. Isaacs, John, 1978, testimony before the Subcommittee on Water Re-

sources of the Committee on Public Works and Transportation, House of Representatives, 95th Congress, May 25 and 25, 1978.

16. National Academy 9of Sciences Report, "Policy Implications of Greenhouse Warming," April 1991, quoting: "For purposes of informed policy choice, it is crucial to acknowledge the limited capability of the atmospheric models."

Recommended Reading

Discussion of environmental issues can be found in literally hundreds of magazine articles, newspaper op-ed columns, special reports from both public and private institutions, and in newsletters. In addition, many books include detailed information on environmental issues. Among these, the following are recommended for further reading.—DLR and LRG.

Aldrich, Samuel R., 1980, *Nitrogen: In Relation to Food, Environment, and Energy*, special publication, Agricultural Experimental Station, College of Agriculture, University of Illinois, Urbana. Authoritative, informative, highly readable, and indispensable!

Arnold, Andrea, 1990, *Fear of Food: Environmental Scams, Media Mendacity, and the Law of Disparagement*, Free Enterprise Press, Bellevue, WA. Contains the most thorough, well documented expose of the Alar hoax and solid information on media handling of issues in science.

Arnold, Ron, 1987, *The Ecology Wars*, Free Enterprise Press, Bellevue, WA. How it all got started, from philosophy to activism.

Balling, Robert, Jr., *The Heated Debate: Greenhouse Predictions Versus Climate Reality*, Pacific Research Institute for Public Policy, 1992, San Francisco. This is one of three books, which, taken together, provide the last word on "global warming." The others, listed below, are by Pat Michaels and Gerd-Rainer Weber. All three are indispensable!

Benedick, Richard Elliot, 1991, *Ozone Diplomacy*. Astonishing revelations on the misuse of science and how foreign relations leading to binding treaties are carried on by mid-level bureaucrats.

Bennett, Michael J., 1991, *The Asbestos Racket*, Free Enterprise Press, Bellevue, WA. Important for dependable information on asbestos. Also a startling expose of the Environmental Protection Agency's role in misleading the public.

Bertels, Sister Thomas More, O.S.F., 1988, *In Pursuit of Agri-Power*, Silver Lake College Press, Manitowoc, WI. Well informed discussion of America's farm problems.

Bettmann, Otto L., 1974, *The Good Old Days—They Were Terrible!*, Random House, NY. *Everybody* should read this one!

Daly, John L., 1989, *The Greenhouse Trap: Why the Greenhouse Effect Will NOT End Life on Earth*, Bantam Books, Sydney, Australia. Lots of interesting information; irreverent but accurate!

Eckard, Jo Kwong, 1990, *Protecting the Environment, Old Rhetoric, New Imperatives*, Studies in Organization Trends, Capital Research Center, Washington, DC. Contains valuable information not otherwise easily available.

Efron, Edith, 1984, *The Apocalyptics*, Simon & Schuster, Inc., New York. Beware the do-gooders!

Greve, Michael S. and Fred L. Smith, Jr., 1992, *Environmental Politics: Public Costs, Private Rewards*, Praeger, NY. Unique insights. Invaluable.

Hage, Wayne, 1989, *Storm Over Rangelands: Private Rights in Federal Lands*, Free Enterprise Press, Bellevue, WA. Remarkable revelations and insights about the attack on ranching.

Health, Lifestyle, and the Environment: Countering the Panic, 1991, ten authors, published by the Social Affairs Unit, Manhattan Institute. Eminently sensible.

Heinz, Agnes, editor, 1991, *Issues in Nutrition*, American Council on Science and Health, New York. Very useful. Full of common sense and facts.

Idso, Sherwood, 1989, *Carbon Dioxide and Global Change: Earth in Transition*, IBR Press, Institute for Biosphere Research, Inc., Tempe, AZ. The most thorough and well documented treatise on the effects of carbon dioxide. It is challenging and convincing. Everyone concerned about carbon dioxide should consider this remarkable book.

Isaac, Rael Jean and Erich Isaac, 1985, *The Coercive Utopians*, Regnery Gateway, Inc., Washington, DC. There are always those who know what's best for the rest of us. The Isaacs reveal them.

Jasper, William F., 1992, *The United Nations and the Emerging New World Order*, Western Islands Publications, Appleton, WI. Thought provoking; makes one wonder if good intentions are enough.

Lamb, H. H., 1982, *Climate History and the Modern World*, Methuen, London and New York. A classic; the starting point for all intelligent discussion of earth's changing climates.

Lehr, Jay H., 1992, *Rational Readings on Environmental Concerns*, Van Nostrand Reinholt. Covers many subjects, all of them expertly.

Maduro, Rogelio A., 1992, *The Holes in the Ozone Scare*, 21st Century Science Association, Washington, DC. An antidote, well documented, to Benedick's *Ozone Diplomacy*.

McGee, Harold, 1984, *On Food and Cooking: The Science and Lore of the Kitchen*, Charles Scribner's Sons, New York. No reason to list this book—except that it's so great! Wonderful reading. See especially Chapter 11 on food fads.

Michaels, Patrick J., 1992, *The Sound and the Fury: The Science and Politics of Global Warming*, CATO Institute, Washington, DC. This is the second of the three "indispensable" books on the subject of "global warming." See also Balling and Weber.

Pesek, John, et al, 1989, *Alternative Agriculture*, National Academy Press, Washington, DC. Although bearing the imprimatur of the prestigious National Academy of Sciences and the National Research Council, this biased, subjective travesty is based on anecdotes and emotion, rather than factual evidence.

Pollot, Mark, 1992, *Grand Theft and Petit Larceny*, Pacific Research Institute for Public Policy. Probably the best thing ever written on private property and the law.

Ponte, Lowell, 1976, *The Cooling*, Prentice Hall. The conventional wisdom of the 1970s—a cooling earth and the coming ice age.

Powell, S. Steven, 1987, *Covert Cadre: Inside the Institute for Policy Studies*, Green Hill Publications, Ottawa, IL. There is often a hidden agenda; Powell reveals some environmental ones.

Sawyer, Peter, 1990, *Green Hoax Effect*, Fraser Publishing Co., Burlington, VT. A solid myth-exploding book. Challenging.

Simon, Julian L. and Herman Kahn, 1984, *The Resourceful Earth*, Basil Blackwell, Inc. Common sense and facts in the area of natural resources.

Simon, Julian L., 1990, *Population Matters*, Transaction Publications, New Brunswick, NJ. One of the few sensible books on human population. An important reference.

Singer, S. Fred, editor, 1989, *Global Climate Change, Human and Natural Influences*, Paragon House, New York. Plenty to consider—and to think about.

Soderberg, K. A. and Jackie DuRette, 1988, *People of the Tongass: Alaska Forestry Under Attack*, Free Enterprise Press, Bellevue, WA. Common sense in the timber controversy.

Weber, Gerd-Rainer, *Global Warming: The Rest of the Story*, Bottiger Verlags-Gmbtt, Wiesbaden, Germany. And this is the third of the three "global warming" books called "indispensable." The others are by Balling and Michaels, above.

Whelan, Elizabeth, 1985, *Toxic Terror*, Jameson Books, Ottawa, IL. Reveals the planned campaign against agriculture and modern living.

Winkless, Nels III and Iben Browning, 1975, *Climate and the Affairs of Man*, Fraser Publishing, Burlington, VT. Unorthodox, and some would say "controversial," but this little volume is a treasury of observations on climate and climate change.

And, finally, the following are a few selections from the activists' literature, a starting point for readers to become familiar with what the extremists really want:

Manes, Christopher, 1990, *Green Rage: Radical Environmentalism and the Unmaking of Civilization*, Little, Brown & Co. The title says it all.

Forman, David and Bill Haywood, editors, 1985, *Ecodefense: A Field Guide* to *Monkey Wrenching*, Ned Ludd Books, Tucson, AZ. Truly a terrorist handbook. Unbelievable.

Kriesberg, Joseph, *Shutdown Strategies, Citizen Efforts to Close Nuclear Power Plants*, Public Citizen's Critical Mass Project, Washington, DC. "We don't want safe nuclear power plants; we want NO nuclear power plants."

Index